ADOLESCENT FATHERHOOD

ADOLESCENT FATHERHOOD

Edited by

ARTHUR B. ELSTER and MICHAEL E. LAMB
The University of Utah

LAWRENCE ERLBAUM ASSOCIATES, PUBLISHERS
1986   Hillsdale, New Jersey   London

Lawrence Erlbaum Associates, Inc., Publishers
365 Broadway
Hillsdale, New Jersey 07642

Library of Congress Cataloging in Publication Data

Adolescent fatherhood.

Includes bibliographies and indexes.
1. Adolescent fathers—United States.   I. Elster,
Arthur B.   II. Lamb, Michael E., 1953–   .
HQ756.A36   1986   306.8′742′088055   86-6354
ISBN 0-89859-540-1

Printed in the United States of America
10   9   8   7   6   5   4   3   2   1

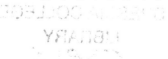

Contents

Preface

Until relatively recently, adolescent pregnancy and parenthood were viewed from a rather narrow perspective. For at least 2 decades, health service providers, psychologists, educators, and researchers speculated about causes and consequences, health care delivery systems, health habits, and an array of sociopolitical issues that affect pregnant adolescents, adolescent mothers, and their infants. Certain "truths" emerged, mostly regarding medical issues, but the majority of psychosocial questions remained unanswered because the available data were inadequate or inconclusive. In part, the problem was that few researchers had studied populations other than the disadvantaged poor. In addition, the changing sociopolitical and legal climate altered both the epidemiology of adolescent pregnancy and the frequency of the various pregnancy outcomes. Further, there were few research teams that benefited from the multidisciplinary backgrounds needed to understand the complex interactions among the physiological, biological, psychological and sociological factors pertinent to adolescent pregnancy and parenthood. Lastly, our understanding of adolescent pregnancy and parenthood was hampered by an exclusive focus on adolescent mothers and their children, without regard for the male role in both pregnancy and parenthood. This research myopia was exemplified in many studies during the 1970s into "the causes of adolescent pregnancy". A conflicting array of personality traits, family factors, peer influences, and psychological characteristics were "causally associated" with adolescent pregnancy, but unfortunately, few consistent results were obtained. In almost every case, teen mothers were studied without regard for their partners.

Times are changing, however, and there is a renewed interest in the role of the father in family life. During the past 10 years, many researchers have investigated paternal influences on child development, from the perspective of both present and absent fathers. In addition, increasing concern has surfaced concerning the financial burdens imposed on society by the need to support single mothers and their infants. This has led to heightened interest in the fathers of infants born to adolescent mothers. The fathers are now seen as an essential component of an important and expensive social problem.

In 1982 there were 523,531 infants born to adolescent mothers; of these, at least 125,305 were fathered by men under 20-years-of-age (*Monthly Vital Statistics Report Advance Report of Final Natality Statistics,* 1982, N.C.H.S., *33* (#6) Suppl.). Thus at least 24% of the infants born to adolescent mothers had two adolescent parents. We say *at least* because in 34% of the cases the age of the father was not stated on the birth certificate. (In no other maternal age category was this information missing for more than 13% of the births.) The high incidence of missing data concerning fathers in this study epitomizes a more general problem: We seem to know little if anything about teen fathers. Who are these young men? What are they like? What happens to them and their infants? Are there characteristics that distinguish between teenage partners and older partners of adolescent mothers? These are just a sampling of the many unanswered questions which stimulated us to organize this conference. Fortunately, others shared our view of the topic's importance, and we were thus able to obtain funding from the Committee on Study Groups and Institutes of the Society for Research in Child Development. Their award to us was made possible by a grant from the Foundation for Child Development, and we are grateful to both organizations for their support.

Because it is necessary to examine adolescent fatherhood from a broad perspective, we purposively invited professionals with diverse interests to participate in the Study Group. Some of the participants were researchers and some were clinicians, but all directly studied or worked with adolescents, families, or developmental issues. At the conclusion of the 2½ day conference, the contents of this volume were outlined and the writing responsibilities were divided. Realizing that the participants were not able to discuss all the issues that had seemed important during our discussions, we subsequently solicited chapters from nonparticipants with expertize in these areas. Unfortunately, three of those who had contributed generously during the Study Group were unable to participate in the preparation of the volume: We salute Larry Bradford of the Menninger Foundation, Ken Robson of Tufts University, and Steve Suomi of the National Institute of Mental Health for their seminal contributions.

The chapters in this book can be divided into four sections, each containing a set of chapters focused on similar themes. We begin with three chapters concerned with those aspects of adolescent development that seem most pertinent to an understanding of adolescent fatherhood. Following an overview of key issues in the study of adolescence by Ray Montemayor (Chapter 1), Teti and Lamb discuss male sex-role development in adolescence (Chapter 2), and Sonenstein reviews research on sexuality and contraceptive use by male adolescents (Chapter 3). These chapters together provide a background against which adolescent fatherhood can be viewed.

In the next three sections, we narrow our focus to those adolescents who become fathers, dealing in turn with the effects of adolescent fatherhood on individual males, their fulfillment of parental and spousal roles, and the intervention strategies likely to be of benefit to them. Section II, which is concerned with the effects of premature fatherhood on individuals, contains one chapter concerned with the stresses perceived by adolescent fathers (Elster and Hendricks, Chapter 4), and one concerned with evidence concerning the devastating effects of fatherhood on their educational and vocational attainment (Marsiglio, Chapter 5).

In section III, we consider the effects of stress and economic constraints on the ability of adolescent fathers to fulfill their family roles and responsibilities. Lamb and Elster (Chapter 6) review the literature on parental behavior, Belsky and Miller (Chapter 7) consider aspects of the transition to parenthood and the likely origins of individual differences in paternal commitment, and Bolton and Belsky (Chapter 8) review the evidence and controversies concerning child maltreatment by adolescent parents.

In the final section, we turn our attention to intervention strategies, reviewing considerations relevant to the behavior of individual clinicians and programs as well as the development of national policies concerning teen fathers. Kahn and Bolton (Chapter 9) draw upon their clinical experiences to suggest effective strategies for programs serving teen fathers, while Klinman, Sander, Rosen, and Longo (Chapter 10) describe the national Teen Father Collaboration, an attempt to encourage adolescent pregnancy programs to serve adolescent fathers. In Chapter 11, Vinovskis reviews historical changes in the perception and response to adolescent fathers.

Our focus on teen fathers was sufficiently narrow that it proved difficult to prepare a useful subject index. Each major topic is addressed in a single chapter, and readers will find that chapter titles and subheadings provide the most useful way of locating discussions of specific issues.

Because the book is designed to synthesize current knowledge and stimulate further research, it closes with a brief epilogue in which the editors summarize some key questions worthy of further research. We hope that this summary, like all the chapters in the book, will be of value to all of those who work with pregnant adolescents and young fathers—be they clinicians, researchers, or policymakers.

List of Contributors

Jay Belsky, Department of Individual and Family Studies, Pennsylvania State University, University Park, PA 16802

Frank Bolton, Coordinator of Psychological Services, Arizona Department of Economic Security, 1400 West Washington, Phoenix, AZ 85007

Arthur B. Elster, Department of Pediatrics, University of Utah Medical Center, Salt Lake City, UT 84132

Leo Hendricks, I.U.A.R., Howard University, 2900 Van Ness St. N. W., Washington, D. C. 20008

James Kahn, Teen Mother and Child Program, Department of Pediatrics, University of Utah Medical Center, Salt Lake City, UT 84132

Debra Klinman, Teen Father Collaboration, Bank Street College of Education, 610 West 112th Street, New York City, NY 10025

Michael E. Lamb, Departments of Psychology, Psychiatry, and Pediatrics, University of Utah, Salt Lake City, UT 84112

Karen R. Longo, Teen Father Collaboration, Bank Street College of Education, 610 West 112th Street, New York City, NY 10025

William Marsiglio, Center for Human Resource Research, Ohio State University, Columbus, OH 43202

Brent Miller, Department of Family and Human Development, Utah State University, Logan, UT 84321

Ray Montemayor, Department of Family and Consumer Studies, University of Utah, Salt Lake City, UT 84112

Jacqueline L. Rosen, Teen Father Collaboration, Bank Street College of Education, 610 West 112th Street, New York City, NY 10025

Joelle Sander, Teen Father Collaboration, Bank Street College of Education, 610 West 112th Street, New York City, NY 10025

Douglas M. Teti, Department of Psychology, University of Utah, Salt Lake City, UT 84112

Freya Sonenstein, Urban Institute, 2100 M Street S. W., Washington, D. C. 20037

Maris Vinoskis, Department of History, University of Michigan, Ann Arbor, MI 48109

ADOLESCENT FATHERHOOD

1

Boys as Fathers: Coping with the Dilemmas of Adolescence

Raymond Montemayor
University of Utah

Little is known about the effects of having a child during adolescence on the later development of teenage fathers, and even less is known about the parental and spouse behavior of these males. Popularly held notions that a pregnancy during adolescence adversely affects the subsequent development of teenage fathers and that these males are poor husbands and inadequate fathers are premature. Although the data that do exist generally support these ideas, the empirical evidence is meager. Males who become fathers during adolescence, in comparison to those who do not, appear to be somewhat more likely to divorce (Kellam, Adams, Brown, & Ensminger, 1982; Moore & Waite, 1981), abandon their partners and babies, and suffer later educational, vocational, and economic losses (Card & Wise, 1978; Lorenzi, Klerman, & Jekal, 1977; Marsiglio, Chapter 5). The magnitude of these group differences is not large, however. Further, much variation exists in the impact that fatherhood has on adolescents, and not all males are adversely affected to an equal degree. Lastly, these findings are neither substantively nor methodologically incontrovertible, and more work is needed to identify the immediate and long-term effects of teenage pregnancy on adolescent fathers.

Besides identifying the consequences of becoming a father during adolescence, explanations are needed that account for the association between fatherhood and its various stresses and problems. One reasonable and commonly held belief among many researchers and practitioners who focus on adolescent parents is that the problems these teenagers experience are to some extent the result of their youth. The following excerpt from Elster, McAnarney, and Lamb (1983) illustrates this point: "Because of the adolescent's age and because of the stressful events that frequently accompany youth pregnancy and parenthood, clinicians and investigators have questioned the ability of adolescents to parent

1

their young in a way that promotes optimal child development'' (p. 494); and, according to Hendricks, Howard, and Caesar (1981): ''Pertinent [stress] factors for the unmarried adolescent father are: the nature and outcome of each father's struggle with . . . [the] dilemmas of adolescence'' (p. 733). Some researchers use phrases such as ''premature parenthood'' (McAnarney, Lawrence, & Aten, 1979) and ''early motherhood'' (Bacon, 1974) to convey the idea that parenthood can occur before an individual is ready to assume its burdens, that is, during adolescence.

The reasonable idea that youth is in some ways its own problem is a hypothesis in need of verification. Yet before this idea can be tested, the adolescent period itself needs to be considered and the various factors that influence adolescent behavior identified. The purpose of this chapter is to examine these issues and to do so in a developmental context. Just what are the ''dilemmas of adolescence,'' and how might they account for the adversity experienced by some adolescent fathers?

What does it mean to be an adolescent? This straightforward question does not have a simple answer. Webster's New Collegiate Dictionary defines ''adolescence'' as ''the period of life from puberty to maturity terminating legally at the age of majority.'' As this definition makes clear, adolescence is a multifaceted concept. Chronological age is one component of the definition of the adolescent period, but adolescence cannot be reduced to the teenage years. Puberty marks the beginning of this period, but the cessation of biological growth is not generally regarded as its end. Many new psychological abilities appear during adolescence, but which ones signal entry into adulthood has not been clearly established. Adolescence is a legal concept, but its beginning and end cannot be legislated. Lastly, adolescence is a sociological concept closely bound with normative expectations about when certain life-course events should occur in a society, but it's end is not merely graduating from high school, full-time employment, and marriage. The definition of adolescence includes all five of these components, and an adequate understanding of the behavior of adolescents and of the problems they experience requires that we examine each.

In this speculative chapter the components of the adolescent experience are briefly discussed and their relevance for understanding the problems of adolescent fathers are considered. In the five sections that follow the possible ways that chronological age, biological development, psychological maturity, legal status, and life-cycle events might affect the behavior of adolescent fathers are examined.

FIVE COMPONENTS OF THE ADOLESCENT PERIOD

Chronological Age

In everyday speech, many people consider adolescents to be teenagers and use the terms synonymously. It is not difficult to understand why. The teenage years are positively correlated with the upfolding of many significant biological and psychological events. For example, in modern societies puberty begins a few years before age 13, on the average about 11.5 years for girls and 12.5 for boys in the United States, and biological growth ceases at about 19 years of age (Tanner, 1978). Further, during the teenage years several advances occur in cognitive development (Inhelder & Piaget, 1958), moral judgment (Colby, Kohlberg, Gibbs, and Lieberman, 1983) and concerns about the self (Erikson, 1968). Also, schools provide institutional support for the notion that 13-year-olds are no longer children and 19-year-olds have entered adulthood, because these are the approximate ages when most students enter junior high school and graduate from high school. Lastly, research and common knowledge reveals the existence of an ''adolescent society,'' with it's own norms, language, and leisure activities (Coleman, 1961), which emerges during the teenage years and centers around high school life.

Although age is correlated with the appearance of many psychological abilities and is used as a basis to group students in age-graded schools, it is a poor developmental concept. The problems of using age as a developmental construct are numerous. First, large individual differences exist in the ages at which an ability first appears. To take just one example, in a longitudinal study of 94 normal females who were teenagers between 1934 and 1946, average age of menarche was reported to be 12.8 years, with a range between 10.5 and 15.8 years of age (Faust, 1977). Using age 13 as the initiation of adolescence includes some girls in this category who are premenarcheal and excludes others who are post. Age 13 is a rough approximation of the beginning of puberty in this group, but, as a scientific construct or as a criterion to decide who is normal and abnormal, the mismatch between marker and event is too great for age to be of much use.

A second limitation of using age to define adolescence is that age does not *cause* the characteristic to appear or the behavior to occur. An individual's age merely marks the passage of time during which genetically controlled biological sequences unfold, and more and different social experiences occur. When biological events such as puberty or psychological characteristics such as identity concerns occur at approximately similar ages among adolescents, it is because of similarities in physical maturation and social experiences.

Individuals of different ages can be justifiably classified into a single age-category only if they are alike. This can occur if the individuals are close to each other in age, if little or no biological change is occurring, and if their social experiences are similar. On all three of these accounts classifying teenagers into a single category is inappropriate. The 6-year age span between 13 and 19 years is long, and this period is marked by rapid biological change and many new social experiences.

The further implication of this line of reasoning is that the term *adolescence* itself may not be a useful scientific concept. Increasingly, developmentalists are finding it necessary to split the adolescent period into ''early'' and ''late'' because of the vast biological, psychological, and social differences between youth who are experiencing puberty and those who are some years past these events but not yet considered adults.

Biologically, youth classified as "early adolescents" are in the midst of sexual maturation and a rapid growth spurt. These biological changes appear to lead to heightened concerns about body image (Hamburg, 1974), self-consciousness (Elkind & Bowen, 1979), and some disruption of self-concept (Dusek & Flaherty, 1981). Relations with parents deteriorate somewhat and adolescents become more powerful vis-a-vis their parents (Steinberg, 1981). Peers take on an added importance and interest in the opposite sex increases (Berndt, 1982). Cognitively, the early stages of scientific thinking appear and adolescents develop more sophisticated information-processing abilities (Keating, 1980). During this period adolescents complete elementary school, with its single classroom learning environment, and stable peer group, and enter junior high school, or middle school, with new social rules, changing classrooms and teachers, and new peers.

The situation in "late adolescence" is different from that encountered earlier. During this period the tempo of growth slows and is completed. Most youth finish their secondary education and many experience an "identity crisis" as they consider their various educational, employment, and life-style options (Offer, Marcus, & Offer, 1979). Achieving independence from parental influence becomes an important issue (White, Speisman, & Costos, 1983). During this time most youth leave home and begin to function more autonomously (Montemayor, in press). A sexual relationship may be entered into for the first time and decisions about marriage are made (Jessor & Jessor, 1975; Miller & Simon, 1974).

The main justification for using age as a definition of adolescence is convenience. A research and service delivery population needs to be identified, and adolescent fathers have been equated with teenage fathers. The point of this discussion about chronological age is that teenagers are not a developmentally homogeneous group. The issues of concern to younger and older teenagers and the biological and social factors that control their behavior are different. Researchers interested in identifying the causes and consequences of teenage fatherhood, and providers of services to teenage parents need to recognize the developmental changes that occur between early and late adolescence.

Biological Development

Adolescence is generally defined as the period of time between the initiation of puberty and the acquisition of the full rights and responsibilities of adulthood (e.g., Lerner & Spanier, 1980; Santrock, 1981). It is the period of life when an individual is sexually, but not socially or legally, an adult. Separating sexual capability from social maturity may have an evolutionary basis. Among the higher orders of nonhuman primates an adolescent period exists during which adult males prevent young postpubescent males from copulating with mature females (Savin-Williams & Montemayor, in preparation). Access to females is not a right but a privilege that male adolescents must earn by demonstrating their physical fitness through combat. Adolescence is a testing period during which weak and puny males are identified and excluded from the reproductive community, thereby eliminating their genes from the gene pool.

Among humans, the most dramatic and visible of all the changes that occur during adolescence are those biological events that prepare individuals for parenthood. Increases occur in height, weight, and strength (Tanner, 1978). Both sexes show increases in muscle bulk and body fat, but the former is more marked for boys and the latter for girls (Tanner, 1962). Secondary sex characteristics appear, such as a widening of hip width and an increase in breast size for girls, and boys' voices deepen and they begin to grow beards.

Considerable change in hormonal secretions also occur during adolescence (Forest, DePeretti, & Bertrand, 1976; Winter, 1978). The first pubertal event is an increase in the secretion of gonadotrophic hormones by the pituitary gland, which causes the ovaries and testes to develop. Estrogen production remains roughly constant in both sexes until about age 7 years and then rises gradually. As adolescence begins in girls, estrogen production rises sharply and becomes cyclic. Estrogen levels also increase slightly in boys during puberty, but the main hormonal change is a large rise in testosterone secretion. In both boys and girls increases take place in the secretion of adrenal androgens, which are responsible for the emergence of some of the secondary sexual characteristics, particularly pubic and axillary hair.

As this brief description indicates, puberty is not a single event but a whole series of events that transform in a relatively short time an immature organism into one capable of sexual reproduction. This transformation is directly responsible for the problem of teenage fatherhood—without reproductive capability there can be no children. Reproductive capability and sexual behavior are not equivalent, however; although the first begins at puberty, the second has a prepubescent history, and most American adolescents have engaged in many forms of childhood sex play (Kinsey, Pomeroy, & Martin, 1948; Kinsey, Pomeroy, Martin, & Gebhard, 1953). Little is known about prepubescent sexual behavior, and one can only wonder whether differences exist in this area between males who do or do not become adolescent fathers. In general, it is not known whether the sexual behavior of adolescent fathers is in any way different from sexually active adolescent males who do not become fathers.

In addition to the relationship between puberty and sexuality, other adolescent behaviors may be affected by the biological changes that occur at puberty. Two models for the relationship between puberty and behavior have been proposed: (1) a *direct effects model,* in which it is thought that biological factors act directly on behavior, and (2) a *mediated effects model,* in which it is postulated that intervening variables exist between biological factors and behavior (Petersen & Taylor, 1980).

The scientific study of behavioral endocrinology has only recently begun, in part because of the difficulty of obtaining accurate endocrinological measurements (Beach, 1975). Some tantalizing findings have been reported on hormone-behavior relations in adolescents, but the literature in this area is not extensive. Sex steroids have been implicated in the intensification of sex drive and sexual activity (Ehrhardt & Meyer-Bahlburg, 1975), and changes in social rank and dominance during adolescence (Lloyd, 1975). High levels of testosterone have been correlated with aggressiveness in adolescent boys (Olweus, Mattsson, Schalling, & Low, 1980). Recent research at NIMH has shown a positive relation between high-for-age pubescent endocrine changes and interest in dating, sexual behavior, spending time with friends, and some types of psychopathology. These results suggest that early endocrine changes may be stressors in the lives of young adolescents (Susman, Nottelmann, Inoff, Dorn, Cutler, Loriaux, & Chrousos, submitted). What is not well understood are the mechanisms through which hormones affect the brain and, in turn, the behavior of adolescents (McEwen, 1976).

A primary pathway by which biological events may indirectly affect behavior is through variation in the timing of puberty, resulting in age differences in physical appearance. Early-maturing boys generally have higher self-esteem, greater athletic ability, and better relations with parents and peers, especially girls, than their late-maturing peers (Clausen, 1975). The physical characteristics that are most strongly associated with these behavioral advantages are height and the presence of facial hair (Petersen, Tobin-Richards, & Boxer, 1983). The findings for girls are more complex but generally show that high self-evaluations and social status are related to being maturationally on time for every physical characteristic except breast development, where earlier is rated better and is related to high heterosexual status (Brooks-Gunn, 1984; Petersen et al., 1983). The explanation for these associations is almost certainly social and psychological rather than directly biological.

Little is known about the association between early puberty and sexuality, but it appears that early maturers become sexually active somewhat sooner and have more sexual experiences than late maturers (Gagnon, 1983). The early onset of sexual experience is not without its consequences, and girls who engage in sexual intercourse early in life are more likely to have premarital pregnancy (Rutter, 1980). Further, early-maturing boys tend to marry earlier than late-maturing boys (Clausen, 1975), perhaps because some of them become teenage fathers.

The relationship between biological change during puberty and aspects of teenage fatherhood has not been explored, although it is potentially significant. Is endocrinological variation in adolescent males directly implicated in the age of onset of sexual activity, its frequency, or the likelihood of impregnating a female, because of high sperm counts or large sperm volume? Are hormonal variations during adolescence directly related to aspects of fathering such as infant care or family violence? Do aspects of pubertal change indirectly affect adolescent fatherhood through variation in pubertal timing and differences in physique? Many questions exist in this area but as yet few answers.

Cognitive and Psychological Development

In addition to biological change many cognitive abilities and psychological characteristics are transformed during adolescence. In this section cognitive development, identity formation, and the capacity for intimate relations are explored during the second decade of life. These three issues are focused on for two reasons: First, mature thought, a clear sense of purpose, and the capacity for intimacy are believed to be characteristics of adults; and second, deficiencies in these capacities may be related to problematic parenting during adolescence (Elster et al., 1983; Rogel & Petersen, 1984).

Cognitive development.   At least four cognitive developmental trends have been found between childhood and adulthood: (1) increases in factual knowledge, (2) improvements in understanding of verbal material, (3) the development of sophisticated scientific deductive reasoning, and (4) the appearance of executive control ability (Sternberg & Powell, 1983). In this short section these developments can only be examined briefly.

Studies of cognitive development are mainly about changes in structure, process, and strategy. Besides transformations in cognitive processing, an enormous increase in knowledge also occurs between childhood and adulthood (Brown, Bransford, Ferrara, & Campione, 1983). The knowledge base includes information about the external world as well as one's internal cognitions. More than any other aspect of cognitive development, increases in knowledge are related to direct and vicarious experience rather than maturation.

Developmental changes have been found for both verbal and scientific reasoning. Distinguishing between the central and the extraneous in reading material is an ability that improves with age. Older adolescents are better able than children to identify the crucial elements of texts (Brown & Smiley, 1978) and as a result have better recall of textual material. Not only do adolescents show increased sophistication in literacy skills but also in the development of scientific and mathematical reasoning (Inhelder & Piaget, 1958; Siegler & Liebert, 1975). The thinking of children is more closely tied to concrete reality, whereas adolescents are able to examine possibilities not immediately present in a situation. Closely related to the separation of the real from the possible is the development of the ability to generate and test hypotheses (Keating, 1980).

In Piagetian theory cognitive development progresses from unconscious to conscious regulation of cognitive activity (Piaget, 1976). According to Piaget, mature learners can reflect on their own thinking and select learning strategies appropriate to a problem, whereas the strategies children employ are largely not accessible to their consciousness. This idea also has been called "metacognition" (Flavell, 1977), i.e., knowledge and control of cognition, or "executive control," by which an individual monitors his or her attempt to solve a problem.

These skills might be related to teenage fathering in several ways. For example, not only do teenagers know little about babies and development (DeLissovoy, 1973), problems in themselves, but also they may be less able to profit as much as adults from printed material. Younger adolescents, especially, may have a difficult time acquiring and using information about child rearing contained in books and may depend more on personal experience and trial-and-error learning, potentially costly strategies when used with fragile infants.

In addition, adolescents have a difficult time keeping schedules and planning for the immediate and long-term future. Both of these deficiencies could interfere with effective infant care. Further, a "sensitive parent" has been described as one who can perceive the child's cues, correctly interpret them, and plan and implement an appropriate response (Lamb & Easterbrooks, 1981). These skills require the abilities to generate and test hypotheses, select a plan of action, and monitor its effectiveness. Most adolescents do not possess these abilities to a high degree.

Identity development.   Erik Erikson's concept of "identity crisis" has been the central theoretical idea used by contemporary writers to organize much of the material on personality and social development during adolescence (Adams & Montemayor, 1983). According to Erikson (1968), the establishment of an identity involves the exploration of life choices and an eventual commitment to a career, an ideology, and a set of values. Erikson suggests that thinking about these issues begins early in life, reaches its ascendancy during adolescence, and is refined during the adult years. The ability to form intimate relationships and to engage in productive adult work is thought to be facilitated by the formation of a mature identity.

Research on identity development reveals that mature commitments are rarely made before early adulthood, and are uncommon even then. Most junior high school and high school students have either engaged in no identity activity or have made premature nonreflective commitments (Archer, 1982; Meilman, 1979). Thinking about one's identity and making choices increase between childhood and adulthood, but only about 20% of college students are classified as having achieved a mature identity (Archer & Waterman, 1983).

Family factors are highly related to the achievement of an identity and the father–son relationship is particularly important for males. For example, LaVoie (1976) reported that identity-achieved males in high school had fathers who were highly masculine, exerted a moderate degree of control, and often praised them. Other work suggests that identity achievers have fathers who are able to accept father–son differences, thereby creating a context conducive to identity exploration (Grotevant & Cooper, 1985).

Identity achievement is positively correlated with several personality characteristics and styles of interaction. Individuals who have achieved a mature identity are less susceptible to the influence of others (Marcia, 1980), have higher internal locus of control (Abraham, 1983), and tend to use postconventional forms of moral reasoning (Podd, 1972). These results suggest that individuals who have achieved an identity are more independent, self-directed, and autonomous.

A teenage father with a diffuse identity may find it difficult to be an effective parent and husband. The lack of clarity about oneself, and the resulting lack of commitment to his baby and wife, could make it hard for the adolescent male to much care about learning how to be effective in his family roles or whether he succeeds. Further, not having a firm sense of self, the adolescent may compete with his own child for his wife's attention and feel threatened by and jealous of the interest she shows in their baby.

Besides the effect that identity diffusion might have on adolescent fatherhood, becoming a father during adolescence may affect subsequent identity development. Becoming a parent and marrying during adolescence close off opportuniites for the adolescent and result in premature commitment, what is referred to as ''identity foreclosure.'' Besides being a commitment without much exploration, adolescent fatherhood may be experienced as a forced choice. It is not known what effect adolescent fatherhood has on later personality development, but this question is important for understanding the effect that different contexts have on developmental trajectories.

Interpersonal development.   According to Erikson, a major outcome of the establishment of a mature identity is the capacity to form intimate relationships. Loving another, in Erikson's view, is possible only after the development of self-knowledge. What little research has been conducted on this issue generally supports Erikson's theoretical prediction that identity achievement is positively related to interpersonal intimacy (Fitch & Adams, 1983; Orlofsky, Marcia, & Lesser, 1973).

Recently, White and her colleagues have argued that relationships vary along a maturity dimension (White, Speisman, Costos, & Smith, 1985). At the lowest level are relationships that are ''self-focused'' in which the individuals are primarily concerned about their own needs. Next are relationships dominated by conformity and conventionality, referred to as ''role-focused.'' Lastly are ''individuated-connected'' relationships in which the individuals are psychologically separate from each other, but with intimate, reciprocal, and mutual emotional bonds. Age is correlated with relationship maturity, and individuals of any age who have not yet achieved an identity are most likely to have marriages of the first type. Couples in self-focused marriages have simple views of each other, expressed in sweeping judgments about right and wrong. Affect toward one's spouse also is simple and undifferentiated—love or hate, good or bad.

A fertile field of research would be to examine the factors related to teenage marital satisfaction and success. Little is known about these marriages, although understanding them should be an important goal in itself and may also lead to a deeper understanding of the problems of teenage parenting. Among adults, husbands who are happily married spend more time playing with their infants and provide them with more emotional support than husbands less satisfied with their marriage (Feldman, Nash, & Aschenbrenner, 1984; Goldberg & Easterbrooks, 1984). The low capacity for intimacy found among most teenagers may be partly responsible for their marital dissatisfaction and discord may result in insensitive parenting.

Legal Status

Between ages 14 and 21 years individuals acquire more and different legal rights and obligations than they had as minors. A short illustrative list of the ages at which states grant seven important rights to individuals is given in Table 1.1 (Guggenheim & Sussman, 1985). Two points are evident from this list. First, much variability exists in the ages when states allow these legally regulated behaviors. This lack of consensus reflects the inability of policy makers and social scientists to arrive at a "best" age to grant any legal right. The ages chosen, therefore, are a reflection of historical and political forces, which differ to some extent from state to state.

A second point evident from Table 1.1 is that legal adulthood is not acquired all at once, but gradually. Legal scholars consider age to be a "proxy" for an underlying attribute thought to be significantly related to the legally regulated behavior (Neugarten, 1981). In a general sense, that attribute might be called *competence* (Melton, 1983). Jurists argue that during the teenage years important improvements occur in the ability of developing individuals to make competent decisions, which make it appropriate to grant then new rights and expect increases in responsibility (Zimring, 1982). These improvements in competence are believed to be correlated with age (Melton, 1983). It is generally recognized by the legal profession that the use of age as a proxy involves a trade-off between expediency and accuracy (Stodolsky, 1981).

Teenage mothers and fathers are beset by a myriad of actual and potential legal problems, which could have important implications for how they behave as parents and marriage partners. For example, under Texas law a "parent" is defined as the biological mother, but a father's parenthood is established through marriage to the mother—the child must be conceived or born while the father is married to the mother (McKnight, 1982). An unmarried father has no legal rights over his illegitimate child. Further, a teenage father is a minor and has no obligations either. Because a teenage male is under no obligation to marry the mother of his child or support them, the decision to marry must be based on other than legal considerations. Research that examines the reasons why teenage fathers marry and the relationship between these reasons and later paternal and spouse behavior could be important for understanding individual behavioral differences. For example, do differences exist in the behavior of males who married either because they wanted to, felt morally obligated, or were pressured by parents?

TABLE 1.1
Ages (in years) At Which States Legally Allow Various Activities

State	A	B	C	D (Male)	D (Female)	E	F	G
Alabama	19	14	14	18	18	16	16	16
Alaska	18	18	a	18	18	16	16	16
Arizona	18	18	em	18	18	18	16	16
Arkansas	18	a	a	18	18	16	16	16
California	18	18	a	18	18	18	16	16
Colorado	18	18	a	18	18	15	16	16
Connecticut	18	18	e	18	18	no law	16	18
Delaware	18	18	12	18	16	16	16	16
D.C.	18	18	a	18	18	16	16	16
Florida	18	18	a	18	18	18	16	16
Georgia	18	18	af	18	18	14	16	16
Hawaii	18	18	14	19	16	14	16	17
Idaho	18	18	a	18	18	18	16	16
Illinois	18	18	a	18	18	18	16	16
Indiana	18	18	18	18	18	16	16	16
Iowa	18	18	18	18	18	16	16	16
Kansas	18	18	16	18	18	16	16	16
Kentucky	18	18	a	18	18	16	16	16
Louisiana	18	18	f	18	18	17	16	15
Maine	18	18	a	18	18	14	17	15
Maryland	18	18	a	18	18	14	16	16
Massachusetts	18	18	a	18	18	16	16	18
Michigan	18	18	18	18	18	16	16	16
Minnesota	18	18	a	17	18	16	16	16
Mississippi	21	a	a	18	15	12	13	15
Missouri	18	18	a	18	18	16	16	16
Montana	18	18	f	19	18	14	16	15
Nebraska	19	19	19	18	19	16	16	16
Nevada	18	a	a	18	18	16	17	16
New Hampshire	18	18	18	18	18	13	16	16
New Jersey	18	18	18	18	18	16	16	17
New Mexico	18	18	18	18	18	13	18	16
New York	18	18	a	18	18	17	16	17
North Carolina	18	18	a	18	18	12	16	16
North Dakota	18	18	18	18	18	15	16	16
Ohio	18	a	a	18	18	15	18	18
Oklahoma	18	18	me	18	18	16	18	16
Oregon	18	15	a	18	18	18	18	16
Pennsylvania	21	18	a	18	18	16	17	17
Rhode Island	18	16	18	18	16	13	16	16
South Carolina	18	16	a	18	18	14	16	16
South Dakota	18	18	18	18	18	15	16	16
Tennessee	18	18	a	18	18	18	16	16
Texas	18	18	16	18	18	17	17	16
Utah	18	18	18	18	18	14	18	16
Vermont	18	18	18	18	18	16	16	18
Virginia	18	18	a	18	18	13	16	16
Washington	18	18	18	18	18	16	18	16
West Virginia	18	18	18	18	18	16	16	18
Wisconsin	18	18	18	18	18	15	16	16
Wyoming	19	19	19	19	19	16	16	16

A--Age of majority
B--Age of consent for general medical care
C--May consent for contraception
D--May marry without parental consent
E--Age at which females may consent to sexual intercourse
F--Age under which school enrollment is compulsory
G--Age at which driver's license available
NOTE: a = any age; e = emancipated; f = female; m = married.
Source: Guggenheim and Sussman (1985).

Consider one further example, again in Texas. Individuals under the age of 18 years need parental consent to marry, even if the girl is pregnant (McKnight, 1982). The desire of two teenagers to marry is inextricably tied up with their relations with their parents. Presumably, parents make their decision based on an evaluation of the characteristics of their own adolescent and the suitability of the other. Ultimately it is the girl's parents who decide whether the boy may become the father of his baby. Parental involvement in the marriage of their teenagers can be a two-edged sword. In-laws may provide financial support and other forms of needed aid (Furstenberg, 1980), but they can be perceived by the teenagers as meddlesome or become a source of marital friction. Adolescent parents interviewed in one study reported that they found the unsolicited advice of parents and relatives to be more stressful than helpful (Barth, Schinke, Liebert, & Maxwell, 1981). Research on the effects that the families of married teenagers have on their marriage and child-rearing practices is needed.

Participation in Adult Life Events

In addition to age, biological maturity, cognitive and psychological development, and legal status, another criterion used to differentiate adolescents from adults is passage through certain events that are generally considered by members of a community to indicate entrance into adulthood. Socially, individuals become adults when they have participated in certain life events and lead lives similar to those of most adults in a society. For example, because most adults in the United States are married and self-supporting, one might use as criteria for adulthood marriage and financial independence from parents. Using social criteria to define adulthood anchors the unfolding of the life cycle to a particular society during an historical period. In other societies or at other times adolescence and adulthood could be defined differently.

It is common to read that the period of transition from childhood to adulthood has been prolonged in recent times (e.g., Hopkins, 1983). For example, Aries (1962) states: "it (adolescence) encroached upon childhood in one direction, maturity in the other" (p. 30). Such statements seem to be based on the fact that on the average young people today are enrolled in school for a longer period of time than ever before. The median age of school departure was 14.4 years in the nineteenth century as compared to roughly 19 years in 1970 (Modell, Furstenberg, & Hershberg, 1976). As important as this life event is for socially defining adulthood, other events such as leaving home, marriage, and setting up a household are equally important. When all these status transitions are examined it does not appear that the period of youth has been lengthened. For example, Modell et al. (1976) studied the age at which five life events occurred for youth living in the nineteenth century and in 1970. The events were exit from school, entrance into the work force, departure from the family of origin, marriage, and the establishment of a household. "Youth" was defined as the period of time between the average age of attainment of one of these life events, and all five. For nineteenth-century Philadelphia males, youth lasted about 22 years, from 12.6 years to 34.3 years. Their counterparts in 1970 entered youth at 14.2 years and completed the series of transitions at 28.6 years, a period of about 14 years. For females the duration of youth was, and is, shorter, because it ends earlier through marriage. The period between childhood and adulthood appears to be shorter today than it was a century ago.

Over the past few years sociologists have paid increasing attention to the study of the life cycle, and the transition to adulthood. Two important conclusions have emerged from these investigations. First, the life cycle is normatively patterned. Age ranges around which many life-course events occur are narrow, and events unfold in a predictable sequence (Marini, 1984). Second, informal social support, and much formal social assistance, is organized around the normative life cycle. Therefore, major deviations in timing or sequence may be problematic for individuals due to a lack of informal and formal support (Elder, 1975; Neugarten & Datan, 1973; Teachman & Polonko, 1984). There is growing evidence that, in general, violating transition norms is related to subsequent nonnormative transitions and later negative consequences such as reduced lifetime earnings and lower social status (Hogan, 1981).

Several interesting implications for understanding adolescent fathers follow from this perspective. Teenage fatherhood is a deviation from two important norms; it occurs early and out of sequence, i.e., before completion of high school and before marriage. Many of the problems associated with becoming a father during adolescence may be the result of these deviations. Specifically, the problems may be the result of the negative sanctions and ostracism of others in the community, and to a lack of real societal support.

There are few social advantages to being a teenage father and one doubts that a young male's social status is enhanced by it. More likely, fatherhood and marriage isolate males from their natural peer group. Preexisting personality and social differences, divergent life-styles, exit from the dating world, and an inability to participate in many afterschool and peer activities because of domestic responsibilities and the need to work would effectively remove adolescent fathers from their teenage social environment. To what degree this occurs and what effects it has on the ability of teenage fathers to adequately carry out their responsibilities as fathers and husbands are questions in need of research.

Besides a lack of social support, little real societal aid and support exist for teenage fathers. For most American men fatherhood occurs after finishing school, starting full-time employment, and marriage. Traditionally, a man's primary responsibility to his family has been to provide financial support. Teenage fathers are severely hampered in this regard because of their lesser educational attainment and poorer job prospects in comparison to males who did not become fathers before completing high school. Research is needed to identify what kinds of assistance teenage fathers are most in need of, and whether receiving this aid increases their immediate effectiveness as fathers and husbands and improves their future prospects.

Intervention

Teenage fathers have many problems. They are young, are capable of sexual reproduction but not considered adults, are cognitively and psychologically immature, possess few legal rights, and are out of life-cycle synchrony with their peers. Clearly, an effective intervention cannot focus on only a single aspect of these multiple-problem individuals and their families. Two of these classes of problems seem especially important as bases for intervention—possible cognitive and psychological immaturity and being out of sequence with their cohort.

Programs designed to facilitate cognitive development, clarify identity issues, enhance the marital relationship, and teach parenting skills are all based on the idea that developmental immaturity is a significant cause of problematic parenting during adolescence. Few programs of these types targeted expressly for teenagers exist. Research on ways of accelerating development, improving relationship skills, and developing parental sensitivity in teenagers is needed.

The additional serious problem that teenage fathers face is early entry into parenthood and marriage before finishing school and developing good job skills. Interventions addressed to these problems have as their goal the eventual attainment of financial self-sufficiency. This would be achieved by providing tangible support, primarily financial assistance and child care facilities, so that adolescents can complete school and acquire marketable job skills. Experimental programs in this area, with an evaluation component, are needed.

SUMMARY

Two broad perspectives have shaped theories and research on adolescence, and of what services need to be delivered to adolescent fathers—developmental and social. The period of adolescence has been defined by characteristics of the developing organism, which have included age, biological development, and cognitive and psychological functioning; and by social criteria such as legal status and participation in adult social experiences. Interventions designed to help teenage fathers and mothers based on the first perspective include clinical attempts to improve individual functioning, accelerate development, and enhance the parent–child and marital relationship. Examples of the second type are large-scale social programs designed to keep teenage fathers in school and teach job skills. To what extent the problems of adolescent fathers are the result of developmental or social factors is the overriding question awaiting further research.

REFERENCES

Abraham, K. G. (1983). The relation between identity status and locus of control among rural high school students. *Journal of Early Adolescence, 3,* 257–264.

Adams, G. R., & Montemayor, R. (Eds.). (1983). Identity formation during early adolescence [Whole Special Issue]. *Journal of Early Adolescence, 3,* 193–292.

Archer, S. L. (1982). The lower age boundaries of identity development. *Child Development, 53,* 1551–1556.

Archer, S. L., & Waterman, A. S. (1983). Identity in early adolescence: A developmental perspective. *Journal of Early Adolescence, 3,* 203–214.

Aries, P. (1962). *Centuries of childhood: A social history of the family.* New York: Random House.

Bacon, L. (1974). Early motherhood, accelerated role transitions, and social pathologies. *Social Forces, 52,* 333–341.

Barth, R. P., Schinke, S. P., Liebert, M. A., & Maxwell, J. S. (1981). *Distressing situations and coping responses for school-age mothers and mothers-to-be.* Paper presented at the biannual Western School-Age Parenthood Conference, Portland, OR.

Beach, F. A. (1975). Behavioral endocrinology: An emerging discipline. *American Scientist, 63,* 178–187.

Berndt, T. J. (1982). The features and effects of friendship in early adolescence. *Child Development, 53,* 1447–1460.

Brooks-Gunn, J. (1984). The psychological significance of different pubertal events to young girls. *Journal of Early Adolescence, 4,* 315–327.

Brown, A. L., Bransford, J. D., Ferrara, R. A., & Campione, J. C. (1983). Learning, remembering, and understanding. In J. H. Flavell & E. M. Markman (Eds.), *Handbook of child psychology* (Vol. 3, pp. 77–166). New York: Wiley.

Brown, A. L., & Smiley, S. S. (1978). The development of strategies for studying texts. *Child Development, 49,* 1076–1088.

Card, J. J., & Wise, L. L. (1978). Teenage mothers and teenage fathers: The impact of early childbearing on the parent's personal and professional lives. *Family Planning Perspective, 10,* 199–205.

Clausen, J. A. (1975). The social meaning of differential physical and sexual maturation. In S. E. Dragastin & G. H. Elder (Eds.), *Adolescence in the life cycle* (pp. 25–48). New York: Halsted.

Colby, A., Kohlberg, L., Gibbs, J., & Lieberman, M. (1983). A longitudinal study of moral judgment. *Monographs of the Society for Research in Child Development, 48*(1–2, No. 200).

Coleman, J. S. (1961). *The adolescent society.* New York: The Free Press.

DeLissovoy, V. (1973). Child care by adolescent parents. *Child Today, 2,* 23–25.

Dusek, J. B., & Flaherty, J. F. (1981). The development of the self-concept during the adolescent years. *Monographs of the Society for Research in Child Development, 46*(4, No. 191).

Ehrhardt, A., & Meyer-Bahlburg, H. (1975). Psychosocial correlates of abnormal pubertal development. *Clinics in Endocrinology and Metabolism, 4,* 207–222.

Elder, G. H. Jr. (1975). Age differentiation and the life course. In A. Inkeles, J. Coleman, & N. Smelser (Eds.), *Annual review of sociology.* Palo Alto, CA: Annual Reviews.

Elkind, D., & Bowen, R. (1979). Imaginary audience behavior in children and adolescents. *Developmental Psychology, 15,* 38–44.

Elster, A. B., McAnarney, E. R., & Lamb, M. E. (1983). Parental behavior of adolescent mothers. *Pediatrics, 71,* 494–503.

Erikson, E. H. (1968). *Identity: youth and crisis.* New York: Norton.

Faust, M. S. (1977). Somatic development of adolescent girls. *Monographs of the Society for Research in Child Development, 42*(1, No. 169).

Feldman, S. S., Nash, S. C., & Aschenbrenner, D. (1984). Antecedents of fathering. *Child Development, 54,* 1628–1636.

Fitch, S. A., & Adams, G. R. (1983). Ego identity and intimacy status: Replication and extension. *Developmental Psychology, 19,* 839–845.

Flavell, J. H. (1977). *Cognitive development.* Englewood Cliffs, NJ: Prentice–Hall.

Forest, M. B., DePeretti, E., & Bertrand, J. (1976). Hypothalamic–pituitary–gonadal relationships in man from birth to puberty. *Clinical Endocrinology, 5,* 551–569.

Furstenberg, F. (1980). Burdens and benefits: The impact of early childbearing on the family. *Journal of Social Issues, 36*(1), 64–87.

Gagnon, J. H. (1983). Age at menarche and sexual conduct in adolescence and young adulthood. In S. Golub (Ed.), *Menarche* (pp. 175–185). Lexington, MA: Heath.

Goldberg, W. A., & Easterbrooks, M. A. (1984). The role of marital quality in toddler development. *Developmental Psychology, 20,* 504–514.

Grotevant, H. D., & Cooper, C. R. (1985). Patterns of interaction in family relationships and the development of identity exploration in adolescence. *Child Development, 56,* 415–428.

Guggenheim, M., & Sussman, A. (1985). *The rights of young people.* New York: Bantam.

Hamburg, B. (1974). Early adolescence: A specific and stressful stage of the life cycle. In G. Coelho, D. A. Hamburg, & J. E. Adams (Eds.), *Coping and adaption* (pp. 101–124). New York: Basic Books.

Hendricks, L. E., Howard, C. S., & Caesar, P. P. (1981). Help-seeking behavior among select populations of black unmarried adolescent fathers: Implications for human service agencies. *American Journal of Public Health, 71,* 733–735.

Hogan, D. (1981). *Transitions and social change: The early lives of American men.* New York: Academic Press.

Hopkins, J. R. (1983). *Adolescence: The transitional years.* New York: Academic Press.

Inhelder, B., & Piaget, J. (1958). *The growth of logical thinking from childhood to adolescence.* New York: Basic Books.

Jessor, S., & Jessor, R. (1975). Transition from virginity to nonvirginity among youth: A social-psychological study over time. *Developmental Psychology, 11,* 473–484.

Keating, D. P. (1980). Thinking processes in adolescence. In J. Adelson (Ed.), *Handbook of adolescent psychology* (pp. 211–246). New York: Wiley.

Kellam, S. G., Adams, R. G., Brown, C. H., & Ensminger, M. E. (1982). The long-term evolution of the family structure of teenage and older mothers. *Journal of Marriage and the Family, 44,* 539–554.

Kinsey, A. C., Pomeroy, W. B., & Martin, C. E. (1948). *Sexual behavior in the human male.* Philadelphia: Saunders.

Kinsey, A. C., Pomeroy, W. B., Martin, C. E., & Gebhard, P. H. (1953). *Sexual behavior in the human female.* Philadelphia: Saunders.

Lamb, M. E., & Easterbrooks, A. (1981). Individual differences in parental sensitivity: Origins, components, and consequences. In M. E. Lamb & L. R. Sherrod (Eds.), *Infant social cognition: Empirical and theoretical considerations* (pp. 127–153). Hillsdale, NJ: Lawrence Erlbaum Associates.

LaVoie, J. C. (1976). Ego identity formation in middle adolescence. *Journal of Youth and Adolescence, 5,* 371–385.

Lerner, R. M., & Spanier, G. B. (1980). *Adolescent development: A life-span perspective.* New York: McGraw–Hill.

Lloyd, J. A. (1975). Social behavior and hormones. In B. E. Eleftheriou & R. L. Sprott (Eds.), *Hormonal correlates of behavior: A life-span view* (pp. 185–204). New York: Plenum.

Lorenzi, M. E., Klerman, L. V., & Jekal, J. F. (1977). School age parents: How permanent a relationship. *Adolescence, 12,* 13–22.

Marcia, J. E. (1980). Identity in adolescence. In J. Adelson (Ed.), *Handbook of adolescent psychology* (pp. 159–187). New York: Wiley.

Marini, M. M. (1984). Age and sequencing norms in the transition to adulthood. *Social Forces, 63,* 229–244.

McAnarney, E. R., Lawrence, R. A., & Aten, M. J. (1979). Premature parenthood: A preliminary report of adolescent mother–infant interaction. *Pediatric Research, 13,* 328.

McEwen, B. S. (1976). Interactions between hormones and nerve tissue. *Scientific American, 235,* 48–58.

McKnight, J. W. (1982). Texas Family Code symposium: Husband and wife. *Texas Tech Law Review, 13,* 611–797.

Meilman, P. W. (1979). Cross-sectional age changes in ego identity during adolescence. *Developmental Psychology, 15,* 230–231.

Melton, G. B. (1983). Toward 'personhood' for adolescents. *American Psychologist, 38,* 99–103.

Miller, P. Y., & Simon, W. (1974). Adolescent sexual behavior: Context and change. *Social Problems, 22,* 58–76.

Modell, J., Furstenberg, F. F., & Hershberg, T. (1976). Social change and transitions to adulthood in historical perspective. *Journal of Family History, 1,* 7–32.

Montemayor, R. (in press). Developing autonomy: The transition of youth into adulthood. In G. K. Leigh & G. W. Peterson (Eds.), *Adolescence in a family context.* Cincinnati, OH: South-Western.

Moore, K. A., & Waite, L. (1981). Marital dissolution, early motherhood, and early marriage. *Social Forces, 60,* 20–40.

Neugarten, B. (1981). Age distinctions and their social functions. *Chicago–Kent Law Review, 57,* 809–825.

Neugarten, B. L., & Datan, N. (1973). Sociological perspectives on the life cycle. In P. B. Baltes & K. W. Schaie (Eds.), *Life-span developmental psychology: Personality and socialization.* New York: Academic Press.

Offer, D., Marcus, D., & Offer, J. L. (1970). A longitudinal study of normal adolescent boys. *American Journal of Psychiatry, 126,* 917–924.

Olweus, D., Mattsson, A., Schalling, D., & Low, H. (1980). Testosterone aggression, physical, and personality dimensions in normal adolescent males. *Psychosomatic Medicine, 42,* 253–269.

Orlofsky, J. L., Marcia, J. E., & Lesser, I. M. (1973). Ego identity status and the intimacy vs. isolation crisis of young adulthood. *Journal of Personality and Social Psychology, 27,* 211–219.

Petersen, A. C., & Taylor, B. (1980). The biological approach to adolescence: Biological change and psychological adaptation. In J. Adelson (Ed.), *Handbook of adolescent psychology* (pp. 117–155). New York: Wiley.

Petersen, A. C., Tobin-Richards, M., & Boxer, A. (1983). Puberty: Its measurement and its meaning. *Journal of Early Adolescence, 3,* 47–62.

Piaget, J. (1976). *The grasp of consciousness: Action and concept in the young child.* Cambridge, MA: Harvard University Press.

Podd, M. H. (1972). Ego identity status and morality: The relationship between two developmental constructs. *Developmental Psychology, 6,* 497–507.

Rogel, M. J., & Petersen, A. C. (1984). Some adolescent experiences of motherhood. In R. S. Cohen, B. J. Cohler, & S. H. Weissman (Eds.), *Parenthood* (pp. 85–102). New York: Guilford.

Rutter, M. (1980). *Changing youth in a changing society.* Cambridge, MA: Harvard University Press.

Santrock, J. W. (1981). *Adolescence: An introduction.* Dubuque, IA: William C. Brown.

Savin-Williams, R. C., & Montemayor, R. (in preparation). *A classification of primate adolescence: An ethological perspective.*

Siegler, R. S., & Liebert, R. M. (1975). Acquisition of formal scientific reasoning by 10- and 13-year-olds: Designing a factorial experiment. *Developmental Psychology, 10,* 401–402.

Steinberg, L. D. (1981). Transformation in family relations at puberty. *Developmental Psychology, 17,* 833–840.

Sternberg, R. J., & Powell, J. S. (1983). The development of intelligence. In J. H. Flavell & E. M. Markman (Eds.), *Handbook of child psychology* (Vol. 3, pp. 341–419). New York: Wiley.

Stodolsky, S. S. (1981). Age related changes in the individual: Childhood and adolescence. *Chicago–Kent Law Review, 57,* 851–857.

Susman, E. J., Nottelmann, E. D., Inoff, G. E., Dorn, L. D., Cutler, G. B., Loriaux, D. L., & Chrousos, G. P. (submitted). Timing of maturation: Social-emotional consequences of hormonal and physical developmental status for early adolescents. *Journal of Youth and Adolescence.*

Tanner, J. M. (1962). *Growth at adolescence.* Springfield, IL: Thomas.

Tanner, J. M. (1978). *Fetus into man.* Cambridge, MA: Harvard University Press.

Teachman, J. D., & Polonko, K. A. (1984). Out of sequence: The timing of marriage following a premarital birth. *Social Forces, 63,* 245–259.

White, K. M., Speisman, J. C., & Costos, D. (1983). Young adults and their parents: Individuation to mutuality. In H. D. Grotevant & C. R. Cooper (Eds.), *Adolescent development in the family* (pp. 61–76). San Francisco: Jossey–Bass.

White, K. M., Speisman, J. C., Costos, D., & Smith, A. (1985). *Relationship maturity: A conceptual and empirical approach.* Paper presented at the Third Biennial Conference on Adolescence Research, Tucson, AZ.

Winter, J. S. D. (1978). Prepubertal and pubertal endocrinology. In F. Falkner & J. M. Tanner (Eds.), *Human growth* (Vol. 2, pp. 183–213). New York: Plenum.

Zimring, F. E. (1982). *The changing legal world of adolescence.* New York: The Free Press.

2
Sex-Role Learning and Adolescent Fatherhood

Douglas M. Teti
Michael E. Lamb
University of Utah

Aside from the unpreparedness for the concrete demands of early parenthood, adolescent parents must contend with varied degrees of ability and willingness to care for their children. At a time when issues of identity formation are paramount, it is not surprising that adolescent parents frequently express feelings of unpreparedness for and inadequacy in the parental roles (Hendricks & Montgomery, 1983; Ross, 1982). Whereas adjustment to parenting is a central concern for adolescent mothers *and* fathers, fathers may have an especially difficult time. As a result, many adolescent males seem ambivalent (at best) about fatherhood. In this chapter, we suggest that the ambivalence manifest by adolescent fathers may be attributed in part to aspects of male sex-role development. We explore this issue and examine the ways in which sex-role learning might predispose adolescent males to avoid situations calling for behaviors like child care that are stereotypically feminine. In our culture, of course, fatherhood is defined by economic and emotional support more than by nurturant caretaking, and here, too, the developmental status of the adolescent limits his readiness for a parental role. These tendencies to avoid feminine behavior and attempt to embrace the masculine role may become exaggerated in adolescence as a result of identity struggles and peer-group pressures, and this may create a special dilemma for adolescent fathers.

We begin the chapter with a discussion of contemporary gender-related stereotypes, with emphasis on those relevant to adolescent fatherhood. We then discuss processes of sex-role learning, before turning to two issues of central concern: The devaluation of femininity and the emphasis on breadwinning as a key aspect of masculine success. Finally, we review evidence concerning the behavior and sex-roles of adolescent males.

SEX-ROLE STEREOTYPES IN CHILDREN

Children develop a sense of their gender and begin making generalizations about masculine and feminine roles as early as 2 to 3 years of age. Weinraub, Clemens, Sockloff, Ethridge, Gracely, and Myers (1984) demonstrated that children as young as 26 months reliably knew their own gender and showed a preference for sex-appropriate toys and an awareness of sex-role stereotypes. Young children's knowledge of masculine and feminine roles develops in part from observing males and females in the culture at large and appears to be part of a normal cognitive process (Martin & Halverson, 1981). It is not surprising, therefore, that children's sex-role stereotypes are patterned after cultural stereotypes (see review by Weinraub & Brown, 1983).

It is not our intention here to discuss the many gender-related stereotypes that abound in American culture. Instead, we focus on those that might influence the behavior of adolescent fathers. One such is the belief, held by adults and children of both sexes, that women are more nurturant, emotional, dependent, and accepting than males (Kagan, 1964; Matteson, 1975; Rosenberg & Sutton-Smith, 1972)—a belief, according to Kagan (1964), that is consistent with evidence obtained by observation and self-report of both males and females of many ages. Erikson (1968) has speculated that these differences may be biologically rooted in females' awareness of an inner body space, the womb, which predisposes females to a sense of "vital inner potential" (p. 275) and a tendency "to include, to accept, to hold on, and hold in" (p. 285). In similar vein, Parsons and Bales (1955) described females as *expressive* by virtue of their tendency to focus upon the emotions and feelings of other family members. Thus, females are expected to be home centered, accepting, nurturant, and closely attuned to the emotional dynamics among family members. Through various means, children internalize this stereotype as they piece together generalizations about the feminine role.

In contrast, the masculine stereotype emphasizes the affairs of the outside world. In Parsons' (1955) view, the externally and goal-oriented *instrumental* masculine role emphasizes social interaction only insofar as it serves as a means to an end (Johnson, 1963). The emphasis is not on nurturance and the preservation of emotive familial ties but on meeting the family's more concrete needs (such as those for shelter, food, and protection). Matteson (1975) notes that instrumentality is associated with strength (males are perceived by young children to be stronger and more powerful than females), rationality (as children get older, they perceive males as less emotional, more logical, and smarter than females), effectiveness (children consider males more worldly, skillful, and decisive than females), and cruelty (children tend to view males as less nurturant, more punitive, and more aggressive than females). Only on this last point do adult males' self-descriptions not agree with children's perceptions. Interestingly, stereotyped male traits are generally valued more highly than female traits by both sexes and at most ages (Broverman, Vogel, Broverman, Clarkson, & Rosenkrantz, 1972; Weinraub & Brown, 1983).

SEX-ROLE LEARNING IN MALES

What are the processes by which children learn these stereotypes and adapt their own behavior accordingly? Among several theories of sex-role development, the two that have received the most attention recently are the social-learning and cognitive-developmental theories. As explicated by Bandura and Walters (1963) and Mischel (1966), social-learning theory stresses environmental reinforcements, punishments, and modeling to account for the acquisition of gender identity and sex-typed behaviors. Children learn both their own gender and the sets of behaviors that are considered gender appropriate by being rewarded for sex-appropriate behaviors, punished for sex-inappropriate behaviors, and by observing their parents and other models in their environment. Parents and peers reinforce sex-appropriate activities and punish sex-inappropriate behavior in children as young as preschoolers (Lamb, Easterbrooks, & Holden, 1980; Lamb & Roopnarine, 1979; Langlois & Downs, 1980; see reviews by Huston, 1983, and Ruble, 1984). In addition, children observe an endless array of sex-stereotyped models portrayed in the media (Ruble, Balaban, & Cooper, 1981; Sternglanz & Serbin, 1974; see review by Weinraub & Brown, 1983).

On the other hand, cognitive-developmental theorists (Kohlberg, 1966; Kohlberg & Zigler, 1967) assign the child a much more active role. Gender identity is believed to involve a cognitive conclusion based on perceived physical differences between males and females. This conclusion is reached around 2 years of age and is linked with naturally and universally occurring trends in cognitive development. Gender identity is seen as the primary organizer of behavior and attitudes, motivating the young child to maintain self-consistency by seeking out gender-appropriate models and engaging in gender-appropriate activities. The organizing role played by cognitive processes of this sort is highlighted by the apparent universality and rigidity of sex-role stereotypes in young children (Kohlberg, 1966; Lee, 1976) and by investigations of the behavior and information-processing tendencies of children high or low in gender constancy and sex-role stereotypy (e.g., Cann & Newbern, 1984; List, Collins, & Westby, 1983; Martin & Halverson, 1983; Ruble et al., 1981; Smetana & Letourneau, 1984).

Although cognitive-developmental theorists believe that the child plays a more active role than do social-learning theorists, they still consider social-learning experiences to be important, especially in early childhood when gender identity is not yet fully established (Kohlberg, 1966). In addition, although self-categorizations serve as primary organizers of sex-typed information, exactly how children categorize information as "masculine" or "feminine" varies depending on how it is presented and who presents it. As Rosenberg and Sutton-Smith (1972) note: "Perhaps . . . we need to distinguish between sex-role typing or labeling . . . and the contents of this basic categorization which may change throughout a lifetime. The early categorizing does seem to be determining of whether one perceives oneself as boy or girl. What this means, however, can take a lifetime to decide" (p. 81).

BOYS AND THE DEVALUATION OF FEMININITY

There is some evidence that boys have more difficulty learning their sex role than girls. This has been related to the matricentric nature of the nuclear family, the relative unavailability of adult male models, and the tendency of adults to restrict and punish boys more than girls for cross-sex behavior. Because American family life is largely dominated by mothers, a number of theorists have followed Freud in assuming that both males and females initially identify with their mothers (Johnson, 1963; Lynn, 1961, 1966; Nash, 1965; Parsons & Bales, 1955). Gray and Klaus (1956), for example, found that, although male and female college students *perceived* their personalities to be more similar to that of their same-sexed than that of their opposite-sexed parent, females were actually more like their mothers than males were like their fathers. Indeed, males were as similar to their mothers as to their fathers, perhaps because an initial identification with mothers presaged many years of growing up under mothers' predominant influence and authority. This is underscored by evidence suggesting that fathers are not nearly as involved as mothers in child rearing, even when they have the opportunity and time to do so (Lamb, Pleck, Charnov, & Levine, 1985). Thus, whereas girls learn the feminine role through personal involvement with female role models, boys must define for themselves the essence of the male role by integrating bits of information provided largely by opposite-sexed adults. In addition, when fathers are available, they tend to punish cross-sex behavior in boys more harshly than in girls (Langlois & Downs, 1980; Lansky, 1967). As a result, boys are pressured more than girls to avoid sex-inappropriate activities, which in turn creates more stereotyping, less flexibility, and more anxiety about sex roles among boys than girls. Hartley (1959) neatly sums up the circumstances under which boys may learn about masculinity as

> practically a perfect combination for inducing anxiety—the demand that the child do something which is not clearly defined to him, based on reasons he cannot possibly appreciate, and enforced by threats, punishments, and anger by those who are close to him. Indeed, a great many boys do give evidence of anxiety centered in the whole area of sex-connected role behaviors, an anxiety which frequently expresses itself in overstraining to be masculine, in virtual panic at being caught

doing anything traditionally defined as feminine . . . This kind of overreaction is reminiscent of the quality of all strong emotion precipitated in life before judgement and control have had a chance to develop. (pp. 7–8)

As children grow older, the outside world replaces the family at the center of children's interests. In the traditional nuclear family, children see the outside world as the proper domain of the father, and this carries a special significance for boys. Lynn (1961) predicts that boys identify more and more strongly with the stereotyped male role as they progress in a society that values the masculine more than the feminine role, whereas girls' identification with the feminine role gradually weakens with age. Unfortunately, however, males' increased identification with the masculine role may be accompanied by feelings of hostility to and rejection of the feminine role (Lynn, 1966). This denigration has its roots in early childhood, as evidenced by children's (especially boys) tendency to assign less powerful, lower status occupations to females than males (Franks & Rothblum, 1983; Weinraub & Brown, 1983). This view is also supported by data demonstrating that preschool and elementary school-aged boys interact less with young babies and behave less nurturantly toward them than girls (Berman & Goodman, 1984; Berman, Smith, & Goodman, 1983; Blakemore, 1981; Frodi & Lamb, 1978).

Like Lynn (1961), Matteson (1975) relates males' rejection of the feminine role to the less-than-optimal conditions in which boys learn the masculine role. Boys are more likely than girls to be punished for cross-sex behavior, which means that boys are allowed much less freedom in the expression of sex-typed behaviors than girls. In addition, where boys are reared largely or exclusively by mothers, they may learn much of the masculine stereotype from adult females who restrict or punish cross-sex behavior. This in turn may lead to anxiety about femininity and hostility toward females. Matteson further suggests that the initial parental identification with mother is suppressed, not extinguished, so as boys indirectly learn the masculine role by dissociating themselves from the feminine role, they remain anxious lest behaviors associated with this initial feminine identification re-emerge. This reinforces the need to suppress any behaviors or feelings that might be considered feminine.

MASCULINITY AND THE BREADWINNER ROLE

The rejection of femininity by males develops alongside the notion that the primary masculine family role is to provide for the concrete, material needs of the family. Traditionally, family work has been sharply divided according to sex, with males as primary breadwinners and females relegated to domestic functions. This division had its origins in the nineteenth century, when women and children were gradually excluded from the labor force by labor unions' demands that men's wages be sufficient to support their families (see review by Pleck, 1983). Bernard (1981) estimates that the traditional male breadwinner role lasted from the 1830s until the late 1970s. As a result of this gender-based division of labor, work and the workplace became linked to the male role. Thus, the masculine breadwinning role became centered outside the home; the feminine or homemaking role became centered within the home, with little overlap between the two (Mason & Bumpass, 1975; Maxwell, 1976; Perrucci, Potter, & Rhoads, 1978; Pleck, 1983).

The breadwinning role has traditionally been considered one of the most important, if not *the* most important, measure of masculinity in American society. In a survey of college and noncollege youth in 1973, Yankelovich (1974) found that being a "good provider" was perceived as a central ingredient of masculinity in both groups. The provider role was also identified most frequently by middle-income black fathers in response to the questions, "What do you think it means to be a man today?" and "What is the most important thing you do for your children?" (Cazenave, 1979). From his study of middle-aged, middle-income fathers, Maxwell (1976) concluded, "There is nothing ambiguous or uncertain about what it means to be a father in middle-class America . . . Like an isolated beacon light, fatherhood seems to pulsate with a singular purpose—to provide for the family" (p. 387). Bernard (1981) points out that "traditional" women and their families of origin often assessed the worth of a potential husband and father not in terms of any expressive qualities but in terms of his potential to meet the future needs of the family. Expressivity, tenderness, and the like were nonessentials in the nuptial agreement; if present, these were "merely icing on the cake."

In this context, men may tend to view their success in providing for the family as the most important index of their manhood and as the most direct way of garnering status and respect from family, peers, and community (Bernard, 1981; Brenton, 1966; Komarovsky, 1940). This view is reinforced by Hollywood moguls and the American media, who have popularized again and again the myth that wealth and success enhances sexiness and virility (Gould, 1973). The intimate link between breadwinning and masculinity is poignantly illustrated by the profound loss of self-esteem and family status experienced by unemployed men and their families. As one wife related in Komarovsky's (1940) study of unemployed men, "I still love him, but he doesn't seem as 'big' a man."

The association between breadwinning and masculinity may be especially strong in males who grow up in matriarchial families in which fathers assume traditional instrumental roles. Even when both parents share the breadwinning role, however, family status is often determined primarily by the father's occupational status (Poloma & Garland, 1971). It is quite likely that most males, whether from traditional families or not, learn that holding a job and providing for the family's needs are core features of masculinity.

SEX-ROLE BEHAVIOR IN ADOLESCENT MALES

The consequences of these lessons about masculinity and femininity may become especially evident in adolescence, during which males and females struggle with, among other things, bodily changes accompanying sexual maturation, identity formation, the achievement of autonomy from parents, and the establishment of mature heterosexual and homosexual relationships. Peers may provide stability and support during a time of newly emerging sexuality and conflicting role choices (Erikson, 1968) and thus may play a special role in shaping and maintaining sex roles. For many adolescents, self-esteem is strongly related to the esteem bestowed by the peer group: Indeed, adolescents' involvement in the peer group is motivated in part by the desire to be judged favorably by peers (Burlingame, 1970).

The tendency on the part of males to embrace the stereotyped male sex role and devalue the feminine may be exacerbated in adolescence by pressures to conform to peer-sanctioned sex-role stereotypes, which are especially rigid during adolescence (e.g., Adams, 1973; McCandless, 1970; Urberg & Labouvie-Vief, 1976). This in turn may create problems with respect to males' response to parenthood. For males in particular, self-esteem and peer-group status may require proving their "masculinity," because, unlike girls, boys may not have had the benefit of a close relationship with a same-sexed adult model. As a result, they enter adolescence with an incomplete and stereotyped perception of what it means to be a male, which in turn may foster an overreliance on peers for clarification about masculinity and gender-appropriate behavior. As Hartley (1959) points out, however, the peer group may simply reinforce existing stereotypes, as many adolescent males have learned about sex roles in very similar ways. Thus, male adolescents tend to value activities that are stereotypically "macho" (e.g., drinking, male-dominated sports, sexual prowess with girls, etc.). Gray (1957) found that boys who were highly esteemed by their peers were characterized by a high degree of peer-sanctioned sex-typed behaviors, and both Lamke (1982) and Massad (1981) found significant relationships between adolescent males' self-rated masculinity and measures of self- and peer acceptance. Interestingly, these same investigations found masculine traits (alone or in conjunction with feminine traits) to be important for adolescent females' self-esteem and self-acceptance as well.

The rigidity of sex typing in adolescent males is also evident in their responses to infants. Both Nash and Feldman (1981) and Frodi and Lamb (1978) reported that 14–15 year-old males were more likely than females to ignore social bids by infants. In addition, when asked to choose their favorite pictures from a variety of different photographs, male adolescents chose fewer baby pictures than females did (Nash & Feldman, 1981). Interestingly, these sex differences disappeared in older adolescents (18–19 years old). These data suggest that the tendency to avoid female-typed behavior and embrace peer-sanctioned "macho" activities may become especially pronounced in early-to-mid-adolescence as a defense against the uncertainties of sexual maturation and identity formation. As these uncertainties are resolved, males may broaden their conception of the male sex role and become less threatened by expressions of stereotypically feminine behavior.

The ambivalence toward parenthood among adolescent fathers may also be influenced by the drive to establish autonomy that typifies the adolescent years. Partially breaking away from parents and achieving a sense of independence are important developmental milestones on the road to adulthood for both males and females (Santrock, 1981; Steinberg, 1985). However, the quest for autonomy may be especially salient in males. Unlike females, males are given less parental supervision and are encouraged to be independent from a very early age (see reviews by Huston, 1983 and Ruble, 1984). Males are also expected to be more independent and assertive than females—at all ages. Thus the drive to establish independence not only from parents but also from any long-term dependent relationships may be a more salient issue for adolescent males than for adolescent females, making adolescent fatherhood a serious impediment to the achievement of autonomy. Although males in American society learn that breadwinning is a core aspect of the male role, many adolescents may be unprepared and unwilling to relinquish their emergent independence by acquiescing to demands that they assume responsibility for their partners and children. As Platts (1968) indicates, this particular attitude toward fathers was typical of many social agencies until fairly recently. For some adolescent males, the assumption of parental responsibilities is perceived to involve knuckling under to parental or societal control at a time when achieving autonomy from such control is a paramount goal. This tendency may be especially prevalent in adolescents whose parents have adopted an overly strict child-rearing mode, which may foster rebellion against adult authority, or in adolescents with overly permissive parents, which may cultivate a detachment from parents and an overreliance on peers (Steinberg, 1985).

Another determinant of the response to fatherhood among adolescent males may be their limited ability to provide successfully for the mother and baby. As indicated previously, the ability to provide for the family is one of the most important indices of masculinity in American society. However, both Steinberg (1984) and Lewin-Epstein (1981) report that adolescents' jobs typically require little skill, provide minimal opportunities for advancement, and pay at the lowest end of the wage scale. According to Lewis-Epstein, 53% of male high school sophomores in 1980 were employed as food service employees, manual laborers, store clerks, babysitters, clerks, or at "odd" jobs. Another 30% placed their jobs in the "other" category, and about 11% did farm work. Only 7% were employed in skilled trade jobs. The mean wage for sophomore males was $3.02 per hour, with one-third of them earning less than $2.90 per hour. Very similar statistics were reported for male high school seniors. It is not surprising that many adolescent males may wish to escape the responsibilities of fatherhood rather than deal with emasculating job prospects.

CONCLUSION

For many adolescents, parenthood comes at a time when they are still struggling with bodily changes, sex-role identity, personal independence, and conflicting choices regarding values, roles, and vocations. The inadequacy and unpreparedness reported by adolescent parents is not surprising, considering that parenthood may force an accelerated and unexpected transition into adulthood world (see review by Russell, 1980). For males in particular, however, this transition may be especially difficult. A sex-role learning history that devalues women and femininity while reinforcing male sex-role stereotypes may leave males not just unprepared, but contraprepared to assume parental roles. These tendencies may become especially prevalent during adolescence, when adherence to male sex-role stereotypes serves as a defense against the insecurities of sex-role identity. As such, adolescent males about to enter fatherhood may have difficulty establishing warm, affectionate relationships with partners and children. In addition, although breadwinning may be viewed as an important aspect of masculine performance, the acceptance of parenthood by adolescent males may be further muted by the perception that fatherhood will impede their growing independence from adult authority or will force them into emasculating, dead-end jobs. As a result, many adolescent males may avoid further contact with their partners or put less effort into maintaining their relationships, even after marriage.

As societal values change, it is reasonable to expect some changes in the circumstances under which boys and girls are socialized. In the last decade, we have witnessed a gradual decline in the number of ''traditional'' families and a substantial increase in the numbers of single-parented and dual-earner families (Lamb, 1982a). Mothers now share the breadwinning role with fathers in about 80% of American households (Pleck & Rustad, 1981), perhaps in response to economic pressures and to attitudinal changes regarding women's rights. Concomitant with these changes, paternal involvement in child rearing appears to be expanding somewhat, although fathers' level of involvement still falls short of mothers' (Lamb et al., 1985). Recent research suggests that children whose mothers are employed and/or whose fathers are at least moderately involved in child rearing tend to hold less stereotyped attitudes about sex roles (Lamb, 1982b; Radin, 1982). For boys, paternal nurturance may be an especially important ingredient in the development of flexibility in sex-role attitudes. Hetherington, Cox, and Cox (1982) found high androgyny in boys when their fathers were dominant yet emotionally expressive toward their sons and spouses. This supports the notion that boys who grow up with nurturant fathers are less rigid and stereotyped in their conception of the male sex role and may be more open to expressions of tenderness. Unfortunately, no one has yet studied the differential response to fatherhood of adolescent males' raised in such nontraditional families.

REFERENCES

Adams, J. F. (1973). *Understanding adolescence.* Boston: Allyn & Bacon.

Bandura, A., & Walters, R. H. (1983). *Social learning and personality development.* New York: Holt, Rinehart, & Winston.

Berman, P. W., & Goodman, V. (1984). Age and sex differences in children's responses to babies: Effects of adults' caretaking requests and instructions. *Child Development, 55,* 1071–1077.

Berman, P. W., Smith, V. L., & Goodman, V. (1983). Development of sex differences in response to an infant and to the caretaker role. *Journal of Genetic Psychology, 143,* 283–284.

Bernard, J. (1981). The good-provider role: Its rise and fall. *American Psychologist, 36*(1), 1–12.

Blakemore, J. E. O. (1981). Age and sex differences in interaction with a human infant. *Child Development, 52,* 386–388.

Brenton, M. (1966). *The American male.* New York: Coward–McCann.

Broverman, I. K., Vogel, S. R., Broverman, D. M., Clarkson, F. E., & Rosenkrantz, P. S. (1972). Sex-role stereotypes: A current appraisal. *Journal of Social Issues, 28*(2), 59–78.

Burlingame, W. V. (1970). The youth culture. In E. D. Evans (Ed.), *Adolescents: Readings in behavior and development.* New York: The Dryden Press.

Cann, A., & Newbern, S. R. (1984). Sex stereotype effects in children's picture recognition. *Child Development, 55,* 1085–1090.

Cazenave, N. A. (1979). Middle-income black fathers: An analysis of the provider role. *The Family Coordinator, 28,* 583–593.

Erikson, E. H. (1968). *Identity: Youth and crisis.* New York: W. W. Norton.

Franks, V., & Rothblum, E. D. (Eds.). (1983). *The stereotyping of women: Its effects on mental health.* New York: Springer.

Frodi, A. M., & Lamb, M. E. (1978). Sex differences in responsiveness to infants: A developmental study of psychophysiological and behavioral responses. *Child Development, 49,* 1182–1888.

Gould, R. E. (1973, June). Measuring masculinity by the size of a paycheck. *Ms.,* 18FF.

Gray, S. W. (1957). Masculinity–femininity in relation to anxiety and social acceptance. *Child Development, 28*(2), 203–214.

Gray, S. W., & Klaus, R. (1956). The asessment of parental identification. *Genetic Psychology Monographs, 54,* 87–114.

Hartley, R. E. (1959). Sex-role pressures in the socialization of the male child. *Psychological Reports, 5,* 457–468.

Hendricks, L. E., & Montgomery, T. (1983). A limited population of unmarried adolescent fathers: A preliminary report of their views on fatherhood and the relationship with the mothers of their children. *Adolescence, 18,* 201–210.

Hetherington, E. M., Cox, M., & Cox, R. (1982). Effects of divorce on parents and children. In M. E. Lamb (Ed.), *Nontraditional families.* Hillsdale, NJ: Lawrence Erlbaum Associates.

Huston, A. C. (1983). Sex-typing. In P. H. Mussen (Ed.), *Handbook of child psychology, Vol. IV: Socialization, personality, and social development.* New York: Wiley.

Johnson, M. M. (1963). Sex-role learning in the nuclear family. *Child Development, 34,* 319–333.

Kagan, J. (1964). Acquisition and significance of sex typing and sex-role identity. In M. L. Hoffman & L. W. Hoffman (Eds.), *Review of child development research* (Vol. 1, pp. 137–167). New York: Russell Sage Foundation.

Kohlberg, L. (1966). A cognitive-developmental analysis of children's sex-role concepts and at-titudes. In E. E. Maccoby (Ed.), *The development of sex differences* (pp. 82–173). Stanford: Stanford University Press.

Kohlberg, L., & Zigler, E. (1967). The impact of cognitive maturity on the development of sex-role attitudes in the years 4 to 8. *Genetic Psychology Monographs, 75,* 89–165.

Komarovsky, M. (1940. *The unemployed man and his family.* New York: Dryden Press.

Lamb, M. E. (1982a). Maternal employment and child development: A review. In M. E. Lamb (Ed.), *Nontraditional families: Parenting and child development* (pp. 45–69). Hillsdale, NJ: Lawrence Erlbaum Associates.

Lamb, M. E. (Ed.). (1982b). *Nontraditional families: Parenting and child development.* Hillsdale, NJ: Lawrence Erlbaum Associates.

Lamb, M. E., Easterbrooks, M. A., & Holden, G. W. (1980). Reinforcement and punishment among preschoolers: Characteristics, effects, and correlates. *Child Development, 51,* 1230–1236.

Lamb, M. E., Pleck, J. H., Charnov, E. L., & Levine, J. A. (1985). A biosocial perspective on paternal behavior and involvement. In J. B. Lancaster, J. Altmann, A. Rossi, & L. R. Sherrod (Eds.), *Parenting across the lifespan: Biosocial perspectives.* Chicago: Aldine, in press.

Lamb, M. E., & Roopnarine, J. L. (1979). Peer influences on sex-role development in pre-schoolers. *Child Development, 50,* 1219–1222.

Lamke, L. K. (1982). The impact of sex-role orientation on self-esteem in early adolescence. *Child Development, 53,* 1530–1535.

Langlois, J. H., & Downs, A. C. (1980). Mothers, fathers, and peers as socialization agents of sex-typed play behaviors in young children. *Child Development, 51,* 1237–1247.

Lansky, L. M. (1967). The family structure also affects the model: Sex-role attitudes in parents of preschool children. *Merrill–Palmer Quarterly of Behavior and Development, 13,* 139–150.

Lee, P. C. (1976). Psychology and sex differences. In P. C. Lee & R. S. Stewart (Eds.), *Sex differences* (pp. 359–370). New York: Urizen Books.

Lewin-Epstein, N. (1981). *Youth employment during high school* (Contract No. OE-300-78-0208). Washington, DC: National Center for Education Statistics.

List, J. A., Collins, W. A., & Westby, S. D. (1983). Comprehension and inferences from tradi-tional and nontraditional sex-role portrayals on television. *Child Development, 54,* 1579–1587.

Lynn, D. B. (1961). Sex differences in identification development. *Sociometry, 24,* 372–383.

Lynn, D. B. (1966). The process of learning parental and sex-role identification. *Journal of Mar-riage and the Family, 28*(4), 466–470.

Martin, C. L., & Halverson, C. F., Jr. (1981). A schematic processing model of sex-typing and stereotyping in children. *Child Development, 52,* 1119–1134.

Martin, C. L., & Halverson, C. F., Jr. (1983). The effects of sex-typing schemas on young children's memory. *Child Development, 54,* 563–574.

Mason, K. O., & Bumpass, L. L. (1975). U.S. women's sex-role ideology, 1970. *American Journal of Sociology, 80*(5), 1212–1219.

Massad, C. M. (1981). Sex-role identity and adjustment during adolescence. *Child Development, 52,* 1290–1298.

Matteson, D. R. (1975). *Adolescence today: Sex roles and the search for identity.* Homewood, IL: Dorsey Press.

Maxwell, J. W. (1976). The keeping fathers of America. *The Family Coordinator, 25,* 387–392.

McCandless, B. R. (1970). *Adolescents: Behavior and Development.* Hinsdale, IL. Dryden Press.

Mischel, M. (1966). A social-learning view of sex differences in behavior. In E. E. Maccoby (Ed.), *The development of sex differences* (pp. 56–81). Stanford: Stanford University Press.

Nash, J. (1965). The father in contemporary culture and current psychological literature. *Child Development, 36*(1), 261–297.

Nash, S. C., & Feldman, S. S. (1981). Sex-role and sex-related attributions: Constancy and change across the family life cycle. In M. E. Lamb & A. L. Brown (Eds.), *Advances in developmental psychology* (Vol. 1). Hillsdale, NJ: Lawrence Erlbaum Associates.

Parsons, T., & Bales, R. F. (1955). *Family, socialization, and interaction process.* Glencoe, IL: The Free Press.

Perrucci, C. C., Potter, H. R., & Rhoads, D. L. (1978). Determinants of male family-role performance. *Psychology of Women Quarterly, 3*(1), 53–66.

Platts, H. K. (1968). A public adoption agency approach to natural fathers. *Child Welfare, 47,* 530–537, 553.

Pleck, J. H. (1983). Husbands' paid work and family roles. In H. Lopata & J. H. Pleck (Eds.), *Research in the interweave of social roles, Vol. 3: Families and jobs.* Greenwich, CT: JAI Press.

Pleck, J., & Rustad, M. (1981). *Wives employment, role demands, and adjustment: Final report.* Unpublished manuscript, Wellesley College Center for Research on Women.

Poloma, M. M., & Garland, T. N. (1971). The married professional woman: A study in the tolerance of domestication. *Journal of Marriage and the Family, 33,* 531–540.

Radin, N. (1982). Primary caregiving and role-sharing fathers. In M. E. Lamb (Ed.), *Nontraditional families.* Hillsdale, NJ: Lawrence Erlbaum Associates.

Rosenberg, B. G., & Sutton-Smith, B. (1972). *Sex and identity.* New York: Holt, Rinehart, & Winston.

Ross, A. (1982). *Teenage mothers, teenage fathers.* Toronto: Personal Library.

Ruble, D. N. (1984). Sex-role development. In M. H. Bornstein & M. E. Lamb (Eds.), *Developmental psychology: An advanced textbook.* Hillsdale, NJ: Lawrence Erlbaum Associates.

Ruble, D. N., Balaban, T., & Cooper, J. (1981). Gender constancy and the effects of sex-typed televised toy commercials. *Child Development, 52,* 667–673.

Russell, C. S. (1980). Unscheduled parenthood: Transition to "parent" for the teenager. *Journal of Social Issues, 36*(1), 45–63.

Santrock, J. W. (1981). *Adolescence.* Dubuque, IA: Wm. C. Brown.

Smetana, J. G., & Letourneau, K. J. (1984). Development of gender constancy and children's sex-typed free play behavior. *Developmental Psychology, 20*(4), 691–696.

Steinberg, L. (1984). The varieties and effects of work during adolescence. In M. E. Lamb, A. L. Brown, & B. Rogoff (Eds.), *Advances in developmental psychology* (Vol. 3). Hillsdale, NJ: Lawrence Erlbaum Associates.

Steinberg, L. (1985). *Adolescence.* New York: Knopf.

Sternglanz, S. H., & Serbin, L. A. (1974). Sex-role stereotyping in children's television programs. *Developmental Psychology, 10*(5), 710–715.

Urberg, K. A., & Labouvie-Vief, G. (1976). Conceptualization of sex roles: A life-span developmental study. *Developmental Psychology, 12*(1), 15–23.

Weinraub, M., & Brown, L. M. (1983). The development of sex-role stereotypes in children: Crushing realities. In V. Franks & E. D. Rothblum (Eds.), *The stereotyping of women: Its effects on mental health.* New York: Springer.

Weinraub, M., Clemens, L. P., Sockloff, A., Ethridge, T., Gracely, E., & Myers, B. (1984). The development of sex role stereotypes in the third year: Relationships to gender labeling, gender identity, sex-typed toy preference, and family characteristics. *Child Development, 55,* 1493–1503.

Yankelovich, D. (1974). *The new morality.* New York: McGraw–Hill.

3 Risking Paternity: Sex and Contraception among Adolescent Males

Freya L. Sonenstein
The Urban Institute
Washington, D.C. 20037

During the past decade there has been increasing public recognition that teenage childbearing is associated with reduced life chances for individual mothers and children and with substantial government expenditures for welfare, health care, and basic social supports. The evidence supporting these conclusions has accumulated in numerous research studies documenting the extent of the problem, its causes and consequences (Chilman, 1983; Moore & Burt, 1982). This research has, however, focused primarily on adolescent females. Whereas adolescent males are obviously an important factor in adolescent fertility behavior, surprisingly little research has documented or sought explanations for patterns of sexual activity, contraceptive utilization, or pregnancy resolution behavior among adolescent males. Similarly service interventions have largely ignored the male partners of adolescent girls.

Other chapters in this volume focus on adolescent males after parenthood is an accomplished fact. This chapter describes the state of current knowledge about the incidence of adolescent fatherhood and the conditions leading up to this status. Research findings about sexual activity and contraceptive utlization among adolescent males are reviewed to identify factors associated with the early onset of sexual activity and the nonuse of contraceptives. In addition potential intervention approaches designed to reduce adolescent pregnancy by involving male partners are discussed.

EVIDENCE ABOUT THE INCIDENCE OF ADOLESCENT FATHERHOOD

The most remarkable fact about the research literature on male adolescent fertility behavior is that there is so little of it compared to the literature on female fertility. Although teenage pregnancy and childbearing is recognized as a pressing social problem and considerable research has been conducted on the fertility behavior of teenage girls, the male role in this process has not received much research attention. Even basic descriptive data are missing. There are few reliable national data on rates of sexual activity or contraceptive utilization among adolescent males, nor on the incidence of pregnancies and births attributable to them.

For instance, although there were over half a million births to females between the ages of 15 and 19 in 1981 (National Center for Health Statistics [NCHS], 1983), it is not definitively known how many of these babies were fathered by teenagers. Largely as a result of the high incidence of out-of-wedlock births, the age of the father is not listed on the birth registration forms for almost one-third (32%) of these births. As a result, the nation's vital statistics data system, the major source of information about the incidence of births to adolescent females, cannot generate comparable information for adolescent males. In 1981, the vital statistics did indicate that 45% of all babies born to teenage women were fathered by men between the ages of 20 and 29 years of age, and men over 29 accounted for another 2% of the births. In only 19% of the cases were fathers recorded as being 15- to 19-years-old (NCHS, 1983). Whereas the proportion of births with no age of father listed is quite large, these data show that the incidence of adolescent fatherhood is not as extensive as the incidence of adolescent motherhood. At least 47% percent of the babies born to females between 15 and 19 years of age have fathers that are 20 years old or older.

These overall statistics mask large racial differences. Among white female adolescents (15-19 years-old) bearing children in 1981, 55% of the babies were fathered by males who were out of their teens, 22% were fathered by teenage males (15-19 years old) and 22% had no stated father's age. Among comparable black women 26% of the babies were fathered by men out of their teens, 14% were fathered by teenagers, and a full 60% did not have an age of father registered. There is no way to determine how many of the fathers with no age designation were actually teenagers, although one suspects that teenagers are overrepresented among these cases. However, over half the babies of white teenage mothers and one quarter of the babies of black teenager mothers were known not to have teenage fathers in 1981 (NCHS, 1983). Clearly the partners of adolescent mothers are not always adolescent males.

In 1981 there were 129,336 babies born to fathers who were registered as under 20 years of age (NCHS, 1983) and there were probably many more teenage fathers for the babies whose fathers' ages were not stated on the birth registration form. Until quite recently no data other than vital statistics were available to describe the fertility patterns of adolescent men. However, a national longitudinal study of over 12,000 youth ages 14 to 21 in 1979 when the survey began (the NLS) has asked both male and female respondents about their birth histories (Mott, 1983). In 1982 the cumulative rates of first births were 2% among 18-year-old men, 4% for 19-year-olds and 7% for 20-year-olds. These rates are clearly lower than birth rates for like-aged women; 9.5% of the 18-year-old women and 15.5% of 19-year-old women reported first births.

Birth rates among the men varied by race and ethnicity. Among 18-year-olds only .9% of white men had first births compared to 3.5% for Hispanics and 6.3% for blacks. By age 19, 11.8% of black males were reporting births compared to 2.5% of whites and 6.3% of Hispanics.

Whereas these data are the best available, Mott (1983) reports that almost half of all the fathers in the sample had at least one discrepancy in their retrospective birth reports when these were compared to information provided in earlier surveys. An important reason for these discrepancies was the high proportion of fathers not living with their children, a situation suspected to generate less awareness about specific birth dates. In addition a substantial proportion (25%) of men not living with their children reported children in 1982 whom they had not acknowledged in earlier surveys. Even men living with their children were not as accurate about reporting birth histories as the women were. Because more children have appeared in the male sample as time has passed, further increases in the number of reported children might be expected in later survey years. In addition an unknown proportion of the men may be unaware of children that they have fathered. Consequently the birth rates for teenage men reported for the 1982 NLS survey may be conservative.

Because no other nationally representative data have been published describing the teenage men who bear children, we must look to the research literature on sexual activity and contraceptive use among teenagers to develop a profile of the likely characteristics of teenage fathers. If a profile of adolescent males likely to engage in early sexual activity without using contraceptives can be generated, then we will be closer to describing those adolescents at risk of becoming fathers. Because 40% of teen pregnancies resulted in abortions in 1980 (Henshaw & O'Reilly, 1983), this approach is far from perfect. However, it must suffice until better data are available.

EVIDENCE ABOUT SEXUAL ACTIVITY AMONG ADOLESCENT MALES

Whereas the dramatic 10-year rise in the proportion of adolescent women experiencing coitus has been documented in detail (Baldwin, 1976; Chilman, 1983; Zelnik & Kantner, 1980), the data on the rates of sexual activity among adolescent males are significantly less complete. For a nationally representative sample of women, Zelnik and Kantner (1980) report a two-thirds increase—from 30 to 50%—in the proportion of metropolitan women ages 15 through 19 who have ever had coitus between 1971 and 1979. Among 15-year-olds, the proportion rose from 11 to 18% for white females and from 31 to 41% for black females.

Comparable data on recent trends in the sexual activity for young men are simply not available. In 1979 the first nationally representative sample of males ages 17 through 21 was surveyed as a counterpart to the national survey of young women. For the first time reliable national data on the incidence of sexual

TABLE 3.1
Percentage of Never-Married Metropolitan Women and Men Ages 17-19 Years
in 1979 Who Have Ever Had Intercourse by Race

Age	Total		White		Black	
	Males	Females	Males	Females	Males	Females
17	55.7	48.5	54.5	44.1	60.3	73.3
18	66.0	56.9	63.6	52.6	79.8	76.3
19	77.5	69.0	77.1	64.9	79.9	88.5

Source: Tables 1 and 2, Zelnik & Kantner, 1980.

intercourse among young men were available. That year 56% of never-married metropolitan 17-year-old men had experienced intercourse as had 66% of 18-year-olds and 77.5% of 19-year-olds (Zelnik & Kantner, 1980).

Table 3.1 provides the percentage with coital experience for men and women by age and race. These data show that although more black women are likely to have had intercourse than their white counterparts, similar differentials between black and white males are not as marked. Among white respondents, males are more likely to have had intercourse than females of the same age; in general among black respondents, females are more likely to have had intercourse than males. The percentage point differences between the sexes are not very large and never more than 13 points.

Although these data present the first nationally representative picture of the incidence of coitus among unmarried male teenagers, the absence of earlier comparable data sets and the exclusion of males under age 17 from the sample limit its utility. Although it is known that proportionately more young women were sexually active in 1979 than in 1970, these comparisons cannot be reliably constructed for adolescent males. In looking at trends in sexual activity some observers have speculated that male adolescents' involvement in sexual intercourse has not changed much since Kinsey and his colleagues collected their data in the 1940s (Diepold & Young, 1979). Others have noted a decline in the proportion of male teens who are sexually active since the Kinsey survey (Miller & Simon, 1974). Yet another researcher reports an increase in nonmarital intercourse rates among white males between 1967 and 1974 (Chilman, 1983). The paucity of data makes it extremely difficult to determine what the trends in male adolescent sexual behavior have been over the past four decades. There is general consensus, however, that the adolescent female rates of coitus have increased and that the male and female adolescent rates of participation in sexual intercourse are converging.

Although there are no nationally representative data on the rates of engagement in sexual activity for males under age 17, there have been a number of scattered studies of sexual behavior, most conducted in specific localities, that have included younger male adolescents as respondents (Chilman, 1983; Diepold & Young, 1979). Table 3.2 lists these studies' findings about the proportion of

15-year-old males who have had premarital coitus. The findings for 17-year-old males are also included because national data for 1979 are available for this group (Zelnik & Kantner, 1980). The table shows that there is no consistent pattern over time or from place to place on reported sexual activity for 15 year-old males. As few as 8% and as many as 89% of 15-year-old males are reported to have had intercourse. The differences undoubtedly reflect variations in meth-

TABLE 3.2
The Findings of Selected Studies Regarding the Percentage of
Adolescent Males Who Have Had Intercourse by Ages 15 and 17

	Age	
Studies Published Since 1970	15 Years	17 Years
Vener, Stewart, & Hager (1972) 3 Michigan communities in 1969 Professional (N = 611) Socioeconomically mixed (N = 989) Blue collar (N = 531)	19 26 25	31 38 31
Vener & Stewart (1974) Resurvey of socioeconomically mixed Michigan community in 1973 (N = 937)	38	34
Sorenson (1973) Nationally representative cluster sample, 1972 (N = 214)	40	55
Miller & Simon (1974) Random sample of Illinois youth in 1969 (N = 990)	8	21[a]
Finkel & Finkel (1975) Three high schools in northeast city (N = 421) White Black Hispanic	 36 79 69	 48[a] 84[a] 75[a]
Jessor & Jessor (1975) Random samples of students in a Rocky Mountain city (N = 186)	21[b]	33[c]
Ross (1979) Availability sample of New York City youth (N = 304)	83	81
Zelnik & Kantner (1980) Nationally representative sample of metropolitan youth in 1979 (N = 843) White Black	 -- --	 54 60
Clark, Zabin, & Hardy (1984) Two inner city, black schools in Baltimore in 1983 (N = 336)	89	

Sources: Table 5, Diepold & Young (1979) and Table 5.1, Chilman (1983).

[a] 16- and 17-year-olds

[b] 10th grade

[c] 12th grade

odology, sample composition and geographic location among the studies, and it is difficult to pinpoint which are the most important sources of variation.

Although conclusions about the typical sexual behavior of U.S. teenage males cannot be drawn from these studies, those that have found high rates of sexual activity among the 15-year-olds are of special interest (Finkel & Finkel, 1975; Ross, 1979; Zabin, Hirsch, Smith, & Hardy, 1984). These studies demonstrate that there are schools especially in some inner cities where most of the males become sexually initiated at early ages. Finkel and Finkel (1975), for instance, report that the males in their northeast city high school sample initiated coitus at a mean age of 12.8 years. Clark, Zabin, and Hardy (1984) report a mean age of 11.8 for black male students in a Baltimore high school and a junior high school. Billy and Udry (personal communication) have communicated their difficulty in studying the sexual initiation of black males because approximately 80% of the seventh graders in their southern city junior high school sample were already sexually active.

National data indicate higher mean ages of first intercourse than these individual city samples. The mean age of first coitus for white males, 17–21 years old in 1979, was 15.9 years; the mean age for black males was more than 1 year younger—14.4 years (Zelnik & Shah, 1983). Clearly the average black teenage male initiates intercourse at an earlier age than a white male. Sexually active women (15–19 years old) reported older ages at first intercourse than the men. The mean age of first intercourse was 16.4 years for white women and 15.5 for black women.

Both male and female teenagers tend to have their first sexual experience with partners older than themselves (Ross, 1979; Zelnik & Shah, 1983). The male partners of both black and white females are on average 3 years older; the female partners of both black and white males are 1 year older (Zelnik & Shah, 1983). The pattern among women is consistent with the finding reported earlier that almost half the babies born to teenage mothers are fathered by men out of their teens.

Other Determinants of Sexual Activity

Although studies indicate that teenagers engage in sexual activity earlier if they are male, and if they are black, there are also a number of other factors associated with the early initiation of sexual activity among adolescents (Chilman, 1983; Moore & Burt, 1982). Some of these factors appear to affect both sexes in the same way, others operate differentially for males and females. Among the factors that have been found to be associated with earlier initiation for both sexes are: less religiosity (Chilman, 1983; Devaney, & Hubley 1981; Moore & Caldwell, 1976; Mott, 1983); lower educational achievement and goals (Devaney & Hubley 1981; Jessor & Jessor, 1975; Miller & Simon, 1974; Mott, 1983); more frequent dating, going steady, or being in love (Chilman, 1983; Delameter &

MacCorquodale, 1979; Sorenson, 1973); and earlier onset of biological puberty (Billy & Udry, 1983; Diepold & Young, 1979; Zelnik, Kantner, & Ford, 1981).

Whereas early pubertal development is associated with early sexual activity, Hofferth (forthcoming) points out that there are probably distinct differences between white and black males in the influence of maturation on the timing of sexual intercourse. For white adolescent males, pubertal development is a very strong predictor of sexual activity; and recent evidence from the work of Billy, Morris, Groff, and Udry (1984) indicates that hormone levels may be the reason for this strong relationship. In contrast, among black males the relationship between pubertal development and sexual activity is weak. Indeed, a large portion of black males initiate intercourse prior to puberty (Westney, Jenkins, & Benjamin, 1983; Zabin, Street, & Hardy, 1983). Hofferth suggests that social influences may be more important in explaining sexual activity among black males than among white males; however, she cautions that social factors are undoubtedly also important in mediating the effects of maturation for white males.

Early premarital sexual activity is associated with low-income status in general, and the association is even stronger when low-income status is associated with being black. Chilman (1983) discusses the interconnectedness of racism, poverty, and the lack of educational attainment in generating high rates of premarital sexual intercourse among black teenagers. Yet another associated factor is living in single parent families. Adolescents from families headed by a single parent are more likely to initiate sex early (Moore & Caldwell, 1976; Ross, 1979; Zelnik, Kantner, & Ford, 1981) and these families are more likely to be poor (Ross & Sawhill, 1975). In addition black families of adolescents are more likely to be headed by single parents.

Few studies have attempted to disentangle the interrelated effects of race, income, single-parent family status, and educational goals and achievement in explaining early sexual initiation. Mott (1983) reports preliminary results from a regression of a sexual activity variable on race, ethnicity, and poverty status as well as a number of other important predictor variables. In his national sample of young men and women he found that "even after controlling for various socioeconomic factors in the model, black male and female respondents have above average levels of sexual activity." Ross (1979) found that coming from a single-parent family had an effect on sexual activity independent of the income and employment status of the parent in a sample of teenagers from New York City.

Moore, Simms, & Betsey (1984) investigated whether lower educational aspirations explain the higher rates of sexual activity, pregnancy, and parenthood among blacks. They conclude that black and white youth have equally high educational aspirations, and therefore differences in aspirations cannot account for higher pregnancy rates among black teenagers. Citing the work of Hogan and Kitagawa (1983) comparing black adolescents growing up in different areas in

Chicago, they speculate that many factors that independently predict early child-bearing are concentrated in poor neighborhoods where many black children are particularly likely to grow up. The effect of these factors—lack of contraceptive information, poorly educated parents, school dropouts, poor employment prospects, and single-parent families—on teenage fertility behavior may be greater when aggregated in a neighborhood than the simple sum of their separate effects would suggest. Clearly much more research and analysis must be conducted before the independent and combined effects of race, poverty, educational attainment, and single-parent family status upon teenage fertility can be adequately described and explained.

Male and Female Differences in Determinants of Sexual Activity

Although a number of factors have been found to predict early sexual initiation for both sexes, there are other dimensions on which sexually active male and female adolescents differ. Many authors have described the differences between the sexual scripts prescribed by society for males and females. For example, Byrne (1983) describes the sexual double standard that socializes males "to seek sexual contact, to evaluate each female as a potential sexual partner, to initiate sexual intercourse whenever possible and to assume that conception and its prevention are for the female to worry about." Females, on the other hand, are taught that love is a prerequisite for sexual intercourse and that they should control how far the male goes.

Early adolescence is the time when these sexual scripts are learned (Gagnon & Simon, 1973). In response to their awakening sexual maturity, boys are encouraged to seek sexual activity and achievement; girls are discouraged from sexual activity and urged to define emerging male–female relationships in terms of romantic love. To the extent that these sexual scripts are actually taught and enforced in society, the act of first coitus will have different meanings for males and females and will undoubtedly be associated with different facilitating attitudes, circumstances, and perceptions.

Nationally representative data about young men's and women's relationships with their first sexual partners provide testament to the vitality of the sexual scripts just described. Among women 15–17 years old at the time of first intercourse, 71% were either engaged or going steady with their partners. Among like-aged men, only 47% were engaged or going steady (Zelnik & Shah, 1983). A similar difference between the sexes has recently been reported in a survey of selected Baltimore schools (Zabin, Hirsch, Smith, & Hardy, 1984).

Whereas the proportion of males having first intercourse within a committed relationship is lower than the proportion of females, the fact that close to half the males were either engaged or going steady does show that the stereotypical view of all males as sexual opportunists is not fully supported by the data. Only 11%

of the males had first intercourse with someone they had recently met. Twenty-two percent were dating their first partners and 20% were friends. Zelnik and Shah (1983) note that considering males were an average 1 year younger than their partners, they were not surprised to find that a substantial group of males had their first sexual encounter with a friend.

There is some evidence that self-confidence or self-esteem operates differentially for males and females in predicting sexual activity among adolescents. For example, Miller, Brown, Crawford, Cvetkovich, Grote, Lieberman, & Poppen (n.d.) found in a three-city study of 16- and 17-year-old adolescents that high self-confidence was positively associated with having had sexual intercourse for both sexes. The correlation was, however, much higher for adolescent males. A somewhat similar finding is reported by Jessor and Jessor (1975). They found that males in their white high school sample who were nonvirgins had significantly higher self-esteem than virgin males. There were no differences between female virgins and nonvirgins on this dimension. Later longitudinal analysis confirmed that significantly higher self-esteen predated the transition to sexual activity for males in the sample. Conversely, Mott (1983) reports that higher self-esteem is a significant predictor of less sexual activity at an early age among a nationally representative sample of young women ages 17 through 20. In this sample self-esteem had no significant independent effect on the sexual activity of males.

Liberal attitudes towards premarital sex were associated with sexual experience and with the intent of virgins to have premarital sexual intercourse for both sexes in a special sample of 16- and 17-year-old respondents interviewed in three urban communities in 1975 (Miller et al., n.d.). There were, however, distinct differences between males and females in how actual sexual behavior related to attitudes toward premarital sex and attitudes towards traditional sex roles. For the males, the respondents were likely to have engaged in sexual intercourse unless they were opposed to premarital sex for moral or family reasons, or unless they had not been able to find a willing partner. These data suggest the importance of social skills in dealing with the opposite sex for males intent on losing their virginity.

For females, several patterns emerged. Nonvirgins held more permissive attitudes towards premarital sex but tended to hold conservative attitudes about appropriate gender roles. Virgins who thought that they might engage in premarital sex at some later point held the least traditional views of gender roles, and virgins opposed to premarital sex held the most traditional attitudes towards gender roles (Cvetkovich, Grote, Lieberman, & Miller, 1978).

Motivation behind first intercourse was also found to be different for male and female adolescents for this same sample (Miller, 1978). Males were more likely to report that "my sexual desire" was very important as a reason for first intercourse, whereas sexually experienced females were more likely to report "my partner's sexual desire" and "deep strong feelings/love for partner" as very important reasons. Differential reactions to first intercourse were also reported. Males, more frequently feld proud and experienced afterward; females more frequently worried about pregnancy. Thirty-four percent of the females reported regret at the time of first intercourse compared to 18% of the males. Twenty-eight percent of females still regretted having had first sexual intercourse at the time they did, compared to 4% of the males. A similar pattern was reported by Sorensen (1973), who found in a national sample of adolescents that boys reacted more positively to the first coital experience than girls. Males reacted more with excitement, females with fear. Forty percent of the females said they wish they had waited compared to 14% of the males.

Although this evidence supports the stereotype of adolescent males socialized to seek intercourse, there is also considerable support for the notion that the stereotype does not apply to all males. Ross (1979) in a survey of New York City teenagers found that both males and females ranked ''having sex'' far behind such other goals as getting a job, preparing for the future, making it on my own, getting good grades, and getting along with my family. Males and females showed remarkable similarities in the proportion agreeing that the latter goals are very important. Although both sexes ranked the importance of having sex below these other goals, only 27% of the females compared to 55% of the males thought ''having sex'' was an important goal. Two studies have reported a somewhat surprising finding that males more than females have engaged in sex mostly because ''the person I was with expected me to'' (Ross, 1979) and because ''it seemed like it was expected of me'' (Miller, 1979a). These studies point to a divergence between the behavior of a significant minority of males and the cultural ''macho'' stereotypes.

Sorensen (1973) distinguished between two types of sexually active adolescents—the serial monogamists and the sexual adventurers. He defined serial monogamy (without marriage) as a ''close sexual relationship of uncertain duration between two unmarried adolescents from which either party may depart when he or she desires, often to participate in another such relationship.'' Twenty-five percent of the sexually active males in his national sample of 13–19-year-olds were categorized as serial monogamists compared to 62% of sexually active females. Forty-one percent of the male nonvirgins in his sample and 13% of the female nonvirgins in his sample were classified as sexual adventurers—seeking many mates without maintaining a sexual relationship. The remaining nonvirgins of both sexes were not currently sexually active.

Serial monogamists of both sexes were older and had an average of 4.2 sexual partners. Nearly half, however, had had only one sex partner. Fifty-two percent had had their relationship with one partner for 1 year or more. Sixty-six percent of the monogamists compared to 46% of the adventurers always used a contraceptive or birth control device during the preceding month. A very large majority of serial monogamists (86%) believed they loved their sex partners.

Ninety-three percent of male monogamists believed it was wrong to tell a girl "you love her—even if you don't—if that's what it takes so she will have sex with you."

Sexual adventurers, on the other hand, had had an average of 16.3 partners; they tended to agree with such statements as "there isn't anything in sex I wouldn't want to try at least once" or "there is no kind of sex act that I would think of as being abnormal, so long as the people involved want to do it." Eighty-two percent of the adventurers agree that it is all right to have sex with someone you "really dig, even if you have only known that person a few hours."

In comparison to serial monogamists, adventurers were found to average lower grades, to be less religious, to be less able to be around their parents, to be more likely to smoke marijuana and to drink, to be less accepting of the idea of obeying laws they do not agree with, and to be less conforming to society in matters of clothing and personal grooming. This complex of factors associated with sexual adventurism is very similar to that found by Jessor and Jessor (1975) to be associated with the transition from virginity to nonvirginity.

Moore and Burt (1982) suggest two patterns of sexual intercourse for teenagers. One involves a high probability of intercourse in a long-term and committed relationship among older teens. The other is the reverse, a high probability of intercourse with a relatively large number of partners associated with precocious dating, home conflict, and participation in other deviant activities such as drug experimentation. The evidence suggests more males follow the latter pattern, whereas the reverse is true for females. Moore and Burt argue that these different patterns should not be treated alike by social policy. More effort should be devoted to identifying different patterns of sexual behavior among teenagers, and among male teenagers in particular.

Existing studies suggest differential patterns of sexual behavior among male adolescents, but they are far from conclusive. A recent survey of young men 17–21 years of age showed that on average white males became sexually active before the age of 16 and black males initiated sex soon after they became 14 (Zelnik & Shah, 1983). Moreover, a few local studies of innercity youth show mean ages of first intercourse as young as 11 years of age. To date no national probability survey has examined the sexual behavior of young men during these critical years of transition.

In addition, theoretical explanations of male adolescent behavior in the absence of data have relied heavily on references to stereotypical gender roles. However, the studies reviewed here suggest that stereotypes do not adequately explain the behavior of many male adolescents. Indeed, many similar factors and motivations have been found to influence the behavior of both male and female teenagers. It is clearly time to conduct a study of adolescent sexual behavior that includes adolescents between the ages of 11 and 16, and which draws a sufficiently large sample so that subgroups of the population can be examined. Adequate explanations of male adolescent sexual activity require an adequate data base. To date this information has not been available.

CONTRACEPTIVE USE

Just as little national data describe the sexual activity of adolescent males, a dearth of information also exists about their use of contraception. The data on women are more complete and provide evidence about male contraceptive usage. Zelnik and Kantner (1980), analyzing two national surveys of young women ages 15–19 for 1976 and 1979, report that among metropolitan women with premarital sexual experience the percentage who said that they always practice contraception increased from 29% in 1976 to 34% in 1979. In addition another 10% in 1976 had used a method at first intercourse but not always after that. By 1979, this proportion had risen to 15%. The information on type of contraceptive method used by young women points to the male role in contraception. In 1979, the most frequently used methods of contraception at first intercourse were the condom (34%), withdrawal (36%), and the pill (19%). Thus at first intercourse 70% of contracepting females were relying on males to do the contracepting.

Differences by race were evident with whites more frequently mentioning withdrawal (42% compared to 12.5% for blacks). Black females, on the other hand were much more likely to rely on the pill, 38% of blacks compared to 15% of whites. The condom was used equally by blacks and whites, 34% for each group. When respondents were asked about the method most recently used, the pill was mentioned by 38% of whites and 31% of blacks; condom usage declined to 23% for whites and 24% for blacks. Withdrawal was even less popular with 21% of whites and 7.5 of blacks using this method. Thus over time there is a transition from the male methods of contraception at first intercourse to female methods such as the pill and in a smaller number of cases the IUD and the diaphragm.

A recent analysis of the National Longitudinal Survey of Work Experience of Youth (the NLS) by Mott (1983) provides information about contraceptive use for a nationally representative sample of males and female ages 17 through 20. Among never-married respondents who were sexually active during the month before the survey, 24% of the males and 15% of the females had not used any contraception. Twenty-four percent of the males reported using a condom, 29% relied on the pill, and 6% used withdrawal. Among the females 56% had used the pill, 8% had used a condom, and 4% had used withdrawal. The somewhat higher reported usage of the pill among females in the NLS sample compared to the Zelnik and Kantner sample of young women is attributed to the older ages of the respondents in the NLS survey.

When contraceptive methods are classified as effective and ineffective, more (60%) of the black and white males used effective methods of contraception than Hispanic males (50%). Similarly about 70% of the black and white females used effective methods compared to 60% of their Hispanic counterparts. Somewhat surprisingly, Mott reports that sexually active young adults over age 20 are only marginally more likely to contracept effectively than their younger counterparts.

Information about contraceptive use among younger male adolescents is provided by Zelnik and Shah (1983), who describe patterns of contraceptive use at first intercourse for men ages 17–21 interviewed as part of the National Survey of Young Men in 1979. These data do not necessarily indicate subsequent contraceptive use. They show that slightly more women (48.9%) than men (44.1%) contracept at first intercourse and the older men and women are at first intercourse, the higher the likelihood of contraceptive use at that time. Among men who had first intercourse before they were 15, 36% of the white males and 28% of the black males had used a contraceptive method. Sixteen percent of the whites and 21% of the blacks had used prescription methods. When first intercourse occurred between 15 and 17 years of age, more had used contraception: 49% of whites and 45% of blacks. Prescription methods were more common among black youth—34% compared to 19% for white youth. First intercourse after age 17 was associated with even higher rates of contraception; 59% of these men had used a contraceptive method and 38% had used a prescription method. (Black and white differentials are not available for this age group.)

At all ages, and especially the youngest ages, black males are less likely to use contraception than white males. They are, however, more likely to use prescription methods when they do contracept. As the age at first intercourse rises, the racial difference in contraceptive use lessens. However, because proportionately more black than white teenagers engage in intercourse before they are 15, the time when the use of contraception is the lowest, their risk of pregnancy is substantially higher.

The Role of the Male Partner in Contraception

Among females the relatively high reliance on male contraceptive methods, especially condoms and withdrawal, underlines the importance of the male partner's role in preventing adolescent pregnancy. Undoubtedly males also play a role in suggesting that female partners seek contraception, but the frequency of this behavior has not yet been documented. Many service providers informally report that the male partner is important in determining which contraceptive method is chosen and how reliably it is used.

Support for the importance of partners' attitudes is provided by data on reasons teenagers give for not using contraceptives. Although Zelnik and Kantner (1979) report that very few young women, 1.4% of whites and 4.2% of blacks, did not use a method because their partner objected, other studies report higher proportions of respondents citing partner objections. Miller (1979c) reports that 21% of noncontracepting females in his three-city sample said they did not use contraception because "my boyfriend didn't want me to use it." Interestingly, over half his male noncontracepting respondents (54%) also cited partner resistance. Ross (1979) found in New York City that among noncontracepting females, 11% of blacks, 16% of Hispanics and 14% of whites didn't use contraception because "my partner didn't like it." As in Miller's three-city sample, male respondents were more likely to select this as a reason for nonuse than female respondents, 23% of black males, 12% of Hispanic males, and 16% of white males.

One study examined the influence of partner relationships and communication on contraceptive use and method of choice among teenage girls (Cvetkovich & Grote, 1981). Because previous research had determined that high school and college women involved in stable relationships were more effective contraceptors (Cvetkovich & Grote, 1979; Foreit & Foreit, 1978; Fugita, Wagner, & Pion, 1971), the researchers hypothesized that the stability of the relationship operates in two ways to promote contraceptive use: (1) through more predictably occurring and more frequent sex, and (2) through the young woman's acceptance of her sexuality. In comparing contraceptors to noncontraceptors, they found that female pill users were distinguished by (1) longer relationships with partners, (2) more negative attitude towards getting pregnant, (3) older at time of sexual debut, (4) more frequent intercourse, (5) more trust in partner, and (6) perception of high pregnancy risk from unprotected intercourse. Female condom users compared to no-method users were more likely to have discussed their sexual debuts with their partners, had slightly lower perceptions of the risk of pregnancy, were older at sexual debut, and were slightly more likely to trust their partner to take care of birth control. In discussing their results the authors suggest that male partners in stable relationships are more likely to care about their partner's well-being and to actively encourage contraceptive use. This thesis is consistent with Sorensen's (1973) finding that serial monogamists were more likely to use contraception than sexual adventurers.

FACTORS ASSOCIATED WITH CONTRACEPTIVE USE AMONG MALES

As Moore and Burt (1982) note in their review of the available studies, our current understanding of the reasons for contraceptive use, nonuse, and ineffective use by teenagers is limited. For example, Mott (1983) applied multiple regression techniques to the NLS data to identify independent predictors of contraceptive use for males and females 17–20 years old. The model included a range of demographic, socioeconomic, and psychological measures. No independent predictors of contraceptive use among males were found. When effective contraception replaced the more generalized "contraceptive use" variable as the dependent variable in the model, a number of meaningful predictors emerged. These were lower religiosity, higher educational goals, and higher self-esteem. These predictors were only associated with the effective use of contraception among men 17–20 years old; they did not hold for men in their 20s nor for young women.

A number of studies have asked noncontracepting teenagers why they do not use contraceptives and consistently the same types of responses are given. The major types of reasons reported for nonuse of contraceptives are inaccurate information about the risks of pregnancy, a belief that contraception interferes with pleasure, spontaneity, or convenience, and a perception that contraception is difficult to obtain (Shah, Zelnik, & Kantner, 1975). Whereas the latter set of reasons emerged from the responses of the nationally representative sample of young women, many of the smaller localized studies of both male and female teenagers find similar sets of reasons.

Miller's (1979) multiple regression analyses, for example, revealed that the following reasons cited by male teenagers best explained their nonuse of contraception: My girlfriend assured me that she was sterile or could not get pregnant; I decided to take a chance and count on good luck; I just put the possibility of pregnancy out of my mind; I had planned not to have any more intercourse for a while; I assumed my girlfriend would take some precautions; I didn't believe that my girlfriend would actually get pregnant; and I wanted to get my girlfriend pregnant. Similarly Finkel and Finkel (1975) found that 62% of the males in their sample agreed that birth control makes sex seem preplanned and 54% agreed that only girls should use birth control. Ross (1979) found that the six most popular reasons that males did not use birth control were: It interferes with pleasure, my partner doesn't like it, it is unnatural, it makes sex seem too planned, it is too embarassing to buy, and it is a hassle to get.

Teenagers' knowledge and beliefs about the probability of pregnancy are clearly related to their reasons for not using contraceptives. Both males and females cite the belief that the female could not get pregnant as a reason for not using contraception. Miller (1976) has found wide variations in the estimates of young women give about the probability of pregnancy. Teenage males have been found to be less knowledgeable about pregnancy risk than teenage girls in a number of localized studies (Freeman, Rickels, Huggins, Mudd, Garcia, & Dickens, 1980; Jenkins, 1983; Ross, 1979). Cvetkovich, Grote, Bjorseth, & Sarkissian (1975) point out that teens' lack of understanding about probabilities of pregnancy are affected by factors other than substantive knowledge about the physiological facts of conception. They describe the importance of personal fables for young adolescents. A teenager engaging in intercourse may develop a belief that he/she is sterile if pregnancy does not occur on the first few occasions of unprotected coitus. Thus teens who don't think they can get pregnant or impregnate may hold these beliefs as a result of ignorance about conception or as a result of their own first sexual experiences when pregnancy did not immediately result.

Lack of information among teens also extends to inadequate knowledge about contraception. Zelnik and Shah (1983) report that 13% of women 15–19 years old and 20% of men 17–21 years old did not use a birth control method at first intercourse because they did not know about contraception. More black than white teenagers of both sexes cited lack of contraceptive information as a reason for not using a method.

Many males and females also believe that contraception makes sexual intercourse seem too planned and not spontaneous. The most common reason cited by teenagers for not using contraception at first intercourse was that the intercourse had not been planned. Only small proportions of men (25%) and women (17%) reported that they had planned their first intercourse, and these planners were more likely to have used contraception (Zelnik & Shah, 1983). Needle (1977) hypothesizes that the episodic nature of sexual encounters when sexual activity is first initiated is a fairly adequate explanation for the failure of many teenagers to use any contraception or to use reliable methods. He suggests that the belief in the value of spontaneity helps the newly sexually active population avoid direct confrontation with conventional morality. In addition, sex viewed as unplanned and spontaneous can be better reconciled with a perception of self as not really sexually active. Teenagers at the beginning of their sexual careers often deny to themselves that they are sexually active (Cvetkovich & Grote, 1981; Cvetkovich, Grote, Bjorseth, & Sarkissian, 1975; Sorensen, 1973).

A third set of factors affecting contraceptive utilization centers on the accessibility of contraception (Needle, 1977). Whereas male methods of contraception pose fewer accessibility problems than female methods, one of the major reasons male respondents in the Ross survey (1979) said they didn't use birth control was because it is too embarassing to buy and it is a hassle to get. Smiklo (1982) reports a similar rationale for nonuse of contraceptives in a sample of middle-class male high school students. Forty-four percent of nonusers said they did not use condoms because of embarassment or the hassle. Many teenage males apparently perceive the use of contraception as problematic.

Another factor that appears to explain the lower incidence of contraceptive use among teenage males compared to females is the belief that contraception is a female responsibility. Two studies report more than half their male teenage respondents thought that the female partner should or would take responsibility for contraception (Finkel & Finkel, 1975; Smiklo, 1982). Conversely, a recent survey in selected Baltimore schools reports that high proportions of males and females thought that *both* partners were responsible ''to see that a girl doesn't get pregnant when having sex'' (Clark et al., 1984). A small proportion of teenagers do not use contraception because they desire pregnancy. In 1979, Zelnik and

Shah (1981) found that 4% of females aged 15–19 and 2% of males 17–21 were trying to become pregnant or did not care whether they became pregnant.

In addition to examining the reasons for nonuse of contraception, several studies have looked at the factors related to successful contraceptive utilization. High school males have been found to use contraception when they have accurate knowledge of the risks of unprotected coitus, when they perceive birth control as available and convenient, and when they disagree with the idea that "it is sometimes okay to have unprotected intercourse" (Cvetkovich et al., 1978). Both males and females report that the main reasons that they sought prescription contraception were "began to have sex more frequently," "began a steady relationship," "pregnancy scare," "discovered easy availability of clinic or physician's office," or "influence from sexual partner"—this latter reason was cited more frequently by males (Miller, 1979b). These findings suggest that many factors predicting contraceptive use by males are similar to those isolated for females. They include the perception of the risk of pregnancy, the stability of the relationship with partner, the frequency of coitus, the communication with the partner, and perception of the availability of the method.

The studies of male contraceptive use reviewed here document the significant role of males in preventing pregnancies. The studies show that male adolescents are only slightly less likely than females to report using contraception, whether the occasion is first intercourse, last intercourse, or during the last month. For both males and females, age at first intercourse is related to the likelihood of using contraception. The older adolescents are at first intercourse, the more likely is the use of contraception. At first intercourse, 70% of contracepting adolescent females reported relying on male methods of contraception, but over time many females make a transition to prescription methods. In addition the factors associated with use and nonuse of contraceptives are remarkably similar for both male and female adolescents. Given these findings, it is clear that the adolescent male's role in contraception has clearly been undersold by policy makers and service providers.

IMPLICATIONS OF THE FINDINGS FOR FUTURE RESEARCH

Although all the evidence is not in, this review of research about adolescent male fertility behavior did uncover more information than expected. Several authors, citing the absence of data, have called for more research about the "forgotten half" of the fertility equation. However, a few nationally representative data bases have collected information about male adolescents (see another chapter in this book for a description of these data), and several smaller scale surveys have also been conducted. Many of the findings about males have been reported in the literature. The problem appears to be one of emphasis. Although information about female fertility behavior is often presented by itself, information about male fertility behavior is most often reported in conjunction with information about female fertility behavior. Few reports concentrate any sustained focus on adolescent males.

There are, however, clear gaps in the research. One is the absence of data about trends in male sexual activity and contraceptive utilization. Since 1971, reliable data have been collected about young women's sexual activity and contraceptive practices. They have shown remarkable changes in these behaviors over the past decade. Comparable information about males is simply not available, and because it cannot be reconstructed, we can only recommend that such omissions should not occur in the future.

Another glaring gap in available information is the absence of good data about pregnancies and births attributable to adolescent males. Surveys of male adolescents could attempt to collect this information. However, males have been shown to be less than reliable informants about these occurrences (Mott, 1983). Perhaps more effort should be made to collect information about male partners from the adolescent women. The birth registration data system could not be the mechanism for this data collection because state laws determine who can be listed as a father on a birth certificate for an out-of-wedlock birth. However, other fertility surveys of adolescent women might ask more questions about male partners. These additions would undoubtedly heighten the sensitivity of an already sensitive interview situation. It is clear, however, that more information is necessary about who the male partners are and how they influence fertility decision making.

An ideal data set would include interviews with both partners. Because sexual activity and contraceptive behavior emerge out of the interaction patterns between males and females, it is perhaps surprising that so much of the research in this area has only focused on one partner. The high costs and complicated logistics of developing such a paired data set have so far discouraged attempts to create it.

There is a definite need to develop a theoretical framework that explains the fertility behavior of adolescent males. The work to date in this area has focused on explaining female behavior and the few studies that have tested models using male subjects have used college students (Delameter, 1983; Reiss, Banwart, & Foreman, 1975; Thompson & Spanier, 1978). A compendium of variables have already been found to be associated with males' early sexual activity and use of contraception. These have been cited earlier in this chapter. Still more variables are suspected of influencing fertility behavior. Effort now needs to be devoted to conceptualizing how these variables operate in concert to produce differing patterns of fertility behavior. Existing data bases could be used to test these models initially. However, new data collection efforts will be necessary so that a full range of the important variables could be available within a single data set.

IMPLICATIONS OF THE FINDINGS FOR PROGRAM INTERVENTION

The data indicate that large numbers of teenagers are sexually active. In 1979 over half of 17-year-old men had experienced intercourse and the mean age of first intercourse was 15.9 years (for men 17–21 years old). More black than white males had experienced intercourse by age 17, and their mean age of initiation was 1 year younger. Because age at first intercourse is negatively related to the use of contraception, the risk of pregnancy is very high among these early initiates. Preventing pregnancies among this group poses a severe challenge. Two potential approaches would be delaying the onset of sexual activity among these teenagers and failing this, ensuring the effective use of contraception when intercourse occurs. These are not necessarily mutually exclusive approaches, although bitter controversy has characterized the debate between supporters of each approach in recent years. In a compromise solution Congress has authorized two federally funded programs representing each of these approaches. The Adolescent Family Life Demonstration Program, established in 1981, funds projects attempting to discourage premarital sexual activity, and the much larger Family Planning Program established in 1970 supports family planning services for teenagers, as well as for older women. Although family-planning services have been proven effective in reducing adolescent pregnancies and births (Forrest et al., 1981), the effectiveness of primary prevention programs such as those funded under the more recent Adolescent Family Life program have not yet been demonstrated.

The patients served by family planning clinics are overwhelmingly female. In the middle and late 1970s the federal government responded to the criticisms that men had been excluded from programs by funding a number of demonstration projects to involve males in family-planning services. Typically, these projects set up male clinics with male staff that operated side by side with female clinics within family-planning agencies. These projects were generally judged to be failures because they were unable to attract men into the clinics. At the federal level the male initiative suffered a quiet death when federal funds for family-planning services were cut.

A recent account of the history of the men's clinic in San Francisco chronicles the evolution of one of these demonstration projects (Gordon & DeMarco, 1984). Although this project was unusually successful in attracting clients, few participants asked for reproductive counseling. The most popular services were job physicals, free condoms, and medical care for the health problems associated with homosexuality. The authors describe how the staff began to realize that the medical model of delivering services was not very successful in involving males, particularly adolescents, in family planning. Pointing out that most male methods of contraception do not require medical services, they concluded that it is difficult to determine a precise role for the organized family-planning movement in the delivery of male birth control methods. Instead they recommend public health campaigns and improved distribution of condoms as approaches to promoting male involvement in family planning.

Male and female youth have been found to participate equally in the educationally oriented prevention programs. In 1983, Adolescent Family Life Demonstration Projects reported equal numbers of both sexes participating. The bulk of family life/sex education, however, is not provided through this small federal demonstration program. A 1982 survey of school districts serving large cities showed that sex education in some form was available in 80% of the districts and 85% of the 9.3 million students enrolled in these districts participated (Sonenstein & Pittman, 1984). Beyond school-based programs there are countless others sponsored by private youth-serving agencies, churches, and other organizations. Although the sex distribution of participants in these latter programs is unknown, the school district survey found that male and female students participated in the programs in equal numbers although classes were not necessarily coeducational. At the elementary and junior high levels 90% of the districts reported equal enrollment by sex; at the senior high level this figure fell to 82%. All districts with unequal enrollments reported more girls than boys. Whereas classes were primarily coeducational at the senior high level (83%), the proportion declined to 70% of junior high classes and 47% of elementary classes. Single sex classes were not associated with differences in topic coverage for boys and girls (Sonenstein & Pittman, 1984).

Although school districts in large cities appear to be providing much more sex education than previously thought, an examination of topic coverage by grade level shows that only 21.5% of all districts provided at least one class period on intercourse and pregnancy probability to at least three-quarters of their students and introduced this topic before the ninth grade, when students are normally 14–15 years old. Even fewer districts provided the same type of coverage for such topics as "the most likely time in cycle for pregnancy" (14%), "contraceptives" (11%), and "sources of family planning services" (7%). Some districts introduced these topics at higher grade levels, but the proportion of schools providing one class period on these topics to most of their students never rose above 25%. Because lack of information about pregnancy risks, contraception, and sources of family-planning methods have been shown to be primary reasons why teenagers do not use contraception, it would appear that school sex education programs could do a lot more to provide this information to students before they become sexually active. The mean age for sexual initiation among white males was 15.9 years in 1979; it was 14.4 for black males (Zelnik & Shah, 1983).

The data show that a substantial number of teenage males are not "sexual adventurers" (Sorenson, 1973). Almost half report that their first intercourse occurred with someone with whom they were either engaged or going steady. These men do not fit the stereotypical view of young men as promiscuous opportunists. Prevention programs need to think about the target groups for their services. Although some men may just need more information and skills to obtain contraception, or to support their partner's contraceptive efforts, others may need a lot more convincing about the necessity of contraceptive responsibility.

Because many males do not face the same consequences as females when an unintended pregnancy occurs, they may not be motivated to take contraceptive action. Some authors have argued that the negative consequences should be equally borne by both sexes, especially now that paternity can easily be determined by laboratory tests. If paternity adjudication and child support enforcement were vigorously pursued, pregnancies would be much more costly to males. Rivera-Casale, Klerman, and Manela (1984) argue that adolescent fathers and their parents should bear more financial responsibility for the progeny of unprotected intercourse. This approach would certainly raise the ante for males who are heedless of the need to be reproductively responsible.

Many teenage males do use contraception or report that their partners use contraception. Sixty percent of black and white males (17-20-year-old) used an effective contraceptive method at last intercourse; 50% of Hispanic males used an effective method. These proportions are only 10 points lower than the percentages for females of the same age (Mott, 1983). Almost half of males initiating sex between the ages of 15 and 17 years used contraception at first intercourse (Zelnik & Shah, 1983). Clearly, getting males to use contraception, even at first intercourse, is not a lost cause. Males can be reached. Although the male family-planning clinics were a disappointment, there is no reason to write off efforts to encourage the use of contraception by males. New approaches need to be developed and tried. For example, school-based adolescent pregnancy clinics serving both males and females show very promising results (Kirby, 1984; Zabin et al., 1983). Other approaches might be devised that focus on some of the other factors that have been found to be associated with the later initiation of sexual activity and the use of contraception once sexual activity commences. For example, programs designed to enhance self-esteem, to raise educational expectations and opportunities, and to improve communication skills should be tested.

At least half the babies born to teenage mothers are fathered by men over 20 years old; on average the first sexual partner of a teenage woman is 3 years older than she is. To prevent unwanted adolescent pregnancies, prevention programs will need to target services to men in their 20s. Whereas thorough preparation of young men when they are in junior and senior high school might preclude the eventual need for programs targeted to older men, there is an immediate need to increase the effective use of contraceptives among sexually active unmarried men in their 20s. Creative approaches to reaching this older population need to be developed. Colleges, universities, job-training programs, and the armed forces are likely places to start. If some of the current restrictions in the broadcast industry could be lifted, the mass media could effectively be used to communicate messages about reproductive responsibility to broad segments of the population.

The finding that the sexual double standard is not as prevalent as cultural stereotypes would predict is a reason for cautious optimism. The incidence of unintended adolescent pregnancies could very well be reduced if school-based programs provided more complete information to adolescents before they become sexually active and if contraceptive services were targeted to males in their teens and 20s. On the face of it, males do not appear to be less willing to use contraception than females. However, to date, most contraceptive programs have only targeted females. Each pregnancy is the result of the behavior of two individuals and only one partner need contracept effectively to prevent the pregnancy. Services, therefore, have at least two chances to prevent each pregnancy. It is clearly time to think again about how to get more male adolescents to use effective contraceptive methods. Although the male family-planning clinic model did not work, there is no reason to believe that other approaches will suffer the same fate.

REFERENCES

Baldwin, W. H. (1976). Adolescent pregnancy and childbearing-growing concerns for Americans. *Population Bulletin, 31.*

Billy, J. O. G., Morris, N. M., Groff, T. R., & Udry, J. R. (1984). *Serum androgenic hormones motivate sexual behavior in adolescent human males.* Paper presented at the Annual Meetings of the Population Association of America.

Billy, J. O. G., & Udry, J. R. (1983). *The effects of age and pubertal development on adolescent sexual behavior.* Unpublished paper. University of North Carolina at Chapel Hill, Carolina Population Center.

Byrne, D. (1983). Sex without contraception. In D. Byrne & W. A. Fisher (eds.), *Adolescents, sex and contraception* (pp. 3–31). Hillsdale, NJ: Lawrence Erlbaum Associates.

Chilman, C. S. (1983). *Adolescent sexuality in a changing American society* (2nd ed.). New York: Wiley.

Clark, S. D., Zabin, L. S., & Hardy, J. B. (1984). Sex, contraception and parenthood: Experience and attitudes among urban black young men. *Family Planning Perspectives, 16*(2), 77–82.

Cvetkovich, G., & Grote, B. (1979). *Psychosocial maturity, ego identity and fertility-related behavior.* Paper presented at the American Psychological Association Meeting.

Cvetkovich, G., & Grote, B. (1981). Psychosocial maturity and teenage contraceptive use: An investigation of decision-making and communication skills. *Population and Environment, 211–226.*

Cvetkovich, G., Grote, B., Bjorseth, A., & Sarkissian, J. (1975). On the psychology of adolescent use of contraceptives. *The Journal of Sex Research, 11,* 256–270.

Cvetkovich, G., Grote, B., Lieberman, E. J., & Miller, W. (1978). Sex role development and teenage fertility related behavior. *Adolescence, 13,* 231–236.

Delameter, J. (1983). An interpersonal and interactional model of contraceptive behavior. In D. Byrne & W. A. Fisher (Eds.), *Adolescents, sex and contraception* (pp. 33–61). Hillsdale, NJ: Lawrence Erlbaum Associates.

Delameter, J., & MacCorquodale, P. (1979). *Premarital sexuality: Attitudes, relationships & behaviors*. Madison: University of Wisconsin Press.

Devaney, B., & Hubley, K. (1981). *The determinants of adolescent pregnancy and childbearing*. Final Report to NICHD. Washington, D.C.: Mathematica Policy Research, Inc.

Diepold, J., & Young, R. D. (1979). Empirical studies of adolescent sexual behavior: A critical review. *Adolescence, 14*(53), 45–64.

Finkel, M. L., & Finkel, D. J. (1975). Sexual and contraceptive knowledge, attitudes, and behavior of male adolescents. *Family Planning Perspectives, 6*(7), 256–260.

Foreit, K. G., & Foreit, J. R. (1978). Correlates of contraceptive behavior among unmarried U.S. college students. *Studies in Family Planning, 9,* 169–174.

Forrest, J. D., Hermalin, A. I., & Henshaw, S. (1981). The impact of family planning programs on adolescent pregnancy. *Family Planning Perspectives, 13,* 109–116.

Freeman, E. W., Rickels, K., Huggins, G. R., Mudd, E. H., Garcia, C. R., & Dickens, H. O. (1980). Adolescent contraceptive use: comparisons of male and female attitudes and information. *American Journal of Public Health, 70*(8), 790–797.

Fugita, B., Wagner, H. J., & Pion, R. J. (1971). Contraceptive use among single college students. *American Journal of Obstetrics, 109*(5), 787–793.

Gagnon, J., & Simon, W. (1973). *Sexual conduct: The social sources of human sexuality*. Chicago: Aldine.

Gordon, P. H., & DeMarco, L. J. (1984). Reproductive health services for men: Is there a need? *Family Planning Perspectives, 16*(1), 44–49.

Henshaw, S. K., & O'Reilly, K. (1983). Characteristics of abortion patients in the United States, 1979 and 1980. *Family Planning Perspectives, 15*(1), 5–16.

Hogan, D., & Kitagawa, E. (1983). *Family factors in the fertility of black adolescents*. Paper presented at the annual meetings of the Population Association of America.

Hofferth, S. (forthcoming). *Research on teen pregnancy and childbearing: A review of the literature*. Bethesda, Maryland: Center for Population Research, National Institute for Child Health and Human Development.

Jenkins, R. (1983). *Final Report to NICHD*. Washington, DC: Howard University Hospital.

Jessor, S. L., & Jessor, R. (1975). Transition from virginity to nonvirginity among youth: A social-psychological study over time. *Developmental Psychology, 11,* 473–484.

Kirby, D. (1984). *Sexuality education: An evaluation of programs and their effects*. Santa Cruz: Network Publications.

Miller, P. Y., & Simon, W. (1974). Adolescent sexual behavior: Context and change. *Social Problems, 22*(1), 58–75.

Miller, W. B. (1976). Sexual and contraceptive behavior in young unmarried women. *Primary Care*.

Miller, W. B. (1978). First sexual intercourse. *Transitions: Perspectives on Today's Teenagers for the Physician, 1,* 7–9.

Miller, W. B. (1979a). Premarital sex: Attitudes and motivations among teenagers. *Transitions: Perspectives on Today's Teenager for the Physician, 2*(1), 7–9.

Miller, W. B. (1979b). Teenagers' decisions to begin and discontinue prescription contraception. *Transitions: Perspectives on Today's Teenagers for the Physician, 2*(2), 4–5.

Miller, W. B. (1979c). The use and non-use of contraception by teenagers. *Transitions: Perspectives on Today's Teenagers for the Physician, 2*(3), 10–11.

Miller, W. B., Brown, S. S., Crawford, F. R., Cvetkovich, G., Grote, B., Lieberman, E. J., & Poppen, P. J. (no date). *Adolescent sexuality and contraceptive use: Some psychological factors*. Unpublished manuscript.

Mott, F. L. (1983). *Fertility-related data in the 1982 National Longitudinal Survey of Work Experience of Youth: An evaluation of data quality and some preliminary analytical results*. The Ohio State University: Center for Human Resource Research.

Moore, K. A., & Burt, M. R. (1982). *Private crisis, public cost: Policy perspectives on teenage childbearing.* Washington, DC: The Urban Institute Press.

Moore, K. A., & Caldwell, S. (1976). *Out-of-wedlock pregnancy and childbearing.* (Working Paper 992-02). Washington, DC: The Urban Institute.

Moore, K. A., Simms, M. C., & Betsey, C. L. (1984). *Information, services and aspirations: race differences in adolescent fertility.* Washington, DC: The Urban Institute.

National Center for Health Statistics. (1983). Advance report of final natality statistics, 1981. *Monthly Vital Statistics Report, 32*(9).

Needle, R. H. (1977, June). Factors affecting contraceptive practices of high school and college-age students. *The Journal of School Health,* 340–345.

Reiss, I. L., Banwart, A., & Foreman, H. (1975). Premarital contraceptive usage: A study and some theoretical explorations. *Journal of Marriage and the Family, 37,* 619–629.

Rivera-Casale, C., Klerman, L. V., & Manela, R. (1984). Child support enforcement programs: Their relevance to school-age parents. *Child Welfare, 63,* 521–532.

Ross, H. L., & Sawhill, I. V. (1975). *Time of transition: The growth of families headed by women.* Washington, DC: The Urban Institute.

Ross, S. (1979). *The Youth Values Project.* Washington, DC: The Population Institute.

Shah, F., Zelnik, M., Kantner, J. F. (1975). Unprotected intercourse among unwed teenagers. *Family Planning Perspectives, 7,* 39–44.

Smiklo, L. (1982). *An exploratory study of aspects of adolescent male reproductive responsibility in a white middle-class sample as reflected by attitudes and intended behaviors.* Unpublished doctoral dissertation. Columbia University Teachers College.

Sonenstein, F. L., & Pittman, K. J. (1984). The availability of sex education in large city school districts. *Family Planning Perspectives, 16,* 19–25.

Sorensen, R. (1973). *Adolescent sexuality in contemporary America.* New York: World.

Thompson, L., & Spanier, G. (1978). Influence of parents, peers and partners on contraceptive use of college men and women. *Journal of Marriage and the Family, 40,* 481–492.

Vener, A. M., & Stewart, C. S. (1974). Adolescent sexual behavior in middle America revisited: 1970–1973. *Journal of Marriage and the Family, 36,* 728–735.

Vener, A. M., Stewart, C. S., & Hager, D. L. (1972). The sexual behavior of adolescents in middle America: Generational and American–British comparisons. *Journal of Marriage and the Family, 34,* 696– 705.

Westney, O. E., Jenkins, R. R., & Benjamin, C. A. (1983). Sociosexual development of pre-adolescents. In Brooks-Gunn & Peterson (Ed.), *Girls at Puberty.* New York: Plenum.

Zabin, L. S., Hirsch, M. B., Smith, E. A., & Hardy, J. B. (1984). Adolescent sexual attitudes and behavior: Are they consistent? *Family Planning Perspectives, 16,* 181–185.

Zabin, L. S., Street, R., & Hardy, J. B. (1983). *Research and evaluation in a university, clinic and school-based adolescent pregnancy prevention program.* Paper presented at the annual meeting of the American Public Health Association, Dallas.

Zelnik, M., & Kantner, J. F. (1979). Reasons for nonuse of contraception in sexually active women aged 15–19. *Family Planning Perspectives, 11,* 289–296.

Zelnik, M., & Kantner, J. F. (1980). Sexual activity, contraceptive use and pregnancy among metropolitan area teenagers: 1971–1979. *Family Planning Perspectives, 12,* 230–237.

Zelnik, M., & Shah, F. K.(1983). First intercourse among young Americans. *Family Planning Perspectives, 15*(2), 64–70.

Zelnik, M., Kantner, J., & Ford, K. (1981). *Sex and pregnancy in adolescence.* Beverly Hills, CA: Sage.

4 Stresses and Coping Strategies of Adolescent Fathers

Arthur B. Elster
University of Utah

Leo Hendricks
Institute for Urban Affairs and Research, Howard University

Clinical and research interest in teenage fathers comes from concern for the impact that this group of young men have on child development, their effect on maternal emotional and financial stability, and the problems that they themselves face as a result of pregnancy and parenthood. In this chapter we investigate this latter concern. Discussion focuses on the various kinds of stresses experienced by young fathers, the manner in which fathers cope with their problems, and the factors that may affect individual differences in stresses and coping behavior.

TRANSITION TO PARENTHOOD

Caplan (1961) perceives a crisis as occurring when someone faces an obstacle to important life goals that is insurmountable to the utilization of customary methods of problem solving. Implicit in this concept is that at least for some interval of time a stressful event overcomes a person's capability to cope. Data from studies on adult fathers demonstrates that men perceive pregnancy and parenthood as stressful situations (Gerzi & Berman, 1981; Miller & Sollie, 1980). Research investigating the behavioral changes associated with the transition to parenthood also imply high level of anxiety experienced by fathers. The development of psychiatric problems (Osofsky, 1982), mild marital instability (Belsky, Spanier, & Rovine, 1983), and even physical symptoms (Trethowan & Conlon, 1965) have all been described in expectant and new fathers suggesting that at least for some fathers pregnancy results in an emotional crisis.

Initially, the transition to fatherhood was viewed in terms of a psychological crisis. Thus the problems and negative feelings experienced by fathers were

55

considered within a pathological context. More recently, however, researchers have come to view the increased level of anxiety felt by expectant and new fathers as part of normal, developmental process (see chapter by Miller and Belsky), with the transition to parenthood expected to engender some degree of stress or anxiety. Under "normal" situations, therefore, the level of stress experienced by fathers should be managed relatively easily without psychological crisis.

There is some indication that young fathers may have difficulty resolving the stresses associated with pregnancy and parenthood. Vaz, Smolen, and Miller (1983) interviewed 41 male partners of pregnant adolescents and young mothers and found that 41% of expectant fathers and 21% of new fathers reported an increase in feelings of depression. Elster and Panzarine (1981), in a study of 16 expectant teenage fathers, found that although 62.5% of young men were judged to be coping well with the stresses of pregnancy, 25% were having moderate difficulty and 12.5% were coping poorly. Thirty-seven percent of the total group were referred for additional counseling because of clinical evidence of depression, two of whom had suicidal ideation.

Even without strong empirical evidence, there is ample reason to speculate that adolescent fathers should have difficulty coping with pregnancy and parenthood. As Caplan (1961) proposed, problems can be insurmountable if they are of excessive magnitude or number or if the individual is inadequately equipped to cope with the stress. Such inadequacy might result from psychological immaturity or inadequate social support. Because of both the timing of the pregnancy and their age, teenage fathers may experience parenthood as a major crisis.

Premature transition to parenthood creates an especially stressful situation for any new parent (Bacon, 1974; Russell, 1980), and thus many of the problems experienced by teenage fathers can be viewed as resulting from the fact that their transition to parenthood, and possibly to marriage, has occurred earlier than is socially expected. Young fathers do not follow the traditional prescribed path whereby they complete formal education, obtain stable employment, marry, and only then enter parenthood. Deviating from this sequence may cause difficulty because it results in social criticism, truncated education, subsequent vocational difficulties, and the assumption of adult roles before the teens are psychologically prepared.

During the past decade our society has come to tolerate, and even actively support, adolescent mothers. No longer are these teens castigated and sent out of the community until they deliver their infants. Federal regulations, enacted in the early 1970s guarantee them the right to continue their formal education and to remain in regular school classes during their pregnancy. School programs for young mothers have been established in many districts to allow these women a chance to meet other adolescents in similar circumstances and thereby reestablish a social network. No such opportunity exists, however, for young fathers. They are frequently blamed by society and the girls' parents for the pregnancy. At times they feel alienated from friends and their usual sources of support. In addition, whereas young fathers are expected to provide for their children financially, they do not have legal participation regarding pregnancy outcome. Society's attitudes toward these teens remains somewhat punitive and harsh.

Premature transition to parenthood also adversely affects educational and vocational attainments. Age of parenthood is inversely related to the amount of formal education a man receives (Card & Wise, 1978). Teenage fathers complete substantially less education than their nonparent peers and, subsequently, are overrepresented in unskilled and semiskilled jobs. Undereducated fathers have become even more vulnerable to financial difficulties, unemployment, and lack of job stability as emphasis on educational attainment has increased during the past decade.

Parenthood may be associated with educational risk for either of two reasons: These teens may be marginal students who would have dropped out of school anyway, or they may drop out of school to obtain employment and support their partner and child. In our clinical experience, we see teen fathers in both situations. Future research is needed to clarify the relationship between educational attainment and fatherhood during adolescence.

Lastly, premature role transition causes stress because teens are required to assume adult responsibilities before they are psychologically prepared. Young fathers may still need to "experiment with their lives" as other adolescents do. The social and physical obligations of parenthood, however, may conflict with their desire for expansive social interactions. These teens often feel tied down, especially if married and after the initial excitement of parenthood as been replaced by the realities of parental obligations. Although it was once assumed that fathers rarely remain involved with their adolescent partners, this is not so today. As many as 70% of fathers in the Teen Mother & Child Program at the University of Utah are either married, engaged, or living with their partner at delivery. Other studies, reporting on more financially disadvantaged populations, have found that over 50–70% of fathers are still involved with the adolescent partner at delivery (Furstenberg, 1976; McCarthy & Menken, 1979; Vaz et al., 1983). Fathers of today appear interested in assuming more responsibility for parenting (Lamb, Pleck, & Levine, 1985). This change in attitude is associated with a social cost, however, in that the fathers must cope with the problems of parenthood.

In addition to the stresses resulting from premature transition to parenthood, teenage fathers also experience normative stresses associated with psychological development. During adolescence, youth establish their personal ethical and moral values, their vocational direction, and their sexual identity (see chapters by Teti and Lamb, and by Montemayor). These tasks are accomplished through "behavioral experimentation," whereby various personal alternatives are evaluated and either eliminated or retained depending on acceptance by parents and peers. The emotional turmoil resulting from this self-exploration can be difficult for both teens and parents. The magnitude of turmoil, however, is probably not as great as once thought (Montemayor, 1983; Offer & Offer, 1974). Some degree of developmental stress can be expected with most adolescent males, whether or not they are fathers.

Other aspects of the adolescent developmental process may also influence how young fathers are affected by their new role(s). Thus, problems in solving interpersonal difficulties may result from social cognitive immaturity or from a normal, high level of adolescent self-centeredness; an inability to effectively plan for future vocational or educational goals may result from the normal adolescent concerns with the "here and now." Unfortunately, although "psychological immaturity" is an attractive concept for explaining the problems and social responses of young fathers, it has not been adequately tested and, therefore, remains speculative.

STRESSES EXPERIENCED BY NEW FATHERS

The nature of the problems or stresses reported by fathers differs dramatically depending on whether the investigation concerns adults or adolescents. Studies on adult fathers have focused predominantly on their general anxiety level, self-esteem, psychological adjustment, and marital satisfaction (see chapter by Miller and Belsky). Work on adolescent fathers, however, has been concerned almost exclusively with identifying the specific stresses experinced by these young men. The most logical explanation for the different approaches is that research on adolescents has usually been performed by social service or health care professionals who wish to develop clinical interventions. Investigations of adult fathers, on the other hand, appear to have been motivated not by concern for the well-being of fathers, but by a search to understand their effect on the family.

What follows is a discussion of the specific types of stresses reported by new fathers. We compare differences between adult and adolescent fathers and speculate why these may exist.

McNall (1976) studied 15 expectant first-time fathers who were between 22–35 years of age, married, and had been or were attending college. A standard list of 34 potential concerns were each rated on a scale of 1 (no concern or positive feelings), 3 (some concern), or 5 (much concern or negative feelings). Selected results are presented in Table 4.1. The areas of major concern appeared to be financial, parenthood, and child health.

Miller and Myers-Walls (1983), in their review of studies concerned with adult parents, present similar conclusions. They identified three major categories of stresses that new parents experience: physical, psychological, and financial. Physical stressors include the demands of caretaking, such as fatigue, exhaustion, and the problem of management of time. Psychological stresses involve

TABLE 4.1
Selected Concerns of Expectant Adult Fathers   (n=15)

Type of Concern	Level of Concern		
	1 Low	2 Moderate	3 High
Financial	40%	33%	27%
Fatherhood	20%	47%	33%
Loss of freedom	80%	7%	13%
Child health	7%	53%	40%
Loss of social leisure time	60%	35%	7%

Note: Data adapted from McNall, 1986.

concerns for the well-being of the child, the adequacy of the parenting role, the impact that the child has on the parents, the loss of personal freedom, and the adverse effects on marital companionship. Financial stressors involve the economics of having a family, such as the rising cost of education, inflation, and the depressed job market.

Adolescent fathers appear to experience some of the same stresses as adult fathers. In addition, however, they have concerns and problems predicated on the premature nature of their transition to parenthood.

Hendricks, Howard, and Caesar (1981) used an open-ended question: ''In your opinion, and from what you have seen yourself, what are some of the problems you have faced as a young father?'' to obtain information regarding the stresses experienced by three groups of young black fathers (see Table 4.2). Fifty-five percent of the subjects indicated that their problems involved interpersonal relationships. These included problems with their family of origin, restriction of freedom imposed by responsibility for their children, the duty of providing for their children, the inability to see their children as much as they would like, and problems with various members of the unwed mothers' family. Another 23% indicated that their problems were related to other external factors, such as lack of employment, lack of money, or the inability to finish school. Fewer than 10% of fathers perceived their problems as the result of some person-

TABLE 4.2
Problems Experienced By Young Black Fathers

City of Residence	Personal Failing N(%)	Interpersonal Relationship N(%)	Other External Factor N(%)	None N(%)	Total N(%)
Tulsa	0(0)	11(55)	6(30)	3(15)	20(21)
Chicago	2(7.5)	14(48)	6(22)	6(22)	27(28)
Columbus	6(13)	28(58)	10(21)	4(8)	48(51)
Total	8(8)	52(55)	22(23)	13(14)	95(100)

Note: From Hendricks et al., 1981).

al failing. Those who did indicated they were having a problem coping with being a father and setting "good examples" in their child's presence. Fourteen percent of the young men indicated they had not faced any problems as fathers.

Hendricks (1984) used the same open-ended question with a sample of young Hispanic fathers ($N = 31$) in Albuquerque, New Mexico. The stresses reported by these men included being told how to raise their children, the responsibility of being a young father, meeting financial responsibilities, getting a job, the health of their children, school, preparation for their children's future, setting goals for their own future, having a place to stay, and interpersonal problems with relatives and partners. Taken together, these data suggest that both black and Hispanic young fathers are likely to experience stresses involving the "self," another person, and other external factors.

Studies involving white adolescent fathers yield similar results. Elster and Panzarine (1983) interviewed 20 male adolescent partners of pregnant teenagers (mean age of 17.6 years) from one to four times during the prenatal period and at 4 to 6 weeks following delivery. Eighteen of the subjects were white and most were from middle-class backgrounds. All pregnancies were conceived out of wedlock, but 15 couples had married by delivery. Stressors reported by the subjects could be grouped into four categories: vocational-educational concerns, concerns about the health of the mother and infant, concerns about future parenthood, and problems with relationships. The intensity of these concerns changed throughout pregnancy and the neonatal period. The vocational-educational concerns were present relatively early during pregnancy and remained at a high level; health concerns peaked in late pregnancy and dropped off after delivery; parenting concerns arose during the middle part of pregnancy, dropped slightly, and then increased again postpartum; problems with relationships were greatest during early pregnancy and declined consistently.

More recent data obtained from 20 expectant fathers seen in the Teen Mother and Child Program further confirms the types of stressors affecting adolescents (Kahn, 1984). The sample again was predominently white; 65% of the men were 18 years of age or less. Subjects were asked to rank order each of 10 potential stressors. Financial concerns were ranked first by 35% of young men followed by concerns with school, health of mother and baby, work, and relationship with partner.

In summary, parenthood and financial concerns (including vocational issues) appear to be stressors for fathers regardless of age or ethnic background. Other issues, such as school and social relationships, however, appear to be uniquely relevant for adolescent fathers. There appear to be no differences in the types of problems expressed by young Black, Hispanic, and white fathers. For adolescents who remain involved as fathers, however, teenagers must also resolve the problems associated with premarital conceptions.

HOW FATHERS COPE WITH THEIR PROBLEMS AND CONCERNS

Miller and Myers-Walls (1983), in their review of research on stress and coping in adult parents, describe three major mechanisms by which expectant and new parents manage stress. Unfortunately, they could only speculate about differences in coping strategies between men and women because of the lack of data on fathers.

The major method of coping with parenthood was thought to involve reliance on social support systems and natural helping networks. Family members, friends, and work companions all may serve to mediate the stress resulting from pregnancy and parenthood. Miller and Myers-Walls point out that, whereas the inclusion of fathers in childbirth preparation classes was expected to help expectant mothers, the social contact with other men might be of major help to fathers also. A second major coping strategy involves methods for balancing multiple role responsibilities. This is especially important for working women who have to resolve and manage a variety of social roles (i.e., wife, mother, and working professional); as fathers become more involved in nuturing and care-giving roles, they too must learn how to balance a variety of roles. The third coping strategy involves seeking assistance from professionals and from the media. This strategy was speculated to be used more by women than by men.

Hendricks (1984), in his studies on black and Hispanic adolescent fathers, investigated where these young men would turn for help and assistance. To the question, "Who would you go to first with a problem," a majority of the young fathers, regardless of their racial identity, said they were most likely to go to their family (Table 4.3). The fathers were also asked: "If you had a personal problem, who or where would you go for advice or help?" Responses of the black fathers indicated that a majority of them would go to their mothers or fathers for advice or help. Further analyses showed that the adolescents were most likely to turn to

TABLE 4.3
Sources of Support for Black and Hispanic Adolescent Fathers

| Race | Choices for Sources of Help | | |
	Family	Friend	Social Service Agency
	n(%)	n(%)	n(%)
Black	84(88)	10(11)	1(1)
Hispanic	22(71)	8(26)	1(3)
Total	106(84)	18(14)	2(2)

Note: From Hendricks, 1984.

TABLE 4.4

Anticipatory Coping Strategies Used by Prospective Adolescent Fathers in Preparation for Parenthood

Type of Strategy	Type of Behaviors	
	Problem-Focused Behaviors	Emotion-Focused Behaviors
Direct action	Assume provider Role (n = 20) Help prepare for baby (n = 18)	Alcohol abuse (n = 20)
Information seeking	Talking with others (n = 14) Observing other parents (n = 4) Reading (n = 4)	
Intrapsychic process	Fantasizing about parenthood (n = 12) Reviewing how they were parented (n = 7)	Changing the meaning of the situation (n = 3)
Inhibition of action	Setitng down (n = 6)	

Note: From Panzarine and Elster, 1983; n = 20.

62

their mothers. This finding was not too surprising as a majority of these young fathers reported being closer to their mothers than to other family members. On the other hand, 45% of Hispanic fathers reported they were more likely to go to a friend for help, followed by 35% who would turn to their parents, and 13% who would turn to siblings. Clergy and school teachers were seldom used as a sources of help by either Blacks or Hispanics. As may be observed in Table 4.3, only two of the fathers (2%) indicated they would seek help from a social service agency.

Hendricks et al. (1981) also asked the young black fathers what types of services they would like to see offered by teenage parenting agencies. These fathers appeared to want information (e.g., on sex education and child development), various kinds of practical help (e.g., finding a job or finishing school), and psychosocial counseling (e.g., on coping with family life). For a more complete discussion on the services needed by young fathers see the chapter by Kahn and Bolton.

Panzarine and Elster (1983) investigated the types of anticipatory coping strategies employed by their sample of 20 expectant teen fathers to prepare themselves for parenthood. The various behaviors and strategies were categorized following Lazarus' model (1980) as involving direct action, information-seeking, intrapsychic process, and inhibition of action (see Table 4.4). Some of these strategies dealt with the potential problem directly, whereas others dealt with the emotional stresses created by the pregnancy. Panzarine and Elster found that fathers were more likely to try to cope directly with the upcoming event rather than try to reduce emotional distress. To prepare for parenthood, all fathers involved themselves in some new or additional activity to improve their financial situation. Most fathers helped to prepare for their baby by engaging in such activities as buying clothes or fixing up rooms. Many teens sought information about pregnancy and parenthood by talking with others or observing and evaluating other parents. Young fathers also tended to fantasize about fatherhood and think about how they had been raised. Only a few fathers coped with upcoming parenthood by redirecting their life away from past social activities. Those who did viewed the change as a sign of "growing up." A few fathers reported alcohol abuse and denial as a means of minimizing their emotional discomfort.

SUMMARY

Although our knowledge of the stresses and coping strategies of young fathers is limited, clinical impressions seem to confirm the results of the few empirical studies that have been done. Together, these data imply that many adolescent fathers remain involved with their children and are concerned about their financial responsibility. In light of their lack of academic achievement, this is certainly a realistic concern. Clinicians must help young fathers pursue formal education or vocational programs in order to provide them with realistic options to unemployment or underemployment.

Problems with relationships are another major and realistic concern of young fathers. To become fully committed to parenthood fathers need to resolve the negative and uncertain feelings about the future of the couple's relationship. Support of the kinship contributes heavily to this resolution; parent's concerns should also be assessed and treated clinically. Feelings of being "tied down" and separated from their normal peer group are concerns that probably accompany many fathers in their transition to parenthood. Young fathers should be helped to realize that if they remain involved with their new family, they must relinquish some of the past. Because adolescents tend to live for the "here and now," it is not surprising that young fathers have relatively few concerns about futuristic issues such as the quality of parenting.

Two major factors appear the most relevant from review of the research and clinical data on coping behaviors of adolescent fathers. First is the importance of the social network in assisting teens to cope with the stresses of parenthood. From a clinical perspective, young fathers who remain involved with their children seem to lack strong social support systems. Fatherhood for these youths may have more personal significance than for other teenagers who abdicate their responsibility as parents. The second relevant factor seems to be that young fathers choose to be action oriented in their approaches to coping with fatherhood. Both of these points may help direct counselors as they work with these young men.

REFERENCES

Bacon, L. (1974). Early motherhood, accelerated role transition, and social pathologies. *Social Forces, 54*, 334–341.

Belsky, J., Spanier, G., & Rovine, M. (1983). Stability and change in marriage across the transition to parenthood. *Journal of Marriage and the Family, 45*, 567–577.

Caplan, J. (1961). *An approach to community mental health* (p. 18). New York: Grune & Stratton.

Card, J. J., & Wise, L. L. (1978). Teenage mothers and teenage fathers: The impact of early childbearing on the parent's personal and professional lives. *Family Planning Perspective, 10*, 199–205.

Elster, A., & Panzarine, S. (1981). Unwed teenaged fathers: Emotional and health educational needs. *Journal of Adolescent Health Care, 1*, 116–120.

Elster, A., & Panzarine, S. (1983). Adolescent fathers: Stresses during gestation and early parenthood. *Clinical Pediatrics, 22*, 700–703.

Furstenberg, F. F. (1976). The social consequences of teenage parenthood. *Family Planning Perspective, 8*, 148–164.

Gerzi, S., & Berman, E. (1981). Emotional relations of expectant fathers to their wive's first pregnancy. *British Journal of Medical Psychology, 54*, 259–265.

Hendricks, L. E. (1984). *Outreach with teenage fathers: A preliminary report on three ethnic groups.* Unpublished manuscript (Available from Howard University, Institute for Urban Affairs and Research, Washington, DC 20008).

Hendricks, L. E., Howard, C. S., & Caesar, P. P. (1981). Black unwed adolescent fathers: A comparative study of their problems and help-seeking behavior. *Journal of the National Medical Association, 73,* 863–868.

Kahn, J. (1984). *Teenage fathers: Perceptions and concerns of adolescent fathers.* Unpublished manuscript (Available from University of Utah, Department of Pediatrics, Salt Lake City, UT, 84132).

Lamb, M. E., Pleck, J. H., & Levine, J. A. (1985). The role of the father in child development: The effects of increased paternal involvement. In B. B. Laney & A. E. Kazdin (Eds.), *Advances in clinical child psychology* (Vol. 8) New York: Plenum.

Lazarus, R. S. (1980). The stress and coping paradigm. In L. A. Bond & J. C. Rosen (Eds.), *Competence and coping during adulthood.* New Hampshire: University Press of New England.

McCarthy, J., & Menken, J. (1979). Marriage, remarriage, marital disruption and age of first birth. *Family Planning Perspective, 11,* 21–30.

McNall, L. (1976). Concerns of expectant fathers. In L. McNall & L. Galleener (Eds.), *Current practices in OB/GYN nursing.* St. Louis: Mosby.

Miller, B. C., & Sollie, D. (1980). Normal stress during the transition to parenthood. *Family Relations, 29,* 459–465.

Miller, B. C., & Myers-Walls, J. A., (1983). Parenthood: Stresses and coping strategies. In H. I. McCubbin & C. R. Figley (Eds.), *Stress and the family: Coping with normative transitions* (Vol. 1). New York: Brunner/Mazel.

Montemayor, R. (1983). Parents and adolescents in conflict: All families some of the time and some families most of the time. *Journal of Early Adolescence, 3,* 83–103.

Offer, D., & Offer, J. (1974). Normal adolescent males: The high school and college years. *Journal of the American College Association, 22,* 209–213.

Osofsky, H. (1982). Expectant and new fatherhood as a developmental crisis. *Bulletin of the Menninger Clinic, 46,* 209–230.

Panzarine, S., Elster, A. (1983). Coping in a group of expectant adolescent fathers: An exploratory study. *Journal of Adolescent Health Care, 4,* 117–120.

Russell, E. S. (1980). Unscheduled parenthood: Transition to parent for the teenager. *Journal of Social Issues, 36,* 45–63.

Trethowan, W. H., & Conlon, M. F. (1965). The couvade syndrome. *British Journal of Psychiatry, 111,* 57–66.

Vaz, R., Smolen, P., & Miller, C. (1983). Adolescent pregnancy: Involvement of the male partner. *Journal of Adolescent Health Care, 4,* 246–250.

5 Teenage Fatherhood: High School Completion and Educational Attainment

William Marsiglio
Center for Human Resource Research

INTRODUCTION

Research on the educational and economic consequences of teenage parenthood has focused predominantly on young women (Bacon, 1974; Dillard & Pol, 1982; Furstenberg, 1976; Hofferth & Moore, 1979; McCarthy & Radish, 1983; Trussell, 1976; Waite & Moore, 1978). Whereas it is now customary to note the paucity of research on males in the fertility and family-planning literature, little is actually known about the social, psychological, and economic factors associated with fathering a child as a teenager. Haggstrom, Blaschke, Karouse, Lisowski & Morrisons'(1981) analysis of males from the National Longitudinal Study of the High School Class of 1972 is a notable exception. This study, though insightful in many ways, is restricted to a sample of high school seniors, thereby excluding dropouts, and focuses on teenage parenthood among youth in their late teens. The types of questions that can be addressed are necessarily limited by this sampling design.

Many of the issues salient to teenage fatherhood are similar to those Hofferth and Moore (1979) raised concerning childbearing among young women. As these authors noted several years ago, the pervasive notion that early childbearing brings about various social and economic hardships for young women was not well grounded empirically. Likewise, little has been done to explore comparable issues for teenage fathers. To what extent, if any, and under what conditions, does fathering a child as a teenager decrease the likelihood that a male will attain a socioeconomic status commensurate with his abilities and aspirations prior to fathering a child? In turn, does a young father's inability to pursue his educational goals have a negative effect on his self-esteem and status aspirations? Are the initial socioeconomic differences between young fathers and their childless peers solely responsible for differences in educational and employment experiences among these two groups of males, or does having a child as a teenager represent an independent factor that curtails young men's opportunities net of other factors, including marriage? How do teenage fathers respond to the birth of their first child in terms of their school and work-related activities during the period immediately following the child's birth? For example, do they tend to drop out of high school and college, and if they do leave high school prematurely, do they eventually receive high school accreditation in the form of a GED. (General Educational Development)?[1] Are there long-term consequences associated with an early first birth for teenage fathers who live with their child, such as lower educational attainment and unrealized employment opportunities, and how is age at first fatherhood related to these outcomes?

The questions noted previously represent only a sample of the varied issues germane to early fertility among males. A few of these questions are dealt with here. First, however, the teenage fatherhood concept must be clarified. It is generally assumed that for physiological and social reasons the consequences of teenage fertility are more direct and pronounced for young women than they are for young men (Card, 1977). This does not mean that males are immune to the consequences frequently associated with early childbearing. However, many of these consequences are contingent upon the father's willingness to assume a degree of responsibility in raising his child. In the context of American society, assuming this responsibility generally entails some type of commitment to the mother, usually in the form of marriage. Teenage fatherhood, as conceptualized here and in contrast to teenage male fertility, requires that the male express a commitment to the child, at least initially. Some teenage fathers may disassociate themselves from their child and the child's mother, thereby minimizing their vulnerability to the types of consequences discussed here. Subcultural variations regarding the tendency to legitimize unplanned births through marriage, frequently measured by using race as a proxy variable, are relevant here. Teenage males socialized within the black subculture, for example, are more likely than youth from other racial/ethnic groups to have children out of wedlock and to live apart from these children after their birth.[2] If the bivariate relationship between

---

[1]The GED, first introduced in 1943 and revamped in 1978, is used to grant credit by examination for an individual's competency in material at the high school level. This test is comprised of five sections: (1) mathematics, (2) social studies, (3) science, (4) reading, and (5) writing skills. High school equivalency diplomas or certificates are issued on the basis of satisfactory test scores and are considered official documents. For a more detailed summary of the GED see Cervero (1983); Swarm (1981) and Ulin (1982).

[2]A recent Digest report (1984) in *Family Planning Perspectives,* using data from the National Center for Health Statistics, noted that whereas out-of-wedlock births among blacks may be declining slightly as similar types of births for whites may be on the rise, black teenagers 15–19 still have about five times as many births out-of-wedlock as do whites. In the same issue, Clark, Zabin, & Hardy (1984) summarize their findings from a survey of innercity, junior high and high school black males by noting that "only a third—say they would be 'very upset' if they got a girl pregnant in the next six months. Two-fifths would be a 'little upset,' and one-quarter either would not be upset or would be happy" (p. 82).

fathering a child as a teenager and subsequent educational attainment were considered without controls, the relationship would probably appear weaker for black teenage fathers compared to young white or Hispanic fathers because there would be a higher relative proportion of black fathers who did not live with their child. The theoretically relevant issue then, particularly because males do not experience the physical side effects associated with pregnancy and childbearing, is whether or not assuming the fatherhood role in the social sense as a teenager curtails young males' educational attainment.

I have two major objectives in this chapter, one descriptive and the other substantive. They are shaped in part by my reluctance to group all teenage fathers together irrespective of their level of commitment to their child and by my desire to portray the human capital potential (in terms of high school completion outcomes) of all teenage males who father children.

On a descriptive level, data are presented that provide some basic information on the background characteristics and high school completion outcomes for teenage fathers and their peers who remain childless throughout their teens. These data, although limited in that they cannot be used to address causal issues in their present form, are useful in documenting some of the distinctive features of the teenage father population as the data highlight the human capital potential for particular categories of teenage fathers. The tabular data permit a comparison of the demographic characteristics and high school accreditation status for individuals who father children at different ages, for those who are married and not married when their child is born, for those who live with their child and those who do not, and more generally for those who experience teenage fertility and those who do not.

My substantive focus deals with the association between living with a child fathered by a teenager and the father's educational attainment. Regression analyses are used to test the hypothesis that living with a child fathered by a teenager will be negatively related to the young father's total years of completed schooling. Separate models are also specified for the total sample of teenage fathers and for the two subsamples of teenage fathers, those who lived with their child at the first observation point after the child was born and those who did not. The association between age at childbirth and educational attainment is of primary interest in these latter models.

Teenage Fatherhood and Educational Attainment

From a life-course perspective (Elder, 1978), an unplanned teenage birth is likely to be a disruptive experience, for the individuals directly involved and for the society at large, because it represents a major life event that has usually occurred "out of the normative sequence for which institutions of education, the family, and the labor market are designed" (McLaughlin, Grady, Billy & Winges, 1984). A teenage birth is quite often problematic because it accelerates a youth's transition to a parental and perhaps spousal role, and it may impede a teenager's future role transitions, for example, completion of school, entrance into the labor force, or enrollment in postsecondary school (Bacon, 1974). A young male confronted with unintended fatherhood is likely to experience stress as he attempts to adjust himself to his newly acquired status and reconcile the competing role demands affiliated with being a parent, spouse, and student. A number of diverse factors will play a role in determining how well a particular teenage father adapts to his new situation, in the future, both short term and long term.

Educational and school activities constitute one realm of a young father's life that is likely to be influenced by an unplanned birth. Some teenage fathers may experience little difficulty attending school and achieving their desired level of education, but many others will find it extremely difficult to pursue their educational career in the manner they would have if they had not fathered and assumed responsibility for a child. Perhaps one of the more important factors that will affect a teenage father's schooling decisions and ultimate educational attainment will be his perception of his competency in educational endeavors. If a young father considers himself to be a good student and his significant others do as well, he will probably value his role as a student more than the student who is pessimistic about his abilities and disenchanted with his school system. Consequently, he will probably make a greater effort to continue his education or at least try to receive some type of formal certification for completing high school, especially if others encourage his efforts.

A young father may attempt to reorganize his priorities independently,or he may alter his educational and career plans to accommodate his new obligations as a father and perhaps husband because he feels pressured into making these changes. He may leave high school or college before graduating in order to enter the labor market. Or, if he has already left school, he may find that the responsibilities associated with his newly acquired status make it exceedingly difficult for him to resume his education. Another scenario involves the young male who is currently attending high school or college and perceives the arrival of a new baby as a legitimate reason to postpone or at least reassess his plans to enroll in college or graduate school but manages to finish his current program. A teenage father may postpone or never realize his educational and career ambitions if he becomes entrenched in an everyday work routine, a life-style that may enable him to feel comfortable momentarily with how well he is fulfilling his role obligations as a "responsible" father and husband. The tendency to postpone ambitions is of utmost concern if educational opportunities foregone early in a young male's life place him at a disadvantage later in life in acquiring human capital.

It seems reasonable to expect that a young father who lives with his child will tend to experience more restrictions on unabated schooling than his male counterpart who does not live with his child because the "committed" father will be more likely to assume responsibilities associated with the traditional provider role, and perhaps even contribute to child care. A young father may be more likely to experience difficulties in continuing his education if he is residing in a dwelling apart from his parents' home or the home of his partner's parents. For the teenage father living with other adults, school completion, especially high school, should be facilitated because a convenient support network may be in place to help him fulfill his obligations. The wife or partner of a teenage father in particular may play an instrumental role in assisting a young father to achieve his educational goals. Similarly, parental expectations and financial resources are likely to be related to a young father's ultimate level of educational attainment.

In terms of high school accreditation, the timing of the birth in relation to the youth's current grade level may influence a young father's decision whether or not to "stick it out" in school. Several findings from Morgan's (1984) study of high school dropouts are pertinent to the present discussion. In general, youth who are attending the 10th or 11th grade are more likely to drop out than are those in 9th and 12th grade; so too, those who are 1 or more years behind their normal age–grade are more likely to drop out than are those who are on time. Morgan also found that even after controlling for a number of nonschool differences, high school completion raised the earnings of youth substantially when dropouts and high school completers were compared. Moreover, a regular diploma was found to have considerably more certification value than the GED, whereas delayed completion was not associated with any notable disadvantages compared to on-time completion. The widespread conviction that school leaving is a more prevelant, as well as a more permanent , phenomena among minority groups was also well supported. These findings buttress the contention that accreditation is an important vehicle for status attainment in our industrialized society and therefore an important outcome measure to consider when discussing the ramifications of male teenage fertility and fatherhood.

It is generally assumed that a high school diploma or its equivalent is the minimum qualification for most jobs. This reality is most salient to a young father who has an interest in, or is coerced into, contributing financially to the support of his child and perhaps the child's mother as well. Young women who have their first child at age 15 or 16 frequently use the GED as a means to receive high school credentials (Mott & Marsiglio, 1985). Data presented here suggest that males who father their first child at age 16 or younger also make extensive use of the GED , earning it more than twice as often as older fathers. The GED thus affords many teenage fathers who would probably not otherwise graduate a better opportunity to gain entry into the labor market and to make a financial contribution to their family.

From a policy perspective, one of the more critical issues in terms of male teenage fertility may simply be: Do males who father children as teenagers on average acquire less human capital than males who do not experience early fertility? If teenage fathers are predisposed to have fewer individual resources, for whatever reason, the consequences of their disadvantaged status are likely to be felt by their child and the child's mother. The indirect consequences of male teenage fertility and teenage fatherhood may be quite severe then even though early fertility may not directly be responsible for suppressing young males socioeconomic status. This reality by itself will no doubt influence how policy makers address the teenage fertility issue in general, and how they attempt to incorporate young fathers into legislative and program initiatives. The other obvious issue is whether or not assuming fatherhood responsibilities attenuates educational attainment for these young fathers. Does a young father take a substantial risk in lessening his chances for acquiring human capital when he "decides" to marry his child's mother and live with his new family?

Research Design

Data set.   Data for the present study were drawn from the National Longitudinal Survey of Work Experience of Youth (NLSY). The NLSY is a nationally representative panel survey that included 12,686 respondents age 14 to 22 in the initial survey year 1979. Respondents have been interviewed each year through 1984 and will be interviewed at least through 1987. Over 96% of the original sample were interviewed in 1983. The sample is a stratified cluster probability sample of male and female youth that includes an overrepresentation of black, Hispanic, and economically disadvantaged white youth. The initial 1979 sample had a special military supplement of individuals who were in the service at that time. These subgroups can be weighted to represent a national cross-section of American youth aged 14 to 22 in 1979. This study is restricted to the 6,144 males, 96% of the 1979 male sample, who were also interviewed in 1983. Readers interested in a more detailed summary of the youth sample and panel design are encouraged to review Frankel, McWilliams & Spencer's (1983) technical sampling report and *The National Longitudinal Surveys Handbook* (Center for Human Resource Research, 1984).

Methodology.   Because the NLSY panel design encompasses a range of age categories, it provides an opportunity for alternative sample definitions to be used when studying various aspects of teenage fatherhood. One of the more challenging tasks in using this data set is to select appropriate subsamples that minimize censorship biases and make the best possible use of available data. Several key sampling decisions for this study are discussed here. In short, four steps were taken to arrive at two subsamples of teenage fathers and a comparison group of males who did not father a child as a teenager. First, only those males interviewed in both 1979 and 1983 were considered. Second, a subsample of 4844 males who were 20 years of age and older when surveyed in 1983 was identified. Third, a subset of teenage fathers was drawn from this group and consisted of 489 males who fathered a child when they were 19 or younger. This subset was used to document high school completion outcomes for teenage fathers by comparing their patterns to those for males who did not report fathering a child as a teenager. Fourth, the subset of teenage fathers was divided into two groups, young fathers who lived with their child shortly after the child's birth and those who did not.

The first two sample restrictions were invoked so that individuals would have sufficient time to complete their high school education. It is important to note that high school accreditation may come in the form of a regular diploma or a GED. If a teenage birth is actually a disruptive life event, some teenage males may elect to drop out of school temporarily and then return for a GED, or perhaps if they are already out of school, they may opt for a GED because they feel they are unable to return to regular school. Grouping all high school graduates together would obscure this pattern. GED recipients are likely to be older than the typical group of students who receive their diplomas in the spring of their senior year. The mean age for GED recipients was 19.5 for the present sample of males 20 and older. Many of the would be dropouts are thus accounted for in the present design; roughly 6% of this 20 and over sample earned a GED by 1983. However, this figure is bound to underestimate the total number of males who earn this form of accreditation because a goodly number will be in their 20's when they finally receive it. Thirty-five% of the GED recipients in this sample received their accreditation after age 20 with 9% obtaining it when they were 22 or older. It should be noted that the relatively youthful age distribution of the present sample, 96.5% were between the ages of 20 and 25 in 1983, restricts my discussion primarily to the short-term association between early fatherhood and educational attainment. A more thorough assessment of the long-term effects of teenage fatherhood on educational attainment should be possible as data are collected from future waves of this panel.

An important feature of this study is the dichotomous variable that differentiates between teenage fathers who live with their child at the first observation point after their child's birth and those who do not. In cases where a respondent was not interviewed in the survey immediately following his first child's birth, data from the next survey in which the respondent was interviewed were used. A shortcoming of this variable is that data from the 1979 survey had to be used for all respondents who had a birth prior to their 1979 survey date; retrospective data on living arrangements were not collected. The living arrangement for a number of teenage fathers whose first child was born before their 1979 survey will therefore reflect a situation as it existed several years after the child's birth. This variable is used as a proxie for a young father's commitment to his child.[3]

---

[3]Conceptualizing this variable as an indicator of a young male's commitment to fatherhood may be misleading at times. In some cases this variable will be a more accurate indicator of a young father's concern for the general well-being of his partner than it is a direct indicator of his intentions for assuming fatherhood responsibilities per se. Living with one's child may simply be an unavoidable consequence that goes hand in hand with maintaining a relationship with one's partner.

Whereas this is a reasonable approach given the objectives of this chapter, the living arrangement variable is only a crude measure of a father's commitment to fatherhood responsibilities.

Commitment to fatherhood is undoubtedly a multidimensional concept with a variety of possible indicators.[4] The measure used here, however, does not directly account for, or distinguish between, a number of dimensions presumed to be relevant to the commitment concept, for example, a father's willingness to make sacrifices on behalf of his child, the intensity with which a father assumes child-care responsibilities, or the time a father devotes to interacting with his child. It is also quite possible that a father may alter his educational plans as a result of fatherhood considerations even though he does not live with his child. His reason for not living with his child may in fact have more to do with his relationship with the child's mother than it has to do with his lack of interest in assuming fatherhood responsibilities. In some cases a young father will be denied an opportunity to live with his child from the outset if the child's mother retains custody of the child and chooses not to live with the child's father. Despite these caveats, this variable serves a useful purpose by identifying a group of young fathers for which the relationship between educational outcomes and early fatherhood in its social sense can be considered. It should be noted that because child custody is generally assumed by the young woman when she and her partner do not marry, it may follow that the living arrangement variable is merely a surrogate for a marital status variable that delineates out-of-wedlock and within-wedlock births among young fathers. The living arrangement variable will differ from a marital status variable empirically to the extent that young fathers live with their partner and child outside of marriage or retain custody of their child without their partner present. If the marital status variable is operationalized in terms of marital status at the child's birth, then the two variables will also differ to the extent that marital status changes between the birth of the child and the subsequent interview.

---

[4]The commitment concept in its most general sense may be conceptualized in a number of ways. Stryker (1968, 1980) has proposed an insightful social psychological approach that goes beyond the NLSY sociodemographic data and warrants future attention. As a major proponent of the structural school of symbolic interactionism within sociology, Stryker emphasizes the importance of social structure for human interaction and relates commitment to identity salience. A person's self is assumed to have a variety of identities, some of which are more salient or central to the person's overall conception of self and are consequently more likely to be invoked in social situations. These identities are developed through a process of social interaction and are embedded in a person's positions and roles. A teenage father, for example, will be faced with an opportunity to develop new identities based on his premature parental and in many cases spousal roles. Future research should determine the extent to which a young father commits himself to these identities, identify the factors that lead him to develop a given level of commitment, and consider how the process of developing new identities and commitment to these identities influence other major life goals, such as the pursuit of accreditation and further education.

A noteworthy data issue for the present study involved the quality of males' fertility reporting. The longitudinal nature of the NLSY provides an opportunity to assess the accuracy with which respondents report their birth histories over time. Mott (1983) found, not surprisingly, that women report their birth histories much more accurately than do men. He also noted that although males are less accurate reporters than women, regardless of the living arrangement of the child in question, misreporting is most pronounced for fathers who live apart from their child. These findings suggest that the overall teenage father subsample may be biased to some extent. Males who were less active in assuming fatherhood responsibilities may have also been less likely to acknowledge their fertility and therefore mistakenly excluded from the subsample. Misreporting the child's correct birth date may have also been more common among fathers who were less involved with their children, but dating discrepancy is probably less systematic than is the failure to report a birth altogether. Consequently, the teenage father subsample may be biased toward young fathers who are above average in their degree of commitment to fatherhood. The obvious implication of this data quality issue is that caution is warranted when generalizing from the descriptive data and analyses for the entire teenage father sample and the subset of teenage fathers not living with their child. At the same time, it can be argued that these data are more reliable than cross-sectional data because misreporting can be resolved in some cases. The present study uses revised fertility variables as noted in Mott (1983).

Results

A summary of selective background characteristics is presented in Table 5.1 for the total sample of 4,844 males, a comparison group of males who had their first birth when they were at least 20 or who had not yet fathered a child by 1983, and the two categories of teenage fathers, those who lived with their child shortly after their child's birth and those who did not. This table illustrates the racial, regional, religious, and socioeconomic heterogeneity of the present sample of American youth who are currently in their early and middle 20s. It also highlights a few of the socio demographic differences among young fathers who live with their child and those who do not. These differences appear to be related to a large extent to racial differentials in the tendency for teenage fathers to live with their child.

A comparison of high school completion outcomes between teenage fathers who fathered their first child at various ages and comparison groups of males who fathered a child when they were 20 or older, or who did not have a child by their 1983 survey, reveals several notable patterns. Descriptive statistics are presented in Table 5.2 that represent a respondent's probability of dropping out of high school, receiving a GED, or earning a regular diploma by his 1983 survey, cross-tabulated by his age when he fathered his first child. Given the relatively

TABLE 5.1

Distribution of Background Characteristics for Overall Sample and Relevant Subsamples
of Males 20 and Older as of 1983 Survey

	Total		Not Teenage Father by 1983		Teenage Fathers Living With Child		Teenage Fathers Not Living With Child	
	N	%	N	%	N	%	N	%
Respondent's age as of the 1983 survey								
20	763	15.5	671	15.3	36	15.6	53	18.9
21	757	16.8	672	16.8	33	15.7	50	18.8
22	774	15.6	695	15.8	28	11.7	48	16.1
23	822	16.9	725	16.5	63	28.2	32	14.8
24	801	16.1	731	16.3	33	11.3	37	19.3
25	769	15.7	700	15.8	38	15.8	28	11.7
26	158	3.5	144	3.6	8	1.8	2	0.3
Race/ethnicity								
Hispanic	712	6.1	630	5.9	50	10.9	29	7.6
Black	1200	13.5	1000	12.1	34	10.0	157	56.8
White	2219	73.9	2088	75.8	94	65.4	34	28.6
Disadvantaged white[a]	713	6.5	620	6.2	61	13.7	30	7.0
Region of residence at age 14								
Northeast	948	21.6	875	22.1	31	13.3	41	16.8
North central	1275	32.0	1141	31.9	63	34.4	69	32.1
South	1654	29.2	1463	28.8	84	31.0	99	36.4
West	767	14.2	677	14.0	49	19.0	36	12.3
Other	30	0.2	27	0.2	3	0.4	0	0.0
NA	170	2.9	155	3.0	9	1.9	5	2.3
Residence at age 14								
Urban	3792	77.6	3385	77.6	180	69.4	214	86.0
Rural	1035	22.1	941	22.1	57	29.7	33	11.8
NA	17	0.3	12	0.2	2	0.9	3	2.2
Religion as child								
Catholic	1598	33.0	1471	33.9	77	34.2	45	18.8
Fund. Protestant[b]	1591	32.8	1345	31.0	95	38.1	142	53.5
Other Protestant	1118	23.1	1045	24.1	37	15.8	34	13.5
Other	516	10.7	457	10.5	29	11.7	29	14.2
NA	21	0.4	20	0.5	1	0.2	0	0.0
Lived with two parents at age 14								
Yes	3738	83.6	3398	84.6	183	82.2	148	58.0
No	1098	16.2	934	15.3	56	17.8	100	39.3
NA	8	0.2	6	0.1	0	0.0	2	2.7
Father's education								
Less than 12 years	1741	29.5	1513	28.5	109	42.4	111	44.0
12 years	1430	32.3	1309	32.8	60	29.4	57	23.7
More than 12 years	1025	28.8	977	28.8	26	15.6	20	10.2
NA	648	9.4	539	8.8	44	12.6	62	22.1
Mother's education								
Less than 12 years	1808	27.8	1551	26.5	118	42.8	129	48.6
12 years	1905	45.8	1749	46.5	76	37.8	75	33.2
More than 12 years	797	20.9	760	22.0	15	7.6	22	8.2
NA	334	5.5	278	5.1	30	11.7	24	9.9

Note: Percentages are weighted and do not add to 100% in all cases due to rounding.

[a]This categorization refers to white respondents who met the Office of Management and Budget's criteria for poverty in 1978 when the sample was selected.

[b]The national Opinion Research Center's (1981) coding scheme was used to differentiate Fundamentalists from non-Fundamentalists. The only exception taken to NORC's classification scheme was that all Babtists were categorized as Fundamentalists. See Chi (1982) for a more detailed discussion of the present coding scheme.

TABLE 5.2
Probabilities for Type of High School Completion Outcome by Father's
Age at First Birth and Males With no Children as of the 1983 Survey

Father's Age at First Birth	N	Graduation Status by 1983 Survey			
		Dropout	GED	Diploma	Total Graduates
16 or younger	54	.44	.23	.33	.56
17	69	.48	.09	.43	.52
18	159	.51	.10	.38	.48
19	193	.37	.11	.52	.63
20 or older	821	.22	.09	.68	.77
No child as of 1983 interview	3426	.12	.05	.83	.87
Total	4722	.16	.06	.78	.85
19 or younger	475	.44	.12	.45	.57
20 or older, or no child as of 1983 interview	4247	.14	.06	.81	.87

Note: Probabilities are weighted: The sample is males 20 and older as of
the 1983 survey, 122 cases (2.5%) were omitted from this table because
their graduation status could not be determined. The omitted cases are
similar to the overall sample in terms of background characteristics.

small number of 16- and 17-year-old fathers in this sample, caution is warranted when interpreting the results for these younger fathers. It is clear, however, that the probability of dropping out of high school for those who had a birth while in their teens (.44) is considerably higher than it is for those who either fathered a child when they were 20 or older (.22), or who were childless as of the 1983 survey (.12). This discrepancy in the probability of completing high school can also be noted by pointing out that whereas 87% of males who had not been teenage fathers had graduated from high school, only 57% of teenage fathers had graduated. Teenage fathers on the average were also more likely to gain their high school accreditation by obtaining a GED than males in the other two groups. Whereas 12% of teenage fathers earned a GED, only 6% of all other males received this form of degree. As noted previously, males who fathered a child when they were 16 or younger were in relative terms the most likely to earn a GED (.23). This group of young fathers actually had a higher overall graduation probability than either 17- or 18-year-old fathers. I suspect that males who father children at very young ages are discouraged from getting married and are not expected to assume responsibilities associated with fatherhood because this life event is clearly "off time." Their ability to complete high school should therefore be enhanced in the absence of new family responsibilities.

An interesting finding in terms of racial differences in dropout and graduation probabilities among teenage fathers and their comparison group can be observed in Table 5.3. Although whites who are not economically disadvantaged have the lowest dropout probability (.10) within the nonteenage father group, blacks have the lowest probability of dropping out (.32) within the teenage father subsample.

TABLE 5.3
Probabilities For Type of High School Completion Outcome For (1) Teenage Fathers,
and (2) Males Who Did Not Father a Child as a Teenager, By Race/Ethnicity

	N		Dropout		GED		Diploma		Total Graduates	
	(1)	(2)	(1)	(2)	(1)	(2)	(1)	(2)	(1)	(2)
Hispanic	75	615	.61	.29	.09	.07	.30	.65	.39	.72
Black	185	970	.32	.24	.13	.07	.55	.69	.68	.76
White	126	2046	.46	.10	.11	.06	.42	.85	.53	.91
Economically Disadvantaged White	89	616	.51	.25	.13	.07	.36	.68	.49	.75
Total	475	4247	.44	.14	.12	.06	.45	.81	.57	.87

Note: Probabilities are weighted: The sample is males 20 and older as of the 1983 survey,
14 cases (2.9%) from the teenage father subsample, and 91 cases (2.1%) from the subsample
of males who did not experience teenage fertility, were omitted from this table because
their accreditation status could not be determined.

This finding reflects the minor differences between the black teenage father and the black nonteenage father subsamples in terms of both dropout and graduation probabilities. Sixty-eight percent of black teenage fathers graduated from high school, whereas 76% of black males not experiencing a teenage birth graduated. This 8% difference among blacks is in stark contrast to the 33, 38, and 26% differences for Hispanics, whites, and poor whites respectively. Perhaps part of the reason why there is only a modest difference between black teenage fathers and their comparison group in terms of high school completion probabilities has to do with the social acceptability of early childbearing within the black subculture, evidenced by the tendency for blacks to have their first child out of wedlock. Only 6% of black teenage fathers reported being married at the time of their first birth, while 56, 67, and 62% of Hispanic, white, and poor white teenage fathers were married when their first child was born.

The relationship between young fathers' marital status at birth and their high school completion outcomes within racial/ethnic groups is presented in Table 5.4. The overall probabilities for the selected outcome measures are very similar for those who were married when their child was born and those who were not. For instance, 43% of the teenage fathers who were married compared to 46% of the teenage fathers who were not married earned a diploma. The similarity between the probability levels for the two marital categories is remarkably consistent within racial/ethnic groups as well. One major departure from this pattern occurs for economically disadvantaged whites. Married teenage fathers within this group were more likely to earn a diploma (.42) than their nonmarried counterparts (.24). The nonmarried teenage fathers, however, used the GED more frequently as a means to receive high school accreditation (.24) than economically disadvantaged whites (.07).

TABLE 5.4

Probabilities for Type of High School Completion Outcome for (1) Married, and (2) Not Married Teenage Fathers (At the Time of Their First Birth), By Race/Ethnicity

| | | Graduation Status by 1983 Survey | | | | | | | | | |
| | N | | Dropout | | GED | | Diploma | | Total Graduates | |
	(1)	(2)	(1)	(2)	(1)	(2)	(1)	(2)	(1)	(2)
Hispanic	42	33	.66	.52	.05	.15	.29	.33	.34	.48
Black	12	173	--	.34	--	.12	--	.54	--	.66
White	84	42	.44	.50	.11	.11	.45	.39	.56	.50
Economically Disadvantaged White	55	34	.50	.52	.07	.24	.42	.24	.49	.48
Total	193	282	.46	.42	.11	.12	.43	.46	.54	.58

Note: Probabilities are weighted: Sample is males 20 and older as of the 1983 survey who fathered a child as a teenager. Probabilities were not presented for blacks who were married at birth given the small sample size. Fourteen cases were omitted from this table because the respondent's accreditation status could not be determined.

The degree of similarity between high school completion patterns produced by using a living arrangement variable rather than a marital status at birth variable can be assessed by comparing Tables 5.4 and 5.5. The patterns are very similar for these alternative methods for identifying young fathers who are more likely to be confronted directly with fatherhood responsibilities.

Whereas it may be tempting to infer causality from the high school completion statistics presented thus far, such a leap of logic would be unwise. The probabilities are merely descriptive summary statistics that do not take into account the possibility that an underlying selection process may be responsible for the observed relationships. Males who have a tendency to drop out of high school may also be more inclined to father a child as a teenager. Many of these

TABLE 5.5

Probabilities for Type of High School Completion Outcome for Teenage Fathers Who (1) Lived With Their Child (2) Did Not Live With Their Child, By Race/Ethnicity

| | | Graduation Status by 1983 Survey | | | | | | | | | |
| | N | | Dropout | | GED | | Diploma | | Total Graduates | |
	(1)	(2)	(1)	(2)	(1)	(2)	(1)	(2)	(1)	(2)
Hispanic	47	28	.63	.57	.08	.09	.28	.34	.36	.43
Black	33	152	.26	.33	.21	.11	.53	.56	.74	.67
White	92	34	.43	.57	.09	.18	.48	.25	.57	.43
Economically Disadvantaged White	59	30	.50	.53	.11	.18	.39	.29	.50	.47
Total	231	244	.46	.42	.11	.12	.43	.46	.54	.58

Note: Probabilities are weighted: Sample is males 20 and older as of the 1983 survey who fathered a child as a teenager. Fourteen cases were omitted from this table because the respondent's accreditation status could not be determined.

teenage fathers may actually be out of school when they father their first child thus negating causality assumptions regarding the temporal ordering of the relevant events.

Four regression models were estimated to examine the relationship between fathering a child as a teenager, living with this child, the father's age when his child was born, and the highest grade a respondent had completed by his 1983 survey. A number of background factors were used in these analyses primarily as controls, including a respondent's age as of his 1983 survey, father's education (mother's education in father's absence), whether or not the respondent was black, and whether or not he was raised as a Fundamentalist Protestant. Three additional dummy variables identified whether or not the respondent lived with two parents, lived in an urban area, or lived in a southern state at age 14.

The first model (see Table 5.6) used all respondents and included dummy variables for fathering a child as a teenager and living with this child at the first observation point after the child's birth. Both of these variables were negatively related to the respondent's highest grade completed by the 1983 interview. Simply fathering a child as a teenager was related more strongly to educational attainment than was living with the child. In a stepwise regression analysis (results not reported here) fathering a child as a teenager was the third variable entered into the model after parental education and the respondent's age in 1983. Its inclusion increased the explained variance of the model by a modest 2%.

In the model estimated only for teenage fathers, the dummy variable used in the first model to identify whether a young male fathered a child as teenager was replaced with a variable representing the age at which the young male fathered his child (see Table 5.6). Age at childbirth was positively related to educational attainment while the living arrangement variable made no significant difference. Father's age at childbirth increased the explained variance by only 2% when a stepwise regression was performed.

Regression analyses for young fathers who lived with their child and those who did not are presented in Table 5.7. Somewhat surprisingly, the respondent's age when he fathered his child was not significantly related to educational attainment for the group of young fathers who lived with their child. Parental education was the most powerful variable in this model; it accounted for all but 2% of the explained variance. Among young fathers who did not live with their child, an older age at childbirth was significantly related to more years of completed schooling net of other factors. Being older in 1983, black, and having a more educated father were also significantly related to higher levels of educational attainment. Relatively speaking, the association between parental education and respondents' completed years of schooling was weaker for the group of young fathers who did not live with their child compared to the group of fathers who did live with their child. This finding may be partly explained by the fact that parental resources, a correlate of educational attainment, may take on greater

TABLE 5.6

Results of Multiple Regression Equation for Highest Grade Completed for Total Sample and Teenage Fathers[5]

Variables	Total Sample		Teenage Fathers	
	b	Beta	b	Beta
Age as of 1983 survey	.206[c] (.015)	.181	.147[c] (.043)	.150
South residence at age 14 coded 1, others = 0	-.026 (.063)	-.006	-.280[a] (.164)	-.079
Fundamentalist protestant as a child coded 1, others = 0[a]	-.101 (.068)	-.022	-.075 (1.169)	-.022
Black coded 1, others = 0	-.019 (.088)	-.003	1.033[c] (.215)	.285
Lived with two parents at age 14 coded 1, others = 0	.345[c] (.074)	.062	.190 (.172)	.050
Urban residence at age 14 coded 1, others = 0	.126[b] (.064)	.026	-.249 (.175)	-.063
Father's education in years completed, mother's level used when father's data was missing	.224[c] (.007)	.404	.154[c] (.021)	.316
Living with first child at first observation point after child's birth coded 1, others = 0	-.464[b] (.209)	-.044	.006 (.178)	.002
Fathered child as a teenager, coded 1, others = 0	-.864[c] (.165)	-.106	-------	
Age at first fatherhood coded 16-19, those younger than 16 were coded 16	------		.226[c] (.076)	.136
Intercept	5.094		2.070	
Adjusted R^2	.245[c]		.174[c]	
F	166.914		11.432	
N	4601		447	

Note: Regression equation is based on weighted data. Sample sizes are not identical with Ns in Table 5.1 because 243 cases from the total sample and 42 cases from the sample of teenage fathers were omitted due to missing values. Standard errors are in parentheses. See appendix for means and standard deviations. [a] $p < .10$, [b] $p < .05$, [c] $p < .01$.

[a] This categorization refers to white respondents who met the Office of Management and Budget's criteria for poverty when the sample was selected.

[5] Because roughly 10.5% of teenage fathers were enlisted in the armed services at the observation point used to determine whether or not they were living with their first child, a separate model was estimated that excluded these servicemen in order to control for the possible confounding effect of father-child separation due to military service. The substantive findings were not altered in any meaningful way by excluding servicemen from the analysis.

81

TABLE 5.7

Results of Multiple Regression Equations for Highest Grade Completed for Teenage Fathers Who Lived With Their Child and Teenage Fathers Who Did Not Live With Their Child

Variables	Teenage Fathers Living With Child		Teenage Fathers Not Living With Child	
	b	Beta	b	Beta
Highest grade completed by 1983 survey	.057 (.059)	.058	.289[c] (.060)	.292
Age as of 1983 survey	-.307 (.228)	-.086	-.134 (.232)	-.039
South residence at age 14 coded 1, others = 0	-.250 (.227)	-.074	.192 (.249)	.057
Fundamentalist protestant as a child coded 1, others = 0	.910[b] (.386)	.161	.964[c] (.264)	.284
Black coded 1, others = 0	.354 (.289)	.078	-.050 (.207)	-.015
Lived with two parents at age 14 coded 1, others = 0	-.467[b] (.216)	-.130	.273 (.304)	.055
Urban residence at age 14 coded 1, others = 0				
Father's education in years completed, mother's level used when father's data was missing	.216[c] (.030)	.437	.061[b] (.029)	.125
Age at first fatherhood, coded 16-19 those younger than 16 were coded 16	.144 (.115)	.078	.261[c] (.095)	.170
Intercept	5.058		-1.279	
Adjusted R²	.244[c]		.199[c]	
F	8.914		8.023	
N	220		227	

Note: Regressions are based on weighted data. N's do not reflect sample size presented in Table 5.1 because 19 cases in "living with child" subsample, and 23 cases in "not living with their child" subsample were omitted due to missing values. Standard errors are in parentheses. See footnote 5 (Table 5.6) for an explanation of alternative models estimated but not reported here. See the appendix for means and standard deviations.

[a] $p < .10$, [b] $p < .05$, [c] $p < .01$

importance to young males who decide to live with their child than they do for males who "choose" not to live with their child.

Summary and Conclusion

Results from this study document quite clearly that males who father children as teenagers are less likely to receive a regular diploma, more likely to receive a GED, and more likely not to receive high school accreditation by age 20, at least 2 years after their age-normal date of graduation, than their peers who did not father children as teenagers. Whereas young fathers are twice as likely as males in the comparison group to earn high school accreditation via a GED, the GED is particularly important for very young fathers. This pattern exists for all racial/ethnic groups, but it is least pronounced for blacks, a finding that suggests that subcultural norms may minimize the disruptive aspects of unplanned teenage fertility, at least for males.

In a multivariate context and using a sample of males 20–26 years-of-age, fathering a child as a teenager, irrespective of whether or not the father lived with his child, was negatively related to respondents' completed years of schooling. A similar though weaker finding was observed between living with a child fathered as a teenager and educational attainment for the total sample of males. Although I suspected that choosing to live with a child would be associated with fewer years of completed education among teenage fathers, no evidence is found here to support this hypothesis. Fathering a child at a younger age is associated with reduced levels of education; however, this finding is only observed for the subsample of fathers who do not live with their child. The tendency for younger fathers to receive a GED may be partly responsible for the relationship between age at fatherhood and educational attainment. As younger fathers capitalize on their opportunities to complete school through the GED route they may complete fewer years of schooling if they earn a GED after leaving school at a young age and do not return for further schooling.

Several notes of caution are warranted when interpreting the findings from this study. Most importantly, the research design is not ideal for resolving complex causality issues since it does not account for the temporal sequencing of educational measures relative to birth events. Teenage fatherhood is operationalized solely in terms of the father's age when his first child was born with no reference to the father's educational aspirations or enrollment status at the time his child was born or during the prenatal period. I have assumed for the sake of simplicity that a teenage birth tends to be a disruptive life event irrespective of the young father's school enrollment status. A more direct analysis of the effects of assuming fatherhood responsibilities on educational attainment could be pursued by focusing only on males whose first child was either born or conceived while the young father was enrolled in high school. This type of design could isolate more readily the causal effects of unplanned births among teenage fathers for a sample of males attending school, although it would fail to consider how a teenage birth could affect the educational experiences of males who dropped out of high school prior to the birth of their first child. An additional shortcoming of the present study is that whereas a number of background factors are accounted for in the regression analyses for completed years of education, no controls are introduced for a respondent's academic abilities and school performance. These are probably key variables and thus should be included in future analyses whenever possible. Finally, the results of this study reflect the association between variables related to early fertility and completed years of schooling in a relatively short-term context due to the current age composition of the NLSY sample. Whether or not similar findings would emerge if the sample respondents were five years older, which would provide some fathers with an opportunity to overcome earlier disruptions in their schooling, cannot be determined at this time.

Future research should attempt to specify more fully the conditions under which fathering a child as a teenager retards a young male's schooling and to explain what factors enhance a young father's chances of fulfilling his educational plans. Whereas I have included a surrogate variable for commitment in the present analysis, whether or not a father's first child was living with him shortly after the child's birth, future research should consider the nature of commitment more directly and in greater depth. The commitment concept should be considered in connection with the child as well as the child's mother. Understanding how the consequences of early fatherhood are mediated will be enhanced by focusing attention on the teenage father's partner and on aspects of his relationship with her. Is his partner supportive of his educational goals, and if so, how does this support manifest itself, e.g., does she assume primary responsibility for financially supporting the family? What are her personal educational and career goals and how inclined is she to lower her expectations or postpone her plans in order to facilitate her partner's education? What kinds of decision-making assumptions and patterns characterize their relationship? For example, is it explicitly or tacitly assumed that the male's educational plans should take precedence?

Another important area for future research involves the role parents play in the educational careers of teenage fathers. Not surprisingly, parental education is found to be an important predictor of educational attainment among teenage fathers in this study. This is particularly true with respect to the group of young males who lived with their child after the child was born. This study, however, does not specify how parental education enhances a young father's educational attainment. Is a teenage father's educational career enhanced because he has developed high educational expectations, or are the financial resources that generally accompany higher parental education levels responsible for providing the young male with key resources? This issue could be clarified if future research included measures of parental assistance and transfer payments so that researchers could assess the extent to which resources are available to a young father and determine to what extent they improve his opportunities to pursue further education. This type of financial assistance would probably be associated with a greater likelihood of completing high school and completing more years of schooling for the group of fathers living with their child. Fathers who received only minimal or no outside financial assistance, but lived with their child, would be more likely to become permanent dropouts, or GED recipients if they did graduate, and complete fewer years of education overall. Educational aspirations and expectations measured for both young males and their parents, before as well as after the young male has fathered a child, would also need to be incorporated into models similar to the ones presented here in order to determine the relative effects of the variables noted previously.

ACKNOWLEDGMENTS

I am indebted to Frank L. Mott, Elizabeth G. Menaghan, and Paula Baker for their helpful comments on early drafts of this chapter. Carol Tomastik Sheet's technical assistance in data management is also greatly appreciated. This chapter was prepared under a contract with the Employment and Training Administration, U.S. Department of Labor, with funds provided by an intergovernmental transfer from the National Institute of Child Health and Human Development. The data in this study have been collected and processed by the National Opinion Research Center. Researchers conducting projects under Government sponsorship are encouraged to express their own judgments. Interpretations or viewpoints contained herein do not necessarily represent the official position or policy of the Department of Labor or the NICHD.

REFERENCES

Bacon, L. (1974). Early motherhood, accelerated role transition, and social pathologies. *Social Forces, 52*, 333–341.

Card, J. J. (1977). *Consequences of adolescent childbearing for the young parent's future personal and professional life*. Palo Alto, CA: American Institutes for Research.

Center for Human Resource Research. (1984). *The National Longitudinal Surveys Handbook*. The Ohio University, Columbis: Center for Human Resource Research.

Cervero, R. M. (1983). *A national survey of GED test candidates: Preparation, performance, and 18 month outcomes,* Educational Resources Information Center, U. S. Department of Education, National Institute of Education, Washington, D.C. (ERIC), ED 229 425.

Chi, K. S. (1982). *Religious affiliation and marital success: Questioning the established viewpoint.* Masters thesis. The Ohio State University.

Clark, S. D. Jr., Zabin, L. S., & Hardy, J. B. (1984). Sex. contraception and parenthood: Experience and attitudes among urban black young men. *Family Planning Perspectives, 16*, 77–82.

Digest (1984). Out-of-wedlock birthrate rising among whites, falling among blacks; overall fertility declining. *Family Planning Perspectives, 16*, 90–91.

Dillard, D. K., & Pol, L. G. (1982). The individual economic costs of teenage childbearing. *Family Relations, 31*, 249–259.

Elder, G. H. Jr. (1978). Family history and the life course. In T. Hareven (Ed.), *Transitions: The family and life course in historical perspective*. New York: Academic Press.

Frankel, M. R., McWilliams, H. A., & Spencer, B. D. (1983). *National Longitudinal Survey of Labor Force Behavior, Youth Survey (NLS): Technical Sampling Report.* Chicago: National Opinion Research Center.

Furstenberg, F. F., Jr. (1976). The social consequences of teenage parenthood. *Family Planning Perspectives, 8,* 148–164.

Haggstrom, G. W., Blaschke, T. J., Kanouse, D. E., Lisowski, W., & Morrison, P. A. (1981). *Teenage parents: Their ambitions and attainments.* Santa Monica, CA.: Rand Corporation.

Hofferth, S. L., & Moore, K. A. (1979). Early childbearing and later economic well-being. *American Sociological Review, 44,* 784–815.

McCarthy, J., & Radish, E. (1983). Education and childbearing among teenagers. In E. R. McAarney (Ed.), *Premature adolescent pregnancy and parenthood.* New York: Grune & Stratton.

McLaughlin, S., Grady, W. R., Billy, J. O. G., & Winges, L. D. (1984). *The effects of the decision to marry on the consequences of adolescent pregnancy.* Final Report to the Office of Adolescent Pregnancy Programs: Battelle Human Affairs Research Centers.

Morgan, W. R. (1984). The high school dropout in an overeducated society. In P. Baker, S. Carpenter, J. Crowley, R. D'Amico, C. Kim, W. Morgan, & J. Wielogosz (Eds.), *Pathways to the future IV: A Final Report on the National Longitudinal Surveys of Youth Labor Market Experience in 1982* (pp. 215–276).

Mott, F. L. (1983). *Fertility-related data in the 1982 National Longitudinal Survey of Work Experience of Youth: An evaluation of data quality and some preliminary analytical results.* Report, National Institute of Child Health and Human Development: Center for Human Resource Research.

Mott, F. L., & Marsiglio, W. (1985). *Early childbearing and completion of high school. Family Planning Perspectives, 17*(5), 234–237.

National Opinion Research Center. (1981). *General Social Survey Cumulative File 1972–1980.* University of Chicago.

Stryker, S. (1980). *Symbolic interactionism: A social structural version.* Menlo Park, CA: Benjamin/Cummings.

Stryker, S. (1968, November). Identity salience and role performance: The relevance of symbolic interaction theory for family research. *Journal of Marriage and the Family,* 558–564.

Swarm, C. C. (1981). *Three studies of general educational development (GED) students—1971–1981.* Educational Resources Information Center, U.S. Department of Education, National Institute of Education, Washington, D. C. (ERIC), ED 211 696.

Trussel, T. J. (1976). Economic consequences of teenage childbearing. *Family Planning Perspectives, 8,* 184–191.

Ulin, R. O. (1982). Equivalent to what? GED high school equivalency test. *English Journal, 71,* 21–25.

Waite, L. J., & Moore, K. A. (1978). The impact of an early first birth on young women's educational attainment. *Social Forces, 56,* 845–865.

APPENDIX I:

Means and Standard Deviations for Regression Models (Tables 5.6 and 5.7)

	Total Sample		All Teenage Fathers		Teenage Fathers Living with Child		Teenage Fathers Not Living with Child	
	x	Std.	x	Std.	x	Std.	x	Std.
Highest grade completed	12.68	10.66	11.17	7.19	11.11	7.79	11.26	6.57
Age as of 1983 survey	22.63	9.38	22.47	7.33	22.60	7.94	22.28	6.63
South residence at age 14	.29	2.38	.33	2.04	.31	2.19	.36	1.89
Fundamentalist as a child	.26	2.31	.43	2.15	.36	2.28	.53	1.95
Black	.13	1.76	.30	1.98	.09	1.38	.58	1.93
Lived with two parents at age 14	.84	1.90	.75	1.90	.84	1.72	.60	1.92
Urban residence at age 14	.78	2.18	.77	1.82	.70	2.17	.87	1.32
Father's education	11.82	19.20	10.25	14.67	10.56	15.73	9.81	13.40
Age at first fatherhood	————————		18.09	4.32	18.24	4.22	17.88	4.28
Lived with child at first observation point	.04	1.02	.59	2.14	————————		————————	
Fathered child as teenager	.07	1.31	————————		————————		————————	
N	4601		447		220		224	

Note: Means and standard deviations are weighted.

6

Parental Behavior of Adolescent Mothers and Fathers

Michael E. Lamb
Arthur B. Elster
University of Utah

Because of the adolescent's age and because of the stressful events that frequently accompany youthful pregnancy and parenthood, clinicians and researchers have long questioned the ability of adolescent parents to care for their children in a way that promotes optimal child development. In this chapter, we critically examine the empirical and theoretical issues that bear on our understanding of adolescent parenting. Although this has become an increasingly popular area of research, our knowledge of adolescent parenting is still surprisingly limited. Among the problems accounting for this are methodological inadequacies (including the failures to employ appropriate comparison groups and appropriate analytic thechniques), atheoretical research strategies, the absence of replication studies, proliferation of measurement instruments (many of which are of unknown reliability and/or validity), and a frequent failure to specify clearly the appropriate group to which findings can or should be generalized. Thus a major goal of this chapter is to provide a conceptual framework that not only helps integrate the available findings but also facilitates the design and interpretation of future researches.

One further limitation is also evident. Although this is a book about adolescent *fatherhood,* most of the studies reviewed in this chapter are concerned with the behavior of adolescent *mothers.* Further, the few available findings suggest that the behavior of adolescent mothers and fathers may not only differ but may also be influenced by different factors. It is important nonetheless to consider the behavior of both parents because together they may form the integral socializing unit.

In the first section, we discuss the characteristics of effective parenting, as understood by contemporary developmental theorists. We then review the limited empirical data on the parental behavior of adolescent mothers and fathers. Finally, we discuss the relationship between adolescent parenthood and a number of socioeconomic, psychological, ecological, and infant factors that are likely to affect the quality of parenting.

CHARACTERISTICS OF EFFECTIVE PARENTING

Despite major differences among the many theorists who have attempted to conceptualize parent–child relationships, there is surprising agreement that a central component of effective parenting is parental sensitivity. By consensus, sensitive behavior involves the ability of a parent to provide contingent, consistent, and appropriate responses to his/her infant's signals—most importantly, the infant's cry (Ainsworth, Blehar, Waters, & Wall, 1978; Lamb & Easterbrooks, 1981). A parent must perceive the child's cues, interpret these cues correctly, and implement an appropriate response in an effective manner. A deficiency at any point in this process would result in insensitive parental behavior. Sensitivity remains crucial in the postinfancy years as well (e.g., Lamb, 1980; Lamb & Baumrind, 1978), comprising a defining feature of effective parenting through adolescence, even though the skills that reflect sensitivity differ depending on the child's age.

Because sensitive parental behavior has been studied in a variety of ways and in relation to children of various ages, it is hard to specify exactly how sensitive parenting affects child development. Nevertheless, there is now a good deal of evidence suggesting that when parents behave in a manner considered desirable by Americans (e.g., tender, promptly responsive, attentive), their infants are more likely to develop trustful or secure attachment relationships and to experience accelerated cognitive development (Ainsworth et al., 1978; Lamb, Thompson, Gardner, Charnov, & Estes, 1984; Lamb, Thompson, Gardner, & Charnov, 1985; Stevenson & Lamb, 1981). Older children whose parents behave in this fashion appear to be more self-confident, assertive, and socially competent (Baumrind, 1975). By contrast, when parents are insensitive, unstimulating, rejecting, or overstimulating, their infants are more likely to develop distrustful, insecure attachments and older children are likely to be dependent and socially incompetent. The nature of the parent–infant relationship thus formed also has important developmental consequences. In the absence of changes in the parent's circumstances, not only is the security of attachment stable over time but so, too, are various aspects of social style and personality that appear to be influenced by this behavior (see Lamb et al., 1984, 1985, for a review). Thus, infants who are securely attached are later more socially adept and friendly with peers and unfamiliar adults as well as more resilient and persistent in the face of challenge and adversity. In addition, continued cognitive benefits seem to be associated with parental behavior that is of consistently high quality (Stevenson & Lamb, 1981; Wachs & Gruen, 1982). These data demonstrate the importance of individual differences in the quality of parent–child interaction and underscore the importance of examining evidence concerning the quality of adolescent parental behavior.

Despite an upsurge of interest in the role of father and parental involvement in child development (e.g., Lamb, 1976, 1981a; Lamb, Pleck, & Levine, 1985), there has been remarkably little research on the effects of *variations* in paternal behavior on child development. Instead, much of the research in the last decade has been descriptive in nature, concerned with the distinguishing characteristics of maternal and paternal behavior. These studies have shown that mothers retain an association with affectionate, "containing," nurturant interaction and stimulation, whereas from infancy fathers are associated with more playful forms of stimulation. It is not known whether these differences have formative significance, although it has been speculated that they may play a role in early gender-role acquisition (Lamb, 1981b). The playfulness of father–child interaction may also make fathers much more salient to their children than would be expected given the amounts of time they spend together, and the special attentiveness of fathers to their sons may play a role in early gender identity formation (Lamb, 1977). For the most part, however, it appears that sensitive stimulation by fathers has the same effect as nurturant stimulation by mothers (Lamb, Pleck, & Levine, 1985; Radin, 1981) and that one of the major ways in which fathers affect their children's development is mediated through their role in and impact on the family system—notably, by their effect on the children's mothers (Parke, Power, & Gottman, 1979). Thus adolescent fathers may have a substantial indirect impact on their children's development depending on the nature of their relationship (or lack of it) with the children's mothers, in addition to whatever direct role they play in their children's lives.

CHARACTERISTICS OF ADOLESCENT PARENTAL BEHAVIOR

Few investigators have directly studied either the responsiveness of adolescent parents or the security of the attachments between adolescent parents and their infants. Some researchers, however, have investigated other characteristics of adolescent parent–child interaction to determine whether adolescent mothers evince unique characteristics. Unfortunately, we know of only one study concerned with the behavior of adolescent fathers, so for the most part we are forced to generalize from research on adolescent mothers.

Parental Sensitivity

Jones, Green, and Krauss (1980) studied responsiveness in 40 primiparous mothers during the postpartum period. Responsiveness was measured by scoring the presence of 14 specific maternal behaviors observed during the infant's discharge examination and during a feeding session. Jones et al. (1980) reported that the 21- to 23-year-old mothers were significantly more responsive to their newborn infants than were the 17- to 18-year-old mothers, regardless of race and socioeconomic or marital status. This serendipitous finding was the first published evidence suggesting that maternal age may actually affect the quality of parent–child interaction.

In a pilot study of 15 healthy, primiparous adolescent mothers who were predominantly black, unmarried, and from lower socioeconomic backgrounds, McAnarney, Lawrence, and Aten (1979) reported a relationship between the chronological age of the mother and her ability to interact with her infant. The younger the mother, the less she demonstrated behaviors such as touching, the use of high-pitched voice, synchronous movements, and closeness to the infant, which are considered by Klaus and Kennell (1976) to be typical of adult mothers. However, these findings were not replicated in a fuller study involving 75 primiparous mothers under 20 years of age (McAnarney, Lawrence, Aten, & Iker, 1984). Nevertheless, McAnarney and her colleagues (Lawrence, McAnarney, Aten, Iker, Baldwin, & Baldwin, 1981), in a study of 30 adolescent mothers, substantiated their clinical impression that some adolescents engage in aggressive, inappropriate behaviors, such as picking, poking, and pinching their infants, which are rarely displayed by adult mothers. The significance of these behaviors is not clear, but if they characterize the interaction, the effects on attachment formation are likely to be adverse. Unfortunately, no comparison group of adult mothers was involved in the study.

Landy (1981) recently compared the quality of parent–child interactions among a group of 14 teenagers (16 years of age and less) and a group of adults (greater than 20 years of age) matched on socioeconomic status, race, marital status, and intellectual ability. When compared to older mothers, teenage mothers were less sensitive and positive in face-to-face interaction with their 4- and 5-month-old infants. Further, at 12 months, the infants of the teenaged mothers were more likely to be insecurely attached than the infants of adult mothers. Unfortunately, these provocative findings are rendered suspect because a large number of measures were employed to compare these small samples, making the probability of false–positive results very large.

Ragozin and her associates (Crnic, Greenberg, & Ragozin, 1981; Ragozin, Basham, Crnic, Greenberg, & Robinson, 1982) assessed maternal–child interactive behaviors at 4 months post partum for 52 full-term dyads. The sample consisted predominantly of white, two-parent families; mothers ranged in age from 16 to 38 years. Regression analysis revealed that maternal age had a significant effect on the quality of parental behavior, even when other demographic and psychosocial variables were controlled statistically. The younger the mother, the less adequate was her observed behavior. This relationship appeared to be continuous across the range of ages studied and stronger among dyads with term than among dyads with preterm infants.

In the most recent study, Levine, Garcia Coll, and Oh (1985) compared 15 white teenage mothers (17 years) with 15 adult mothers from comparable lower to middle-class backgrounds. When observed in face-to-face interaction with their 8-month-old infants the teenage mothers showed less positive affect than did the adult mothers, but three other measures (including verbalization, mutual gaze, and contingent responding) showed no group differences. In a teaching context, the adolescent mothers were less verbal, showed less positive affect, and demonstrated less. Interpretation of these findings is unfortunately clouded by large group differences in mental status, family status, and educational attainment.

Similar problems were not evident in a study by Toberg, Howell, and Wingert (1983) in which 26 low-income Hispanic teenage mothers ($M = 15$ years) were compared with 30 older mothers ($M = 26$ years) from comparable backgrounds. The older mothers engaged in more effective eye-to-eye, verbal, and physical interaction, and infants manifested a limited ability to cope with stress. Such differences in infant behavior might be expected to accompany deficient maternal behavior (Ainsworth et al., 1978). Because the mothers were very young (averaging 14 years or younger at delivery), these differences may be characteristic only of this group, rather than teenage mothers in general.

Physical Versus Verbal Modalities

The results of three studies suggest that adolescent mothers tend to engage in more physical rather than verbal exchanges with their infants (Epstein, 1980; Osofsky & Osofsky, 1970; Sandler, Vietze, & O'Connor, 1981). Epstein (1980) explored the attitudes and behavior of 80 young primiparous mothers, most of whom (57%) were white, from middle-class families (50%), and unmarried (80%). Epstein identified three styles of parent–child interaction when the mothers were observed interacting with their 6-month-old children. The most frequent style was "nonverbal interaction." Mothers who demonstrated this type of interaction provided for the infants' basic physical needs but did not vocalize much to their babies. The second most common behavioral style was "shared interaction" in which the mothers tended to provide their infants with verbal explanations of actions, thus providing both verbal and physical signs of affection. The third and least frequent of the interactive styles involved "directing." Adolescents characterized by this style verbally ordered their infants to do things, instead of allowing them to explore independently. Nonverbal interaction was most commonly seen in younger teens and those who underestimated infant needs and abilities, whereas the shared style was most common among older teens who had strong family support systems. Although it seems reasonable to consider the shared style to be the most sensitive and appropriate of the three interactional forms, Epstein did not provide any evidence to support this assumption. Recall, however, that Levine et al. (1985) reported that teenage mothers engaged in less verbal interaction than did adult mothers.

Somewhat earlier, Osofsky and Osofsky (1970) studied 60 teenage mothers who attended a special young mothers' program. Infants and mothers were observed and videotaped both before and during all routine pediatric examinations in the first year of life. Assessment of these interactions revealed that the mothers exhibited a fairly high level of physical interaction and warmth but engaged in relatively little verbal interaction. The infants scored high on ratings of activity and low on ratings of affectivity and responsivity. In the absence of comparisons with the behavior of older mothers, however, these findings are hard to interpret. It is possible, for example, that young mothers are especially intimidated by health care professionals, and that this accounts for their verbal passivity.

Sandler and his associates (1981) compared the parental behavior of 225 adolescent mothers (mean age 17 years) with that of 80 adult women (mean age 22.2 years). All women participated in the same prenatal clinic and were primiparae; unfortunately, other demographic characteristics of the two groups were not described. Parent–child interactions during a feeding and playing sequence were observed in the hospital during the immediate postpartum period. Overall, there were few differences between groups. When compared with older mothers, however, young mothers engaged in more frequent physical and less frequent verbal interactions with their children. Thus all three of these studies suggest a tendency, especially on the part of the younger teenage mothers in least satisfactory circumstances, to provide unusually low levels of verbal stimulation. If persistent, this pattern of behavior seems likely to have adverse effects on the children's cognitive and linguistic development.

Mother Versus Father Comparisons

In none of these studies, unfortunately, was father–infant interaction investigated. Indeed, we believe that our own recent study, involving home observations of adolescent mothers, their partners, and their 6-month-old infants, is the only one to have involved observations of adolescent fathers (Lamb & Elster, 1985). The mothers in this study were all teenagers (average age = 17.7 years), but their partners ranged in age from 16.5 to 29.9 years. Despite this age range, we found no difference between fathers of different ages, and a pattern of findings indicating that the behavioral styles of these mothers and fathers differed in a fashion consistent with results obtained in comparable studies of adult parents and infants (Belsky, Gilstrap, & Rovine, 1984; Lamb, 1981b; Yogman, 1982). In general, adolescent mothers engaged in more interaction of all types with their infants (affectionate, stimulative, and care related) than fathers did. We did not specifically record playful parental behavior in our study, but this is the preferred interactive mode of American although not Swedish adult fathers (Lamb, 1981b; Lamb, Frodi, Hwang, Frodi, & Steinberg, 1982), and nonsystematic observations suggested that it was in this regard that the adolescent fathers were distinguished as well. As far as relative patterns of interaction with infants are concerned, therefore, adolescent mothers and their partners appear very much like adult parents. Because we did not include a comparison group of adult parents and did not focus on some of the characteristics discussed previously, however, we do not know whether the young parents in our study resembled those observed by McAnarney, Epstein, and Jones et al., or whether adolescent fathers resemble adolescent mothers in the use of inappropriate parental behaviors.

The parents in our study also resembled the adult parents studied by Belsky, Gilstrap, and Rovine (1984) where correlations between behavioral measures of parent–infant and parent–parent interaction were concerned. As in Belsky's study, the quality of father–infant interaction was significantly correlated with almost all measures of mother–father interaction, whereas few (in our case only one) of the measures of mother–father interaction were significantly related to either of the measures of mother–infant involvement. This suggests that the behavior of adolescent and adult fathers is sensitive to variations in other dimensions of their lives and current interactions, whereas the behavior of both adolescent and adult mothers is somewhat buffered from influences of this sort. As shown in the next section, however, maternal behavior does vary depending on several exogenous and endogenous factors.

Summary

Overall, there is suggestive evidence that adolescent mothers tend to engage in behaviors that are likely to foster suboptimal socioemotional and cognitive development, and that these tendencies may be especially pronounced among the youngest mothers and those from the most stressful circumstances—an association that we explore further in the next section. We do not know whether adolescent fathers tend to behave similarly. In other respects, however, it appears that adolescent maternal and paternal roles differ from one another in the same ways that adult maternal and paternal roles differ. In both cases, however, there is great variability within groups; not all (or necessarily most) adolescent mothers and fathers behave in a particular fashion. This underscores the need to explain the variability in patterns of parenting, which is the goal of the next section.

FACTORS INFLUENCING PARENTAL BEHAVIOR

Originally, theorists assumed that the ability to provide high-quality parental care was an intrinsic characteristic of the parent, with individual differences in sensitivity constituting enduring personality characteristics or traits (see Lamb & Easterbrooks, 1981, for a review). It has become increasingly clear, however, that although some enduring personality characteristics may be correlated with tenderness or sensitivity parental competence may vary substantially depending on the parent's circumstances and the child's characteristics (Belsky, 1984; Lamb & Easterbrooks, 1981). Differences between the behavior of adolescent and adult parents can thus be explained by considering the impact of several situational, psychological, and infant factors that may adversely effect the ability of young mothers and fathers to behave sensitively and appropriately in interaction with their infants. In this section, we discuss the association between these factors and adolescent parental behavior. We first discuss four individual characteristics (cognitive development, attitudes toward child rearing, knowledge of child development, infant characteristics), before proceeding to interpersonal factors (stress, social support).

Adolescent cognitive development.   During adolescence, children acquire the ability for logical and abstract thought that allows adolescents to handle a variety of complex social and psychological dilemmas (Elkind, 1974; Keating, 1980). For adolescents to solve such dilemmas, they must not only have the ability to think of alternate solutions to these problems but must also be sensitive to the problems of everyday life, be ready to view the possible consequences of each possible solution, and have the capacity to appraise the causes and effects of behavior (Spivack, Platt, & Shure, 1976). All these skills are likely to benefit from experience, and adolescent parents are thrust into a parental role before they have had much experience solving complex social problems. To date, no researchers have specifically investigated the relationship between social cognitive abilities and parental behavior in adolescents, but it seems reasonable to hypothesize that parents must acquire the cognitive ability to accept and perform the parenting role before they can fulfill that role optimally.

In addition, the cognitive immaturity of adolescents and the other developmental tasks of the adolescent years (Elkind, 1974; Sadler & Catrone, 1983) produce a self-centeredness (Adams & Jones, 1981) that may prevent them from placing their infants' needs ahead of their own desires. This inability could influence parents' attentiveness to their infants, their evaluation of the infants' needs, and, therefore, the quality of their parental behavior. Finally, it is likely that the relative cognitive immaturity of adolescent parents inhibits or retards the development of realistic expectations and attitudes toward child rearing. Research on these topics is discussed in the next subsections.

Attitudes toward child rearing.   In a study of 139 primiparous women who were predominantly from lower socioeconomic families, Green, Sandler, Altemeier, and O'Connor (1981) found that young adolescent mothers, when compared to older adolescent and adult mothers, had less appropriate attitudes toward child rearing. DeLissovoy (1973) found teenage parents whose children were at least 2 years old to be impatient and intolerant with their children. He attributed this to the tendency of teen mothers and fathers to overestimate the rate of child development. Unfortunately, however, no comparison group was used, so the findings are speculative at best. The same is true of the attempt by Wise and Grossman (1980) to assess the factors affecting the child-rearing attitudes of 30 teenage mothers, most of whom were unmarried, black, and from lower socioeconomic backgrounds. The ability to plan for the pregnancy realistically and to have a positive attitude toward the pregnancy was associated with more positive feelings about babies and more realistic views of infant behavior.

Field and her associates (Field, Widmeyer, Stringer, & Ignatoff, 1980) compared the combined impact of prematurity, maternal age, and an intervention program on maternal behavior in a group of 90 adolescent mothers and a group of 50 mothers aged 20 to 29 years, all of whom were black and from families of lower socioeconomic status. Using scales that they developed, Field and her associates found that at 2 days, 4 months, and 8 months postpartum younger mothers had less desirable (i.e., more punitive) child-rearing attitudes than adult mothers. However, whereas the teens were all unmarried and living at home, most adult mothers were married. In addition, the mean parity was greater for the adult group. Thus we do not know whether maternal age, parity, or marital status accounted for the reported group differences.

Mercer, Hackley, and Bostrom (1984), in a study of 294 primiparous mothers ranging from 15 to 42 years of age, found that the 15- to 19-year-old mothers (N = 66) derived greater gratification from the maternal role through the first 8 months, whereas the 20- to 29-year-old mothers ranked highest on this dimension when the infants were 12 months of age. There were no group differences in feelings of love for the infant.

Finally, Zuckerman and his associates (Zuckerman, Winesmore, & Alpert, 1979) compared the attitudes and social support systems of 23 inner-city primiparous adolescent mothers (19 years of age), 24 primiparous adult mothers (20 years of age), and 17 multiparous adult mothers. When interviewed 2 weeks and 3 months postpartum, all mothers perceived their babies as temperamentally easy and expressed a high level of enjoyment. Most mothers were not bothered by caretaking activities and were not concerned about spoiling their children. Three months postpartum, however, more of the adolescent mothers perceived their infants as greedy and expressed insecurity about their maternal roles. In contrast with the other studies mentioned in this section, however, Zuckerman et al. concluded that there were no major attitudinal differences between adolescent and adult mothers.

Overall, most studies suggest that teenage parents (usually mothers) tend to have more negative and punitive attitudes toward their children than do adult mothers. These attitudes may reflect the self-centeredness and cognitive immaturity of adolescents. In addition, the less appropriate attitudes of teenage parents may have their origins in less realistic knowledge of children and of the rate of behavioral development.

Mothers' knowledge of child development.   The more knowledgeable parents are about normal infant development and behavior, the more likely they are to interpret their children's cues and needs correctly and thus to respond appropriately or initiate appropriate interactions. In addition, as intimated previously, the parents' knowledge may affect their child-rearing attitudes as well as the perceived stressfulness of the parenting role. Chamberlain, Szumoski, and Zastowny (1979) found that a gain in mothers' knowledge of child development was significantly correlated with the reported occurrence of more positive contact with their children. In addition, positive mother–child interaction was strongly correlated with the child's level of development as measured by the Minnesota Child Development Inventory (a maternal self-report scale). Unfortunately, all data were gathered by interview, so it is possible that the mothers tried to provide socially desirable responses regarding their parental behavior.

Because they have had less formal education and fewer informal experiences with children, teenage parents seem likely to have less accurate knowledge of child development than do adult parents. Epstein (1980) reported that teens provided consistently inaccurate answers to questions about cognitive, social, and language development. In general, these mothers underestimated the rate of mental development, leading Epstein to conclude that young mothers tend to assume that their infants have only physical needs and limited mental capacities. Epstein also found that the more the teenage mothers *underestimated* child development, the less observant they were of their infants' skills and of various maternal teaching strategies shown on a series of video tapes. Between the prenatal and postnatal assessments, the knowledge of older adolescents tended to improve, whereas no such improvement was evident in the younger teens. In a 3-year longitudinal study of 48 predominantly rural, married adolescent couples of lower socioeconomic status, however, DeLissovoy (1973) found that both parents consistently *overestimated* the rate of child development. Although the studies of Epstein and DeLissovoy reveal different sorts of errors, both suggest that teenage parents may have inaccurate ideas about the rate of child development. Unfortunately, neither study included a comparison group of adult parents, so we do not know whether teenage parents are better or worse informed than adult parents.

In their recent study, Parks and Smeriglio (1983) studied the parenting knowledge of 45 primiparous, black adolescent mothers and compared it to that of a group of primiparous adult mothers (60% black) from somewhat comparable socioeconomic backgrounds. There were no differences between the two groups of mothers, but because most mothers answered the questions correctly, it is possible that a ceiling effect obscured any real differences in parenting knowledge. Unfortunately, in the only other study in which the parenting knowledge of adolescent and adult mothers was compared, Field et al. (1980) failed to control for differences in parity and marital status (the teenagers were single and primiparous; many of the adults were multiparous and married). Thus it is hard to interpret the finding that the adult mothers had more realistic expectations re-garding developmental milestones. However, the results of most of the studies reviewed here point in that direction.

Characteristics of the infant.   In addition to psychological factors (cognitive development, knowledge of child development, and parental attitudes) the be-havioral characteristics of the infant also influence parental behavior (Lamb & Easterbrooks, 1981). Infants have innate behavioral characteristics that facilitate social interaction, and these capacities improve as the infant develops (Bowlby, 1969). Individual differences in the behavioral propensities of infants affect how they respond to parental behavior. Conversely, some infants demonstrate a more positive mood and employ more clearly "readable" signals than others, thus influencing the manner in which parents respond to them. When parent–infant interactions are mutually satisfying, parents may develop feelings of self-worth and effectiveness that enhance the overall quality of their parental behavior (Goldberg, 1977; Lamb & Easterbrooks, 1981). Temperamentally difficult in-fants, likewise, may have an adverse effect on sensitive responsiveness. It is not clear, however, whether neonatal characteristics are affected by maternal age. Thompson, Cappleman, and Zeitschel (1979) found that infants of adolescents differed from infants of adult mothers on the Brazelton NBAS but Sandler et al. (1981) and Lester (as reported by Baldwin & Cain, 1980) found that when medical risk factors were controlled maternal age did not significantly affect scores on the Brazelton examination. Nevertheless, studies by Field et al. (1980) and Green et al. (1981) indicate that adolescent parents view their infants as more temperamentally difficult than do adult mothers. Unfortunately, we do not know whether objective differences existed, but whether or not they do, one would predict that the quality of interaction would be adversely affected by the negative parental perceptions.

Stress and coping.   We switch now from consideration of intrapersonal fac-tors, such as attitudes, knowledge, temperament, and stage of cognitive develop-ment to broader societal factors, most importantly stress, coping, and social support. There is both conceptual and empirical justification for believing that parental stress adversely affects parental sensitivity and thus the quality of par-ent–child relationships (Crnic et al., 1981; Lamb & Easterbrooks, 1981; Ragozin et al., 1982; Thompson, Lamb, & Estes, 1982; Vaughn, Egeland, Sroufe, & Waters, 1979). Vaughn et al. (1979) and Thompson et al. (1982) have indepen-dently demonstrated, in adult populations, that stress and major changes in family circumstances lead to changes in the security of infant–mother attach-ment, whereas Belsky (1980b), Crockenberg (1981), Goldberg and Easterbrooks (1984), and Garbarino (1977) have reported relationships between levels of stress and quality of parenting. These findings are important because, for reasons that are elaborated in the chapter by Elster and Hendricks, adolescent parents may not only face major stresses but may be less well equipped socially and psychologically to cope with them. Among the stresses faced by young parents and parents-to-be are social disapproval and rejection, isolation, vocational-educational, economic, and "marital" problems (or more correctly, problems with the quality of their relationships with heterosexual partners).

Despite the many reasons to expect that stress should be a major factor in studies of adolescent parents, however, empirical investigation of this issue has been meager. Ragozin et al. (1982) found a significant relationship between stress, as measured by a life-events scale administered at 1 month postpartum, and maternal sensitivity to infant cues as measured by behavioral observation at 4 months postpartum. When other variables such as maternal age and social support were included in the regression, however, the effect of stress was greatly minimized. Likewise, in our own research we found that degree of stress accounted for only a small portion of the variance in maternal sensitivity in a feeding task, and a nonsignificant portion of the variance in sensitivity in a teaching task once variations in age and SES were statistically controlled (Elster, Montemayor, & Gilbride, 1984). Further, in our later study of mother–father–infant triads, we found no relationship between measures of mother–infant engagement or responsiveness and measure of marital quality, stress, and social support (Lamb & Elster, 1985). This may well be because our observations were made in a triadic context, whereas all other studies involved dyadic observations. There is other evidence to suggest that the correlates of parental behavior in dyadic and triadic contexts are different. Belsky, for example, found that whereas the quality of maternal behavior in a dyadic context predicted later infant behavior in Ainsworth's Strange Situation procedure (Belsky, Rovine, & Taylor, 1984), the quality of maternal behavior in a triadic context did not (Belsky, personal communication). If this finding is replicated in other studies, it would underscore the need for multisituational assessments of parent–infant interaction in studies designed to explore the effects of stress, social support, and the like, as well as care in the generalization and interpretation of findings obtained in studies sampling a narrow range of situations.

In our later study of adolescent mother–father–infant triads, furthermore, only the measures of *paternal* engagement and involvement were related to measures of social support and social stress. Thus both the quality of ongoing interaction with the partner (see earlier) and social context factors (e.g., stress and social support) appeared to have much less influence on maternal than paternal behavior. As aforementioned, Belsky et al. (1984) reported similar patterns of correlations in their research on adult parents. Perhaps this is because traditional parental roles make paternal involvement discretionary whereas maternal involvement is mandated by the maternal role (Russell, 1978). If anything, paternal involvement is more discretionary and less universally and unambiguously encouraged among adolescent than among adult parents.

Our findings were also consistent with results reported in the only other study concerned with father's age (Nakashima & Camp, 1984): There were essentially no differences among fathers of different ages or their partners with respect to observed behavior, reported stress, social support, and dyadic quality. Thus, at least within the demographic groups (white, middle class, partnered) and the range of ages represented in our study (16 to 29 years), age of father does not appear to have a significant impact on the early social experiences of infants with adolescent mothers. This finding is, of course, inconsistent with the assumption that adolescent parents are "at risk" for inadequate parenting because of the unusual degrees of stress they experience.

Social support.   Although it has long been known that the availability of social support helps to maintain mental health, researchers have only recently started asking whether social support affects parental behavior (Cochran & Brassard, 1979; Hendersen, Byrne, & Duncan-Jones, 1980; Hirsch, 1980). Social support can serve a variety of functions, such as cognitive guidance, social reinforcement, tangible assistance, social stimulation, and emotional support (Hirsch, 1980). These functions may affect parental sensitivity by alleviating stress, increasing the parent's knowledge of child development, enhancing maternal self-esteem and perceived effectiveness, or providing practical assistance (e.g., with housekeeping), thus allowing mother and child more time together (Lamb & Easterbrooks, 1981). Reports in the literature also suggest that frequent contact with supportive health care professionals can have a significant impact on the parental behavior of new mothers (Chamberlain et al., 1979; Gutelius, Kirsch, MacDonald, Brooks, & McErlean, 1977).

Among a group of adolescent mothers, Colletta and Gregg (1981) found a positive correlation between social support and the frequency of appropriate maternal behavior. Of the various kinds of perceived supports, the most important was emotional support, especially when provided by the mother's family of origin. Crnic and his associates (1981) also found that the amount and quality of perceived support was directly related to mothers' responsiveness during interactions with their infants. Levine et al. (1985) found that teenage mothers reported less social support than did adult mothers, and that variations in the amount of support were associated with various measures of maternal behavior. Crockenberg (1981) reported that level of support was influential only in the context of high social stress, as one might expect, but Bates and his colleagues (Bates, Maslin, & Frankel, 1985) were unable to replicate this. Both Crockenberg and Bates et al. studied adult mothers.

The role of family support in helping adolescent parents was also studied by Furstenberg and Crawford (1978) in their 5-year logitudinal investigation of adolescent mothers. Major differences were found in the socioeconomic advantage between never-married women who lived with parents or relatives and those who lived alone. The former were more likely to have returned to school, to have graduated from high school, to be employed, and to be independent of welfare support. Furstenberg and Crawford concluded that there is a strong relationship for never-married young mothers between their residential situation and their vocational-educational outcomes. Apparently more material support and help with child care are available to those mothers who live at home. No relationship was found, however, between where the teen mothers lived and either their child-rearing patterns or the developmental status of their infants.

As mentioned earlier, however, we have failed to find strong associations between reported social support and quality of mothering in two studies of parental behavior on adolescent parents, even when we attempted to look at the combined impact of stress and social support (Elster et al., 1984; Lamb & Elster, 1985). In the second study, however, scores on some measures of social support were correlated with indices of *paternal* but not maternal behavior.

Another aspect of the association between social support and adolescent parental behavior has to do with the degree of support provided by males to their adolescent partners. The lack of appreciation by health providers, social service workers, and the girls' parents for the problems experienced by teen fathers often results in their total exclusion from prenatal care and, in some cases, the denial of opportunities to see their female partners or children. Furstenberg's (1976) longitudinal study of adolescent mothers indicated that parenthood frequently led teens, regardless of marital status, to establish their own households, thus separating them from potentially useful social supports. Five years after delivery, 26% of the teen mothers (11% never married and 15% previously married) were living alone. This is not to imply that the children of teenaged parents are necessarily better off when their parents marry: Couples who marry during adolescence are more likely to experience marital discord than are couples who marry later (Burchinal, 1965; Moore, Waite, Hofferth, & Caldwell, 1978). This is a source of concern because poor relationships between parents seem to have a more predictably negative effect on child development than any other family event, including divorce and single parenthood (e.g., Rutter, 1973; Rutter, Cox, Tupling, Berger, & Yule, 1975).

When teenage fathers remain with their partners and children, some of the stresses experienced by young mothers are alleviated, particularly if the fathers have stable employment. Thus, under favorable circumstances, the fathers' presence may indirectly improve the quality of their children's lives by facilitating better maternal care. Overall, however, the problems experienced by teenage couples in general and teenage fathers in particular may increase the likelihood that they will provide suboptimal rearing environments for their children.

SUMMARY

In summary, there is some evidence that adolescent mothers may provide less appropriate forms of stimulation and care for their young infants, although as Bolton and Belsky point out in their chapter, there is no evidence that adolescent mothers are more likely than adult mothers to abuse or neglect their infants. The fact that adolescent parents may provide less appropriate care for their children than adult parents do is not surprising. As noted in this chapter, there are several reasons for concern that the psychosocial circumstances of teenage parents may adversely affect the quality of their parental behavior. Psychological immaturity, lack of parenting skills, economic stress, and stresses implicit in premature role transitions are problems that psychological and vocational counselors have to address. Furthermore, the quality of parenting is likely to depend not only on the individual parent's circumstances, but on those of his/her partner as well, because each person's behavior is influenced indirectly by the other's emotional state inasmuch as that infringes on the quality of their dyadic relationship. It is important to remember, however, that some teenage parents cope effectively and responsibly, and that many children develop perfectly well despite stressful family circumstances. Further research is necessary to determine more clearly what factors distinguish these individuals and families from those whose adaptations are not so favorable.

REFERENCES

Adams, G., & Jones, R. M. (1981). Imaginary audience behavior: A validation study. *Journal of Early Adolescence, 1,* 1–10.

Ainsworth, M. D. S., Blehar, M., Waters, E., & Wall, S. (1978). *Patterns of attachment.* Hillsdale, NJ: Lawrence Erlbaum Associates.

Baldwin, W., & Cain, V. S. (1980). The children of teenage parents. *Family Planning Perspectives, 12,* 34–43.

Bates, J. E., Maslin, L. A., & Frankel, K. A. (1985). Attachment security, mother–child interaction, and temperament as predictors of behavior problem ratings at age three years. In I. Bretherton & E. Waters (Eds.), *Growing points in attachment theory and research. Monographs of the Society for Research in Child Development, 50,* (Serial No. 209).

Baumrind, D. (1975). *Early socialization and the discipline controversy.* Morristown, NJ: General Learning Press.

Belsky, J. (1980a). A family analysis of parental influence on infant exploratory competence. In F. A. Pedersen (Ed.), *The father–infant relationship: Observational studies in a family context.* New York: Praeger.

Belsky, J. (1980b). Child maltreatment: An ecological integration. *American Psychologist, 35,* 320–335.

Belsky, J. (1984). Characteristics, consequences and determinants of parental competence: Toward a contextual theory. In M. Lewis & L. Rosenblum (Eds.), *Social connections—beyond the dyad.* New York: Plenum.

Belsky, J., Gilstrap, B., & Rovine, M. (1984). The Pennsylvania Infant and Family Development Project, I: Stability and change in mother–infant and father–infant interaction in a family setting at one, three, and nine months. *Child Development, 55,* 692–705.

Belsky, J., Rovine, M., & Taylor, D. G. (1984). The Pennsylvania Infant and Family Development Project, III: The origins of individual differences in infant–mother attachment: Maternal and infant contributions. *Child Development, 55,* 718–728.

Bowlby, J. (1969). *Attachment.* New York: Basic Books.

Burchinal, L. G. (1965). Trends and prospects for young marriages in the United States. *Journal of Marriage and the Family, 27,* 243–254.

Chamberlain, R. W., Szumoski, E. K., & Zastowny, T. R. (1979). An evaluation of efforts to educate mothers about child development in pediatric office practices. *American Journal of Public Health, 69*, 875–885.

Cochran, M. M., & Brassard, J. A. (1979). Child development and personal social networks. *Child Development, 50*, 601–616.

Colletta, N. D., & Gregg, C. H. (1981). Adolescent mothers' vulnerability to stress. *Journal of Nervous and Mental Disease, 169*, 50–54.

Crnic, K. A., Greenberg, M. T., & Ragozin, A. S. (1981). *The effects of stress and social support on maternal attitudes and the mother–infant relationship.* Presented at the Biennial Meeting of the Society for Research in Child Development, Boston.

Crockenberg, S. B. (1981). Infant irritability, mother responsiveness, and social support influences on the security of infant–mother attachment. *Child Development, 52*, 857–865.

DeLissovoy, V. (1973). Child care by adolescent parents. *Children Today, 2*, 23–25.

Elkind, D. (1974). *Children and adolescents: Interpretive essays on Jean Piaget.* New York: Oxford University Press.

Elster, A. B., Montemayor, R., & Gilbride, K. M. (1984). *Factors influencing the parental behavior of adolescent mothers.* Unpublished manuscript, University of Utah Medical Center.

Epstein, A. S. (1980). *Assessing the child development information needed by adolescent parents with very young children.* Final Report, U.S. Dept. of Health, Education & Welfare.

Field, T. M., Widmayer, S. M., Stringer, S., & Ignatoff, E. (1980). Teenage, lower class, black mothers and their preterm infants: An intervention and developmental follow-up. *Child Development, 51*, 426–436.

Furstenberg, F. F. (1976). The social consequences of teenage parenthood. *Family Planning Perspective, 8*, 148–164.

Furstenberg, F. F., & Crawford, A. G. (1978). Family support: Helping teenage mothers to cope. *Family Planning Perspectives, 10*, 322–333.

Garbarino, J. (1977). The human ecology of child maltreatment. *Journal of Marriage and the Family, 39*, 721–736.

Goldberg, S. (1977). Social competence in infancy: A model of parent–infant interaction. *Merrill–Palmer Quarterly, 23*, 163–177.

Goldberg, W. A., & Easterbrooks, M. A. (1984). Role of marital quality in toddler development. *Developmental Psychology, 20*, 504–514.

Green, J. W., Sandler, H. M., Altemeier, W. A., & O'Connor, S. M. (1981). Child rearing attitudes, observed behavior, and perception of infant temperament in adolescent versus older mothers. *Pediatric Research, 15*, 442.

Gutelius, M. F., Kirsch, A. D., MacDonald, S., Brooks, M. R., & McErlean, T. (1977). Controlled study of child health supervision: Behavioral results. *Pediatrics, 60*, 294–304.

Henderson, S., Bryne, D. G., & Duncan-Jones, P. (1980). Social relationships, adversity, and neurosis: A study of associations in a general population sample. *British Journal of Psychiatry, 136*, 574–583.

Hirsch, B. J. (1980). Natural support systems and coping with major life changes. *American Journal of Community Psychology, 8*, 159–172.

Jones, F. A., Green, V., & Krauss, D. R. (1980). Maternal responsiveness of primiparous mothers during the postpartum period: Age differences. *Pediatrics, 65*, 579–584.

Keating, D. P. (1980). Thinking processes in adolescence. In J. Adelson, (Ed.), *Handbook of adolescent psychology.* New York: Wiley.

Klaus, M. J., & Kennell, J. H. (1976). *Maternal–infant bonding.* St. Louis: Mosby.

Lamb, M. E. (1976). *The role of the father in child development.* New York: Wiley.

Lamb, M. E. (1977). The development of parental preferences in the first two years of life. *Sex Roles, 3*, 495–497.

Lamb, M. E. (1980). What can "research experts" tell parents about effective socialization? In M. D. Fantini & R. Cardenas (Eds.), *Parenting in a multicultural society*. New York: Longman.

Lamb, M. E. (1981a). *The role of the father in child development* (revised ed.). New York: Wiley.

Lamb, M. E. (1981b). The development of father–infant relationships. In M. E. Lamb (Ed.), *The role of the father in child development* . 459–488). New York: Wiley.

Lamb, M. E., & Baumrind, D. (1978). Socialization and personality development in the preschool years. In M. E. Lamb (Ed.), *Social and personality development*. New York: Holt, Rinehart, & Winston.

Lamb, M. E., & Easterbrooks, M. A. (1981). Individual differences in parental sensitivity: Origins, components, and consequences. In. M. E. Lamb & L. R. Sherrod (Eds.), *Infant social cognition: Empirical and theoretical considerations*. Hillsdale, NJ: Lawrence Erlbaum Associates.

Lamb, M. E., & Elster, A. B. (1985). Adolescent mother–infant–father relationships. *Developmental Psychology, 21,* in press.

Lamb, M. E., Frodi, A. M., Hwang, C.-P., Frodi, M., & Steinberg, J. (1982). Mother– and father–infant interaction involving play and holding in traditional and nontraditional Swedish families. *Developmental Psychology, 18,* 215–221.

Lamb, M. E., Pleck, J. H., & Levine, J. A. (1985). The role of the father in child development: The effects of increased paternal involvement. In B. B. Lahey & A. E. Kazdin (Eds.), *Advances in clinical child psychology* (Vol. 8). New York: Plenum.

Lamb, M. E., Thompson, R. A., Gardner, W., & Charnov, E. L. (1985). *Mother–infant attachment*. Hillsdale, NJ: Lawrence Erlbaum Associates.

Lamb, M. E., Thompson, R. A., Gardner, W. P., Charnov, E. L., & Estes, D. (1984). Security of infantile attachment as assessed in the "strange situation": Its study and biological interpretation. *Behavioral and Brain Sciences, 7,* 127–147.

Landy, S. (1981). *An investigation of teenage mothers, their infants, and the resulting mother–infant dyads*. Doctoral Dissertation, University of Regina, Regina, Saskatchewan.

Lawrence, R. A., McAnarney, E. R., Aten, M. J., Iker, H. P., Baldwin, C. P., & Baldwin, A. L. (1981). Aggressive behaviors in young mothers: Markers of future morbidity? *Pediatric Research, 15,* 443.

Levine, L., Garcia Coll, C. T., & Oh, W. (1985). Determinants of mother–infant interaction in adolescent mothers. *Pediatrics, 75,* 23–29.

McAnarney, E. R., Lawrence, R. A., & Aten, M. J. (1979). Premature parenthood: A preliminary report of adolescent mother–infant interaction. *Pediatric Research, 13,* 328.

McAnarney, E. R., Lawrence, R. A., Aten, J. M., & Iker, H. P. (1984). Adolescent mothers and their infants. *Pediatrics, 73,* 358–362.

Mercer, R. T., Hackely, K. C., & Bostrom, A. (1984). Adolescent motherhood: Comparison of outcome with older mothers. *Journal of Adolescent Health Care, 5,* 7–13.

Moore, K. A., Waite, L. J., Hofferth, S. L., & Caldwell, S. B. (1978). *The consequences of age at first childbirth: Marriage, separation, and divorce*. Washington, DC: The Urban Institute.

Nakashima, I. I., & Camp, B. W. (1984). Fathers of infants born to adolescent mothers: A study of paternal characteristics. *American Journal of Diseases of Children, 138,* 452–454.

Osofsky, H. J., & Osofsky, J. D. (1970). Adolescents as mothers: Results of a program for low-income pregnant teenagers with some emphasis upon infants' development. *American Journal of Orthopsychiatry, 40,* 825–834.

Parke, R. D., Power, T. G., & Gottman, J. (1979). Conceptualizing and quantifying influence patterns in the family triad. In M. E. Lamb, S. J. Suomi, & G. R. Stephenson (Eds.), *Social interaction analysis: Methodological issues*. Madison: University of Wisconsin Press.

Parks, P. L., & Smeriglio, V. L. (1983). Parenting knowledge among adolescent mothers. *Journal of Adolescent Health Care, 4,* 163–167.

Radin, N. (1981). The role of the father in cognitive, academic, and intellectual development. In M. E. Lamb (Ed.), *The role of the father in child development* (rev. ed.). New York: Wiley.

Ragozin, A. S., Basham, R. B., Crnic, K. A., Greenberg, M. T., & Robinson, N. M. (1982). Effects of maternal age on parenting role. *Developmental Psychology, 18*, 627–634.

Russell, G. (1978). The father role and its relation to masculinity, femininity, and androgyny. *Child Development, 49*, 755–765.

Rutter, M. (1973). Why are London children so disturbed? *Proceedings of the Royal Society of Medicine, 66*, 1221–1225.

Rutter, M., Cox, A., Tupling, C., Berger, M., & Yule, W. (1975). Attainment and adjustment in two geographic areas, I: The prevalence of psychiatric disorder. *British Journal of Psychiatry, 126*, 493–509.

Sadler, L. S., & Catrone, C. (1983). The adolescent parent: A dual developmental crisis. *Journal of Adolescent Health Care, 4*, 100–105.

Sandler, H. M., Vietze, P. M., & O'Connor, S. (1981). Obstetric and neonatal outcomes following intervention with pregnant teenagers. In K. G. Scott, T. Field, & E. Robertson (Eds.), *Teenage parents and their offspring*. New York: Grune & Stratton.

Spivack, G., Platt, J. K., & Shure, M. D. (1976). *The problem-solving approach to adjustment*. San Francisco: Jossey Bass.

Stevenson, M. B., & Lamb, M. E. (1981). The effects of social experience and social style on cognitive competence and performance. In M. E. Lamb & L. R. Sherrod (Eds.), *Infant social cognition*. Hillsdale, NJ: Lawrence Erlbaum Associates.

Thompson, R. A., Lamb, M. E., & Estes, D. (1982). Stability of infant–mother attachment and its relationship to changing life circumstances in an unselected middle-class sample. *Child Development, 53*, 144–148.

Thompson, R. J., Cappleman, M. W., & Zeitschel, K. A. (1979). Neonatal behavior of infants of adolescent mothers. *Developmental Medicine and Child Neurology, 21*, 474–482.

Toberg, A. J., Howell, V. V., & Wingert, W. A. (1983). Attachment interaction behavior between young teenage mothers and their infants. *Journal of Adolescent Health, 4*, 61–66.

Vaughn, B., Egeland, B., Sroufe, L. A., & Waters, E. (1979). Individual differences in infant–mother attachment at 12 and 18 months: Stability and change in families under stress. *Child Development, 50*, 971–975.

Wachs, T. D., & Gruen, G. (1982). *Early experience and human development*. New York: Plenum.

Wise, S., & Grossman, F. K. (1980). Adolescent mothers and their infants: Psychological factors in early attachment and interaction. *American Journal of Orthopsychiatry, 50*, 454–468.

Yogman, M. W. (1982). Development of the father–infant relationship. In H. Fitzgerald, B. Lester, & M. W. Yogman (Eds.), *Theory and research in behavioral pediatrics* (Vol. 1). New York: Plenum.

Zuckerman, B., Winesmore, G., & Alpert, J. J. (1979). A study of attitudes and support systems of inner city adolescent mothers. *Journal of Pediatrics, 95*, 122–125.

7

Adolescent Fatherhood in the Context of the Transition to Parenthood

Jay Belsky
Pennsylvania State University

Brent C. Miller
Utah State University

INTRODUCTION

There is a need to acknowledge at the outset of this chapter that males who impregnate adolescent females are not always themselves adolescents. In fact, the issues concerning fatherhood and fathering of the children of adolescent mothers can be very complex and confusing. Gershenson (1983) reported that "fathering" roles might be performed by former husbands/boyfriends who *are* biological fathers, by current husbands/boyfriends who are *not* biological fathers, and by the mothers' own father/stepfather (who in some cases might even be the biological father). In fact multiple fathering of the children of adolescent mothers, occurring simultaneously and/or serially, might be the rule rather than the exception in such families. Although defining fatherhood in cases of adolescent pregnancy is very complex and problematic, our more specific focus in this chapter is on fathers who themselves are adolescents.

We attempt to shed light upon the experience of the adolescent father in two ways. First, we provide a brief summary of what is known about the transition to parenthood in general and then highlight what makes this transition different for male adolescents. It is unfortunately the case that the data base on adolescent fathers is so meager that we are left to discuss the topic from a mostly speculative standpoint. The same can be said about the second way in which we attempt to illuminate the nature of adolescent fatherhood—by considering individual differences. When it comes to the consideration of individual differences in the males who are adolescent fathers, we discover that, beyond factors like age and ethnicity, little work has been done. Because we believe an individual-difference perspective is essential from the standpoint of science as well as service delivery, we offer a speculative analysis of factors we consider to be important in distinguishing between adolescent fathers and the relationships they may have with the mothers of their offspring and with their children. Much of the analysis focuses upon the nature of the relationship that existed between the adolescent mother and father prior to the birth of the child.

There are two reasons that we adopt this focus. The first is that evidence on nonadolescent parents experiencing the transition to parenthood indicates that the nature of a couple's relationship is strikingly stable across the transition (Belsky, Lang, & Rovine, in press; Belsky, Spanier, & Rovine, 1983). The second is that there is evidence indicating that the quality of the couple relationship is systematically, and even possibly causally, related to the way in which fathers treat and feel toward their offspring. Gibaud-Wallston and Wandersman (1978), for example, found that men who perceive their wives as supportive are highly skilled as fathers, regardless of their infant's temperaments. Consistent with such data are those recently reported by Goldberg and Easterbrooks (1984) indicating that more maritally satisfied fathers were less aggravated by parenting and provided greater emotional support to their toddlers when observed in a laboratory playroom. Finally, Feldman and her colleagues (Feldman, Nash, & Aschenbrenner, 1984) reported that the quality of the marital relationship was a strong predictor of fathers' play patterns in both structured and free play situations. The fact, then, that couple relationships may remain remarkably unchanged across the transition to parenthood, and that they may affect the kind of father a man is, leads us to focus upon relationship factors when considering individual differences in adolescent fathers in the second part of this chapter.

THE TRANSITION TO PARENTHOOD

The transition to fatherhood has no distinct beginning. One author has reported qualitative phases of expectant fathers' active involvement in pregnancy, ranging from announcement, through a kind of moratorium, to a final focusing and redefinition phase (May, 1978, 1979). When men are aware of the impending birth of their child, most are likely to engage in a process of becoming fathers by making plans and physical preparations several months before delivery. However, expectant parents, especially prospective fathers, often remain unaware that conception has occurred until several weeks or even months after conception. The beginning of fatherhood is also less certain because a substantial proportion of pregnancies do not result in live births but end in spontaneous or induced abortion. Given these uncertainties about the beginning of pregnancy and its continuation, the transition to fatherhood most concretely begins with the birth of the first child; a male becomes a father when his first child is born. His responsibilities and activities are likely to change with subsequent children, but he is already a father.

Although we can say that fatherhood begins with the first birth, it is more difficult to specify when the transition to fatherhood is completed. Parental roles are acquired abruptly with the birth of a child, but parental skills and routines are acquired gradually over an extended period of time. Perhaps a helpful distinction can be made here between father*hood,* the distinct status attained by having a child, and father*ing,* the long-term and intensive activities fathers are expected to perform.

Early retrospective studies of the transition to parenthood focused on the "crisis" of role reorganization as the marital dyad became a family triad, concluding that the amount of crisis usually experienced was "extensive or severe" (Dyer, 1963; LeMasters, 1957). Conceptual critiques of this work by Rappoport (1963) and Rossi (1968), and a series of studies by Hobbs (1965, 1968; Hobbs & Cole, 1976; Hobbs & Wimbish, 1977) began changing the view from parenthood as crisis to a normal developmental event that is only sightly or not at all bothersome to most parents, and some researchers (Russell, 1974) began reporting gratifications of new parents as well. Most of the data from these retrospective surveys of new parents showed that mothers and fathers reacted similarly to the birth of the first child but perhaps that new mothers were stressed and changed somewhat more than new fathers.

Two recent longitudinal studies carried out by Belsky (Belsky, Lang, & Rovine, in press; Belsky, Spanier & Rovine, 1983), as well as recent work by others (Cowan & Cowan, 1983; Grossman, Eichler, & Winickoff, 1980; Miller & Sollie, 1980; Waldorn & Routh, 1981), clearly show, at least insofar as the marital relationship in traditional families is concerned, that wives do, in fact, experience greater stress than do husbands; that is, women's reports of how their marriages are functioning and how they are feeling about their spouses change more negatively over time than do those of husbands. Thus, whereas feelings of love and marital satisfaction decline for both men and women from the time before to the time after the baby's arrival, this decline is more pronounced for women.

Across the many investigations of the stress experienced by couples in adjusting to the transition to parenthood, four general classes of problems have been identified (Sollie & Miller, 1980). The first of these involves the physical demands associated with caring for a child. More specifically, new parents routinely report an experience of stress caused by loss of sleep and constant fatigue that results from the extra work required in caring for a highly dependent child, especially that associated with caring for the baby in the middle of the night during normal sleeping hours. Mothers, not surprisingly, seem to be more susceptible than fathers to problems involving physical demands because they are more likely to experience the "role strain" associated with adding primary caregiver to the preparenthood roles of spouse, homemaker, and employee.

A second negative theme that emerges from investigations of the transition to parenthood focuses attention on strains in the husband–wife relationship. Frequent complaints of new parents highlight reductions in time spent together as a couple, changes in the sexual relationship, and the belief that the child's needs take priority over their own. Some of this stress, it should be evident, results from the physical demands of caregiving. As a case in point, consider how fatigue resulting from waking in the middle of the night to care for the infant might dampen one's interest in sex.

A third negative theme that emerges from inquiries into the transition to parenthood centers around the psychological stresses experienced by parents. One such source of emotional strain is having total responsibility for the care and well-being of the child, especially as parents come to realize, often quite slowly, that the responsibilities of parenthood last forever. Doubts regarding one's competence as a parent, which even the most skilled parents experience at one time or another, represent another source of emotional strain.

The final set of negative feelings experienced by parents adjusting to the addition of a child to the family involves opportunity costs and restrictions. Parents frequently comment about limits placed upon their social lives, particularly on their freedom to travel or to decide to do something on short notice. Most new parents discover that doing things while they are responsible for young children is far more complicated than they ever imagined. In addition to such social restrictions associated with parenting, there are also financial costs. The loss of income and career opportunities experienced when one parent remains home as a primary caregiver can be very important. The sheer expenses of raising a young child are also economically significant.

This description of the transition to parenthood might seem to be overly negative. It would be a mistake, however, to conclude that there are no gratifications and rewards associated with it. Indeed, there are, including feelings of personal fulfillment, joy and pride from watching ones own child grow and develop, and a sense of wonder and awe at the miracle of birth (Russell, 1974; Sollie & Miller, 1980). For a variety of reasons these have simply not been studied as extensively.

To a great extent, the study of the transition to parenthood has emphasized the role of mother and wife much more than that of father and husband. In many respects the emphasis is understandable, even if not desirable. Mothers have always been more available for scrutiny than fathers and, in addition to this pragmatic research consideration, mothers usually experience the most profound and dramatic change upon becoming parents. Evidence in support of this claim can be found in the work cited earlier indicating that wives experience a more negative change in their marital satisfaction than do husbands across this transition period. Undoubtedly, this finding results from the fact that women are more likely to assume primary responsibilities for child care, especially in the early postnatal months, and it is they who are more likely to remain at home with the baby or be responsible for finding and maintaining child-care arrangements when and if they return to paid employment outside the home.

There are two studies of which we are aware that have focused specifically on men's reactions to becoming fathers. Fein (1976) interviewed 30 men before and after the birth of their first child and found significant decreases in their infant-related and general anxiety following fatherhood. On the average, however, new fathers were still moderately anxious about parental roles and responsibilities 6 weeks after delivery. In retrospective interviews with 46 fathers, Wente and Crockenberg (1976) found that men's adjustment to fatherhood was related to the quality of their husband–wife relationship but not, apparently, to their participation in Lamaze classes or to the age of the infant at the time of the interview. The association between marital problems and parenthood difficulties is intriguing but inconclusive; because the interviews were all retrospective it is not possible to determine if marital problems lead to parenting difficulties or if both are a reflection of a more general tendency to report problems with life.

It is important to recognize that both of these studies, like those dealing with the transition to parenthood more generally, have focused upon men experiencing a normative transition to parenthood. What is it that makes the transition normative? Several major elements of a normative transition can be identified. Marriage is fundamental in the normative experience of fatherhood because it is the legally recognized relationship between a man and woman that legitimizes their childbearing. Simply put, men who become fathers are expected to be married. Childbearing is expected to occur within this relatively enduring adult heterosexual relationship. By law and by more subtle social sanctions both parents are held accountable to provide for and socialize their offspring.

Another important element in the normative transition to fatherhood is that fathers are expected to be adults. In the normative sequence of major life events, becoming a father is one of the later markers of leaving youth and entering adulthood. In other words, parenthood is normatively expected to occur in young adulthood. Perhaps this is because, by its very nature, parenthood implies major responsibilities. Nurturing an infant requires a certain level of maturity and providing the economic support expected of a father usually requires the completion of school or other training and obtaining a job. In sum, fatherhood normatively includes expectations that the father will provide economic support for his offspring and be mature enough to participate with his partner in caring for and nurturing their child.

The social context of fatherhood and fathering for adolescent males differs importantly from the normative fatherhood experience. The most obvious departure from the normative situation is the *timing* of adolescent fatherhood. Parenthood in adolescence is off schedule, too soon, earlier in the life course than is expected. The phrase "children having children" is often used to describe this accelerated or precocious parenthood. There are several ways that early timing of parenthood is likely to be more problematic than fatherhood for older fathers.

First, fathers are expected to provide the physical necessities of life for their children. Before this century early fatherhood might have meant little difference in a young man's occupational planning or preparation. Meeting this economic expectation of fatherhood is especially difficult for contemporary adolescent fathers, however, because the occupational structure has changed immensely, and adolescents today are not yet fully prepared for continuous lifetime employment. Nowadays, completing high school and attending college or some other vocational training program are prerequisites for obtaining better paying jobs in our highly technical advanced society. An analysis of project TALENT national longitudinal data showed that young fathers were more likely to be employed and to be making more money at first than their peers, but men who become parents when they were older quickly made up this initial difference and were better off occupationally and financially (Card & Wise, 1978). In sum, if they try to fulfill the role of economic provider, adolescent fathers are at a distinct disadvantage.

Secondly, if fatherhood normatively presumes a relatively stable marital relationship, then adolescent fathers are clearly out of step. In 1981, 63% of births to 15–17-year-old mothers, and 41% of births to 18- and 19-year-old mothers were nonmarital (illegitimate) births (National Center for Health Statistics, 1984). It is not known in what percentage of these nonmarital births to teenage mothers the partners were adolescent fathers, but the data are strongly suggestive that relationship stability in the case of adolescent parenthood departs substantially from normative expectations. And, of course, marital status at childbirth does not tell the whole story about relationship stability. Adolescent parents do marry— sometimes to legitimize the birth and sometimes in hopes of beginning an enduring family life—but marriages between young partners have a high probability of early dissolution (Kellam, Adams, Brown, & Ensminger, 1982; Moore & Waite, 1981). So, even if marriage precedes adolescent parenthood as it is normatively expected to, adolescents are much more likely than older couples to divorce, placing them again in a less advantageous parenting context.

Finally, although the data are less clear-cut, it could be argued that adolescent fathers are also psychologically less ready to become parents. Compared to older fathers, adolescents might be less rational in decision making, less capable of making cognitive and moral judgments, less knowledgeable and realistic about the behavior of infants and children, and less advanced in their own psychological identity formation. Data show that younger adolescent development is not yet complete in these respects, but what this means relative to the actual fathering behaviors of adolescents has yet to be established.

A number of studies of adolescent fathers have been reported in the literature, but they are based on clinic populations (Barret & Robinson, 1981, 1982; Connolly, 1978; Earls & Siegel, 1980; Pannor & Evans, 1975; Parke, Power, & Fisher, 1980). Studies of adolescent fathers based on clinic samples are difficult to interpret and generalize because the samples are almost certain to be biased. Sample biases are likely to arise because clinic samples leave out fathers who are literally unknown, or who have deliberately distanced themselves from "the problem.'' In addition, adolescent mothers are usually the gatekeepers through whom adolescent fathers are (or are not) identified, and adolescent mothers have many motives and pressures in making this decision.

Relative to what we know about the normative transition to parenthood, and even the situation of ''on-time fathers,'' our knowledge of teenage fathers is meager at best. Longitudinal studies of this population, which are difficult even with families experiencing a normative transition, are particularly hard to implement. We are aware of no work that has followed a sample of nonclinic teenage men, even as part of couples, from before to after the transition. Is it safe to say, then, that the kinds of difficulties that nonadolescent couples face are experienced in just the same way by adolescent fathers and their mates? We suspect not. As we have noted, the off-time transition of adolescent fatherhood catches the male in a situation for which he is particularly unprepared. Probably lacking any kind of positive career trajectory with sufficient income, and limited psychological resources of his own, we suspect that this transition is much more stressful for adolescent than older fathers—if the male remains involved. In such cases, given the equally challenging situation of the teenage mother, it is likely that stress is heightened and that the gratifications of parenthood are diminished. In short, compared to older men, an adolescent father probably has an especially difficult time in the transition to parenthood.

There may be, however, developmental benefits that accrue from the experience. Relationships may become strengthened and demands placed upon the adolescent father may foster psychological maturation. Although such developments may occur, we suspect they are more likely to be the exception than the rule. If different types of transitions could be distinguished, that would invariably prove useful. The very possibility of such distinctions raises the second major issue that this chapter addresses, namely, individual differences.

INDIVIDUAL DIFFERENCES

Our discussion of the transition to parenthood to this point has focused on the normative changes in family life that the birth and rearing of the first child occasions. In addition, we have reflected upon the implications of the process for teenagers in general, and teen fathers in particular. We must not lose sight of the fact, however, that terms like teenager, or father, refer to classes or groups of individuals, and so far we have been considering just that, *classes* of individuals. Our discussion up until now has focused on the average individual that every reader knows does not exist.

Teenagers, fathers, and teen fathers are not all alike. Thus, the normative trends that we have discussed characterize general experiences that undoubtedly mask a great deal of variability. Individuals and the lives they lead vary immensely—and in functionally very important ways. The ''same'' event for two different persons is, in actuality, two distinct events. As citizens, we need to be careful not to stereotype persons who are the same race, religion, or gender; as scientists, service providers, and policy makers we need to be careful not to stereotype life-course events, like teenage fatherhood. All this is not to say that there are no commonalities across such events; our preceding discussion most certainly demonstrates that there are. But in the face of such shared experience there are also important individual differences.

Each way of looking at a phenomenon provides a different perspective on it. As implied previously, a focus on central tendencies highlights what is general, normative, or average about an experience. In contrast, a focus on individual differences reveals what is variable about the phenomenon. Only by consideration of each of these perspectives can we hope to achieve a more complete understanding of the phenomenon. It is in this spirit that we now turn our attention to consideration of individual differences among teenage fathers.

A focus upon individual differences is important because it helps us to think not only about the characteristics of a phenomenon (i.e., how variable is it), but also about its causes and consequences. In the case of teenage fatherhood and the teenage father's transition to parenthood, we need to ask whether different experiences of this life-course situation result from different antecedent conditions, and whether they result in different effects for the individuals experiencing them. Only by considering variation in the experience is it possible to address such issues. Obviously such issues are pressing concerns to those obligated to provide services or to those desirous of promoting certain policies. Unless individual differences are appreciated, it is unlikely that intervention, particularly that geared toward prevention, will be successful; and unless developmental derivatives are appreciated, it is difficult to determine what the goal of intervention and policy ought to be. Further, because it is clear that resources for services are not, and are not likely to become, unlimited, there is a growing need to provide them strategically so that they will be available to, and used by, those most likely to benefit from them. Who are these individuals? Without an orientation toward individual differences, this question cannot be answered. Clearly, then, a focus upon individual differences is an imperative for both science and service.

The dimensions that can be employed to think about individual differences are unlimited, because persons, including teen fathers, vary in a myriad of ways. Investigations of teenage parents, be they of mothers or fathers, have focused principally upon such factors as age and ethnicity of the teenager. This focus is not surprising, given the sociological foundation of most work in this area. That this foundation has value is evident in the fact that we are no longer likely to think about the needs of 13- to 18-year-old parents or of Anglo and Hispanic teenage parents in exactly the same way. These sociological dimensions help to characterize different contextual niches.

Our mostly speculative analysis of individual variability will focus attention on the relationshps between teenage mothers and teenage fathers. Consideration of individual differences in such relationships brings us to a more psychological level of analysis—one that requires that we think about what the parents mean to each other. In our view, such consideration is essential if we are to plan services for parents who are teenagers. Consideration of characteristics of the teenage mother–father relationship will not necessarily lead to basic decisions about services. But we feel that such a focus is essential if we are to determine which teenage fathers might benefit most from services. As part of our discussion we intend to demonstrate that other factors, in addition to characteristics of the mother–father relationship, need to be considered, especially the attitudes of the mother's kin toward the father. It should be pointed out at the outset that our strategy of examining aspects of the teenage mother–father relationship before considering the social (i.e., kin) context of teenage parenthood is not meant to imply that what goes on within teenage couples is independent of what transpires between teenagers and their kin. In fact, these contextual aspects of teenage parenthood are likely to be dependent on one another. Nevertheless, for heuristic purposes we consider each of these aspects of the social context separately, pointing out, when appropriate, the interrelations that invariably exist.

Relationship Dimensions

Not only are dimensions of individual differences in general unlimited, but so too are dimensions of individual differences in relationships. There are three, however, that we want to consider before discussing types of teenage fathers and the relationship they have with the mothers of their babies. The first dimension is that of *time,* especially the *duration* of the relationship between the teenage male and female. It would be useful to know, for example, how long have they known each other, how long have they "dated," and how long have they been sexually active together? It should be obvious that answers to this set of questions will be different for each couple, and, in fact, one can anticipate a very different situation for couples that have a long history of familiarity and intimacy (with or without comparable length of sexual relations) from one in which the length of time on each aspect of relationship duration is brief. Imagine a couple, for instance, in which sexual intercourse and impregnation occur early in the relationship's history.

A second relationship dimension that seems particularly significant in terms of prognosis involves the *exclusivity* of sexual relations. We need to ask whether the teenage father was and is sexually active with other women during the same period that he was having sexual relations with the adolescent who became pregnant; that is, was the teenage father having intercourse with a variety of females and is he still, or is his sexual behavior restricted to the one who is to be a teenage mother?

The third and final dimension we want to mention is intricately related to the other two and may indeed be defined by them. It involves *commitment.* How committed was the teenage father to the teenage mother prior to the pregnancy and what has been his commitment since? Was theirs a relationship of convenience and opportunity, or had they considered their relationship beyond the immediate present?; that is, did the relationship have a future irrespective of the pregnancy, at least in the eyes of the individuals participating in it?

In certain respects the duration and sexual exclusivity of the relationship implies something about commitment, though by no means is it necessary to think in terms of commitment to marry. Here we are simply speaking in terms of commitment to each other so that the relationship is recognized to be enduring, as opposed to transient. The very fact that the three factors under consideration are not likely to be totally independent of each other, but rather causally connected, leads us to consider several types of teenage relationships, and particularly teenage fathers, which are worth distinguishing if our ultimate goal is to acquire knowledge and to serve programs and policy.

Types of Teen Fathers and Teen Relationships

If the three relationship characteristics described previously were independent of one another, then we could generate a list of eight single relationship subtypes by simply characterizing each dimension in binary terms (duration: long/short; exclusivity: yes/no; commitment: yes/no) and detailing all possible combinations. As noted earlier, these dimensions or characteristics of a relationship are unlikely to be totally independent and indeed are probably causally interrelated such that, for example, enduring, sexually exclusive relationships tend to be characterized by high levels of commitment. For purposes of exposition, then, it seems helpful to think in terms of two extreme types of teenage fathers and their relationships, and two others that fall somewhere in between, while simultaneously recognizing that we may be dealing with a continuum or even a more complex multidimensional configuration of which our discussion only characterizes a few prototypes.

In the example just offered we have already summarized one type of father and the relationship he is involved in. The father who is involved in an enduring relationship that is characterized by sexual exclusivity and some sense of commitment may be viewed as the victim of the probabilistic character of procreation. Unprotected intercourse does not always lead to pregnancy, but repeated unprotected intercourse increases the likelihood that eventually the steady partner will become pregnant. The sexual exclusivity of this relationship, coupled with its enduring quality, suggests that men and women who engage in unprotected intercourse repeatedly are, to some degree, willing to run the risk of pregnancy, because from some vantage point they see themselves as having a future together. In the enduring and exclusive relationship, partners are likely to be least reasonably aware of the risks they are running. In this context, teenage fatherhood would seem to be a distinctly different phenomenon than when it occurs at the other end of the spectrum.

We can imagine the case of a teenage male who has few, if any, enduring relationships, and who is sexually active with a number of partners with whom he has no sense of commitment. Such a potential father is unlikely to think in terms of the future of these partnerships. His sexual activity is likely to be mostly self-centered with only very limited concern for others. One sexual partner may be as good as another and again, on a probabilistic basis, such promiscuous males risk pregnancy when they engage in intercourse with multiple partners on a short-term basis, without engaging in preventive actions (i.e., contraceptive use).

Unlike the first type of teen father we described, the uncommitted, promiscuous male probably would have not much real interest in the role of father. Nor would it seem to be in either the mother's or the child's long-term developmental best interests that he be encouraged to become involved in other than a financially supportive manner. For such a male there would seem to be little evidence of factors that make being a mate and parent a high-quality experience for all involved, namely, nurturance and consideration of the other.

The teen male in an enduring relationship, in contrast, would seem to be potentially available for the establishment of an enduring relationship with his offspring. This is not to imply that he would make an ideal father or that his relationship with his mate, if it led to marriage, would be stable and fulfilling; nevertheless, at least some of the seemingly important building blocks for a relationship would appear to be present. Policies and services to foster family formation in these instances, relative to the other situation, would seem to have a greater likelihood of success, especially when success is measured in the teenage father's life-course availability to his offspring, whether or not he marries, or remains married to, the child's mother.

In some communities and peer groups there is likely to be a third type of teenage father, who, although not randomly promiscuous, is by no means restricted in his sexual activity to a single partner. Indeed, we can imagine a male who has somewhat enduring sexually active relationships with several women, either simultaneously or serially, that are characterized by a modest or low level of commitment. Whether or not these teenage males could become participative fathers would seem to rest on their ability, once their partner becomes pregnant, to make a commitment to her and their child. This would seem to be true also of another possible type of teenage father—the one who is not yet committed to his partner, who has been involved with her for just a short time, yet who "gets" her pregnant early in the course of their relationship. In both cases the possibility exists for turning a somewhat tentative relationship into a committed one.

It seems possible, however, that these may be the kinds of relationships that are all too frequently encouraged or pressured to endure, but which have the least likelihood of success. In such cases, commitment would seem to develop largely as a function of the pregnancy and, thus, it would be impossible to know if these relationships had the potential for commitment if pregnancy had not occurred. Invariably some would, and these would probably be the ones that might actually have looked like the first kind described (enduring, exclusive, committed) had pregnancy not occurred so early in the relationship.

A basic assumption guiding the preceding discussion is that it is difficult to separate the father role from the role of mate. Except in very unusual cases, the teenage mother will have responsibility for the child and will thus serve as gatekeeper to the father's involvement. It is difficult for an involved father role to develop unless there is some degree of commitment in the mother–father relationship. This is not to deny that father–child relationships can and do develop in the case of noncustodial divorced fathers, but to emphasize the extreme difficulty of such relationships developing in the case of adolescent parenthood. Unless the minimum requirements for a relationship are met, it will be difficult for the father to gain access to and spend time with his child. In the absence of such contact, fatherhood remains solely biological without apparent psychological meaning and significance.

Individual Differences in Context

If the types of fathers we have described really do exist, and even if our prognosis about their involvement as fathers are relatively accurate, we still need to recognize that the broader context of teenage fatherhood is likely to exert a powerful influence upon how the father–child relationship develops and how the transition to fatherhood is experienced. In this regard, perhaps the most important dimension of context is likely to be the teenage mother's kin network.

In the large majority of cases of teenage pregnancy, the mother has custody and control over the child, and her own family of origin provides most of the support she receives; the mother's extended family may even be principally responsible for rearing the child and providing for it financially. In many cases the father's contribution relative to the maternal grandmother's, for instance, is miniscule. It would seem, then, that the quantity and quality of father involvement may well be as dependent on the mother's kin network as on the mother herself.

In the same way that there are important individual differences in teen fathers and in their relationship with the child's mother, we must recognize that there is variation in the relation between teen fathers and the families of the child's mother from both the child's, the mother's, and even the father's perspective; the salience and significance of such variation cannot be overemphasized. As we have already noted, exactly what transpires between teenage parents and their kin, especially the mother's, is not likely to be totally independent of the nature of the teen male–female relationship. This needs to be kept in mind as we consider various types of kin relations. It may be helpful to think again in terms of prototypic relationships, this time between teen fathers and the mother's kin. On the one hand one can imagine a supportive set of grandparents who welcome, or at least accept, the pregnancy and the father. The teenage male, in such situations, is recognized as having a continuing place in both the child's and the mother's life. Such a father is unlikely to be excluded from coming to visit the child if mother and child reside in the maternal grandparent's household. Or, if the child and mother live separately, or with the father, the mother's parents are less likely to be critical and may even be supportive of the father, and the mother's and the child's relationship with him. This situation is probably most likely to arise when commitment and sexual exclusivity characterize the relationship between teenage parents.

An extremely different situation is easy to imagine, one in which open hostility is expressed by the mother's kin toward the teen father. Under such circumstances it is likely that efforts will be made to deliberately prevent the father from visiting the mother and baby, especially if the mother lives with her family of origin. If she does not, she is likely to be continually berated for having anything to do with him. If she or he persists in trying to maintain some form of male–female or father–child relationship, it is not unlikely that grandparents providing financial support for the child will threaten to cut off such assistance unless relations with the father are terminated.

The consequence of these types of extended family relationships, and of the variation in types of father–mother relations discussed earlier, are likely to be greatly influenced by the interaction of these conditions of individual differences—as suggested before. When there is no love lost between father and mother as when their coupling resulted from self-interest with little commitment, and when the mother's kin are adversely disposed toward the father, few problems with him are likely to develop—because he is not likely to remain in the picture very long. Here we see consistency in the interests of the father, the mother, and her family. Unless the father develops a desire to be involved with the mother and/or child, it is unlikely that he will have much access to his offspring, and there will be little conflict between the parents.

The situation also seems viable when both mother and father desire to continue their relationship and the mother's kin are relatively supportive of the father and of his relationship with the mother and child. Love and pride need not characterize the feeling of the extended family toward the father; acceptance is likely to be sufficient to enable an involved father–child relationship to develop.

Obviously, the situation is likely to be most complicated and conflicted when the mother and father seek to continue their relationship, but the extended family actively opposes the father, either in his involvement with the child or the mother. In such situations the teenage mother is clearly caught between two competing interests. And it is here that the problems of service providers and policy makers are most apparent. Does one adopt policies and provide services in such situations to encourage father involvement, thereby putting the mother at odds with her own family? Or, does one do something else (possibly nothing) and, thereby, fail to support the mother's own choice and the father's personal interest?

Obviously these are difficult questions to answer. The major point we are trying to make in this speculative analysis is that variation characterizes all aspects of the teen father's situation, and that it is the interrelation of these sources of variation that are likely to be the major determinants of how the role of the father develops. In our view, the two critical dimensions are the nature of the relationships between mother and father *prior* to the pregnancy and the orientation of the mother's family of origin toward the pregnancy and the father. When variation across these situations are consistent, father involvement will either not be an issue or it will be supported. But when the interests of the mother–father relationship are in conflict with those of mother and her family, then serious difficulties are likely to arise for everyone involved, including parents, grandparents, and child(ren). There will likely be great costs associated with such a situation. And for service providers and policy makers concerned with the father's tie to the child, the situation seems almost unresolvable. It is no doubt such situations that make agencies wary of involvement in family matters unless the child's physical well-being is at risk.

SUMMARY AND CONCLUSION

Consideration of the transition to parenthood underscored two important facts that possibly enhance our understanding of the situation of teenage fatherhood. First, for most couples who experience the transition to parenthood normatively, this life event is somewhat stressful. And even if the stress may be greater for women than for men, it is no doubt part of men's experience. In view of the off-time nature of this transition for teenage males, it is likely to be especially stressful for them—at least insofar as they desire to maintain a relationship with the child and/or teen mother.

Exactly how this transition is likely to be experienced is suggested by still a second fact having to do with the transition to parenthood as normatively experienced. Because individual differences in young adult couple relationships are quite stable across the transition, even as levels of couple functioning change, it seems likely that the nature of the relationship between teenagers before conception and the birth of the child would be important to understanding the nature of the mothers' and fathers' transition to parenthood. At least this logic seems warranted to the extent that adolescent couple relationships are like the relationships of young adults—they might, in fact, be quite different. But because so little attention has been paid to teen fathers (to say nothing of teen couples that become pregnant), little is known about the individual differences about which we have speculated so extensively. Thus, the notion that relationship difference between couples will prove important to understanding and providing services to teenage fathers must remain a hypothesis waiting to be tested.

Once individual differences are pursued, a wide variety of important questions can be raised and, hopefully, answered. First, we need to know whether, as clinical experience suggests, there are different types of teen fathers and mother–father relationships. If there are, we can seek to determine whether or not they have different developmental histories that, when understood, may actually enable us to develop more effective prevention strategies. Whether or not our typology captures the true range of variation or even characterizes effectively that variation that does exist is not as important as whether we can meaningfully conceptualize and measure the variability.

As we noted throughout our speculative analysis, we believe strongly that an individual-difference perspective is essential for the development of social policy and service provision in this area. To presume that all teen fathers should be encouraged to participate in the child's development is to assume that biological and psychological investments are one and the same. The task for policy and service would seem to be to facilitate the development of social ecologies that foster healthy individual and family development. In some cases this will require inclusion of the father in service delivery. In others it will invariably be better not to include him. But unless variation in the very experience of teenage fatherhood is systematically investigated, this discrimination may prove quite difficult to make.

REFERENCES

Barret, R. L., & Robinson, B. E. (1981). Teenage fathers: A profile. *Personal and Guidance Journal, 60*(4), 226–228.

Barret, R. L., & Robinson, B. E. (1982). A descriptive study of teenage expectant fathers. *Family Relations, 31,* 349–352.

Belsky, J., Lang, M., & Rovine, M. (in press). Stability and change in marriage across the transition to parenthood: A second study. *Journal of Marriage and the Family.*

Belsky, J., Spanier, G., & Rovine, M. (1983). Stability and change in marriage across the transition to parenthood. *Journal of Marriage and the Family, 45,* 567–577.

Card, J. J., & Wise, L. L. (1978). Teenage mothers and teenage fathers: The impact of early childbearing on their personal and professional lives. *Family Planning Perspectives, 10,* 199–205.

Connolly, L. (1978, January). Boy fathers. *Human Behavior,* 40–43.

Cowan, P. A., & Cowan, C. P. (1983, April). *Quality of couple relationships and parenting stress in beginning families.* Paper presented at the Biennial Meeting of the Society for Research in Child Development, Detroit.

Dyer, E. (1963). Parenthood as crisis: A restudy. *Marriage and Family Living, 25,* 196–201.

Earls, F., & Siegel, B. (1980). Precocious fathers. *American Journal of Orthopsychiatry, 50,* 469–480.

Elster, A. B., & Panzarine, S. (1983). Teenage fathers: Stresses during gestation and early parenthood. *Clinical Pediatrics, 22.*

Fein, R. (1976). Men's entrance to parenthood. *The Family Coordinator, 25,* 341–348.

Feldman, S. S., Nash, S. C., & Aschenbrenner, D. (1984). Antecedents of fathering. *Child Development, 54,* 1628–1636.

Gershenson, H. P. (1983, August). Redefining fatherhood in families with white adolescent mothers. *Journal of Marriage and the Family,* 591–599.

Gibaud-Wallston, & Wandersman, L. P. (1978). *Development and utility of the parenting sense of competence scale.* Paper presented at the Annual Meeting of the American Psychological Association, Toronto.

Goldberg, W. A., & Easterbrooks, M. A. (1984). The role of marital quality in toddler development. *Developmental Psychology, 20,* 504–514.

Grossman, F., Eichler, L., & Winickoff, S. (1980). *Pregnancy, birth, and parenthood: Adaptations of mothers, fathers, and infants.* San Francisco: Jossey-Bass.

Hobbs, D. (1965). Parenthood as a crisis: A third study. *Journal of Marriage and the Family, 27,* 367–372.

Hobbs, D. F., Jr. (1968). Transition to parenthood: A replication and an extension. *Journal of Marriage and the Family, 30,* 413–417.

Hobbs, D., & Cole, S. (1976). Transition to parenthood: A decade replication. *Journal of Marriage and the Family, 38,* 723–731.

Hobbs, D., & Wimbish, J. (1977). Transition to parenthood by black couples. *Journal of Marriage and the Family, 39,* 677–689.

Kellam, S. G., Adams, R. G., Brown, C. H., & Ensminger, M. E. (1982). The long-term evolution of the family struture of teenage and older mothers. *Journal of Marriage and the Family, 44,* 539–554.

LeMasters, E. (1957). Parenthood as crisis. *Marriage and Family Living, 19,* 352–355.

May, K. A. (1978). Active involvement of expectant fathers in pregnancy: Some further considerations. *Journal of Obstetric and Gynecological Nursing, 7,* 7–12.

May, K. A. (1979). *The male pregnancy trajectory: Development of father involvement in pregnancy by first-time expectant fathers.* Unpublished manuscript.

Miller, B. C., & Sollie, D. (1980). Normal stresses during the transition to parenthood. *Family Relations, 29,* 459–465.

Moore, K. A., & Waite, L. (1981). Marital dissolution, early motherhood, and early marriage. *Social Forces, 60,* 20–40.

National Center for Health Statistics. (1984, September). S. J. Ventura: Trends in teenage childbearing, United States, 1970–81. *Vital and Health Statistics.* Series 21, No. 41. DHHS Pub. No. (PHS) 84-919. Public Health Service. Washington, DC: U.S. Government Printing Office.

Pannor, R., & Evans, B. (1975). The unmarried father revisited. *The Journal of School Health, 45,* 286–291.

Parke, R. D., Power, T. G., & Fisher, T. (1980). The adolescent father's impact on the mother and child. *Journal of Social Issues, 36*(1), 88–106.

Rappoport, R. (1963). Normal crises, family structure, and mental health. *Family Process, 2,* 68–80.

Rossi, A. S. (1968). Transition to parenthood. *Journal of Marriage and the Family, 30,* 26–39.

Russell, C. (1974). Transition to parenthood: Problems and gratifications. *Journal of Marriage and the Family, 36,* 294–301.

Sollie, D. L., & Miller, B. C. (1984). The transition to parenthood as a critical time for building family strengths. In N. Stinnett, B. Chesser, J. Defain, & P. Draul (Eds.), *Family strengths: Positive models of family life.* Lincoln: University of Nebraska Press.

Waldron, H., & Routh, D. (1981). The effect of the first child on the marital relationship. *Journal of Marriage and the Family, 43,* 785–788.

Wente, A., & Crockenberg, S. (1976). Transition to fatherhood: Lamaze preparation, adjustment, difficulty and the husband–wife relationship. *The Family Coordinator, 27,* 351–357.

8 The Adolescent Father and Child Maltreatment

Frank G. Bolton, Jr.
Arizona Department of Economic Security

Jay Belsky
Pennsylvania State University

The identification of factors that forecast instability in the adolescent parent–child relationship is a common quest among scientists and practitioners interested in adolescent pregnancy/parenthood. Consideration of the individual and contextual factors that predict relationship failure among *adult parents* and their children provides a starting point for considering determinants of maltreatment by adolescent parents. Unfortunately, the literature on adolescent parenthood suffers from a virtual absence of solid data on the characteristics, consequences, and determinants of adolescent fatherhood. Nevertheless, negative stereotypes are still widely held and current theoretical and empirical work to be examined in this chaper suggests the possibility that even researchers have been too willing to adopt popular assumptions about the adolescent parent–child relationship.

At the outset, it should be made clear that all is not well in the world of adolescent parents. It is well documented that the adolescent mothers and children are at risk for many reasons. Klein (1978) has described the pregnancy and parenthood experience of the adolescent mother as one of "failure": The teenage mother *fails* to establish a vocation, *fails* to remain in school, *fails* to control family size, *fails* to find personal stability, and *fails* to establish an environment in which a child is likely to grow and prosper. As a result, the child of such a parent is also likely to experience failure; his/her childhood is likely to be marked by deficits in cognitive development, overactivity, hostility, resistiveness, lack of impulse control, and reduced school achievement (Baldwin & Cain, 1981). As if these risks were not sufficient, the child of an adolescent parent is also likely to enter parenthood prematurely. Clearly, the psychosocial environment of the adolescent parent and child presents multiple obstacles to both mother and child as well as to their relationship (Menke, 1972). But even in the face of such problems, it seems that family researchers may have been too ready to assume a high potential for extremely negative outcomes, like child maltreatment, in the absence of corroborative evidence.

The current focus on adolescent parenthood began with intense examination of adolescent pregnancy with respect to the physiological dangers posted to mother and child (Lincoln, Jaffe, & Ambrose, 1976). More recent work indicates that the physiological danger is brought within expected limits through adequate prenatal care (Baldwin & Cain, 1981). This finding has allowed those concerned with adolescent pregnancy/parenthood to concentrate upon psychological and social risks in adolescent parenthood, and to consider the *parenting* rather than the *pregnancy* experience in greater detail. The first step in the examination of the adolescent parenting experience was to apply knowledge of adult parenting experiences upon adolescent parent–child relationships. The results have been only moderately successful and, in some cases, has led to erroneous beliefs and conclusions.

Interest in the psychosocial risks associated with adolescent parenting emerged as researchers were developing "ecological" models of child maltreatment risk (Belsky, 1980). As these parallel issues in the study of the family evolved, it became increasingly apparent that the adolescent mother–child relationship disturbingly resembled those adult parent–child relationships that seemed to be at extreme risk for child maltreatment (Bolton, 1980). In short, the resemblance between elements described in etiological models of child maltreatment and the realities of adolescent parenthood served to foster the belief that the adolescent mother and child were at extreme risk for child maltreatment. Even in the absence of authoritative epidemiological data, being an adolescent mother became synonymous with "being at high risk for child maltreatment" at least in the practitioner's belief system (Bolton & Laner, 1981). This belief, however "logical," is not substantiated by the available scientific evidence.

MALTREATMENT AND THE ADOLESCENT PARENT

The level of maltreatment anticipated within the population of adolescent parents has not materialized. Despite the presence of multiple factors that predict risk in adult parents, far fewer adolescent parents are found within officially reported samples of maltreating parents than would otherwise be predicted. Early studies of officially reported child maltreatment cases (Bolton, Laner, & Kane, 1980; Kinard & Klerman, 1980) described the presence of adolescent perpetrators in 37.5 to 51.7% of the substantiated cases examined. Although impressive at first, consideration of the high rates of adolescent birth in the socioeconomic groups most susceptible to "official" reporting of child maltreatment led these researchers to conclude that absolute evidence of increased risk could not be established through these studies.

Most recently, the relationship between adolescent parenthood and child maltreatment has been examined through a secondary analysis of the National Study of the Incidence and Severity of Child Abuse and Neglect (Miller, 1983). This work was an important first step in examining officially reported child maltreatment cases (i.e., known to child protective agencies) and cases known to other community agencies but not necessarily reported. Because (1) adolescent mothers who both bore their children and also were child-abuse perpetrators during adolescence were overrepresented by only about 3%, and (2) mothers who bore children during their adolescence but were not identified as perpetrators of maltreatment until their 20s were overrepresented by about 7%, Miller only concluded that adolescent mothers were ''at least slightly overrepresented'' in maltreating populations when compared to national age rates. Again, the expected ''epidemic'' of maltreatment perpetration by adolescent parents simply failed to materialize.

Recognizing that adolescent parents are not at uniform risk for perpetration of child maltreatment, researchers have begun examining vulnerabilities in those adolescent parents who do perpetrate maltreatment. To facilitate our discussion of this recent research, a brief review of etiological factors implicated in the maltreatment process is presented.

THE ETIOLOGY OF CHILD MALTREATMENT

Three general accounts of the etiology of child maltreatment have been offered (Belsky, 1978; Parke & Collmer, 1975). The explanation most widely held by the lay public focuses attention on the individual abuser and thereby highlights disturbances in the psychological well-being of the maltreating parent. The psychological or psychiatric orientation also underscores the influence of the abusive parent's own child-rearing history. By contrast, the sociological explanation of abuse focuses attention upon the family, community, and societal stressors to which abusive parents are exposed (e.g., poverty, unemployment, social isolation, marital discord). In essence, this sociological orientation assumes that the maltreating parent is as much a victim as s/he is a villain. Indeed, from this perspective, the psychiatric perspective ''blames the victim.''

Neither the psychiatric nor sociological points of view consider that what transpires within the parent–child relationship is a function not only of the parent's psychological makeup and the social context of child rearing, but also of the attributes and behavior of the child; that is, what transpires between parent and child both affects and is affected by the child. And, in the case of child abuse, children may play a role, usually inadvertently, in contributing to their own mistreatment.

Whereas these three perspectives on child abuse have been, by tradition, considered separately, it is clear that they are by no means mutually exclusive

(Belsky, 1980). Consideration of disturbances in parents' psychological functioning and development in no way precludes consideration of social stressors, and neither of these foci preclude consideration of the child's contribution. In point of fact, consideration of all three perspectives provides a means of enhancing understanding of the etiology of child abuse and, more generally, the determinant of parental functioning (Belsky, 1984). A graphic representation of Belsky's model is depicted in Fig. 8.1. As can be seen from the diagram, the model presumes that adult personality functioning is, at least in part, a result of one's history as a developing psychological agent. Individuals who have been nurtured and supported in their families of origin are presumed to develop into psychologically mature adults. Such individuals, because of their greater social skills, their abilities to detect and consider the point of view of others, and their capacities to control impulses and to be nurturant, are expected to be especially capable of caring for their offspring in a growth-promoting manner.

The model displayed in Fig. 8.1 also suggests that parenting is a function of the contextual stresses and supports to which parents are exposed. Parents who are engaged in a harmonious marriage, who are embedded in a reciprocally supportive and satisfying social network, who find satisfaction and limited stress in their occupations, and whose children have easy temperaments, are also likely to provide sensitive, growth-promoting care to their offspring. As the model implies, the qualities of the marriage, social network ties, and occupational experience are themselves viewed as being a function of enduring dispositional characteristics of the person, and thereby derivative of the adult's developmental history. Moreover, these aspects of the social context are presumed to influence parenting directly, as well as indirectly, by affecting the general psychological well-being of the parent.

Is this model, based as it is on studies of adult parents, applicable to teenage parents? Evidence that it is comes from a variety of studies of adolescent parents that implicate many of these same factors (See Table 8.1 for a summary). In what follows, we considered each of three general domains of influence, characteristics of the parent, child, and social context in somewhat more detail.

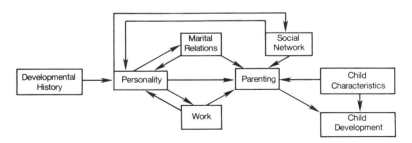

FIG. 8.1.   A process model of the determinants of parenting.

TABLE 8.1
The Adolescent Mother and the Maltreating Parent: Shared Psychological,
Contextual, and Offspring Characteristics

A. DEVELOPMENTAL HISTORY AND PERSONALITY VARIABLES

1. Deprivation, indifference, rejection, and hostility in family-of-origin (Cheetham, 1977)
2. Unfulfilled dependency needs (Daniels, 1977)
3. Childhood atmosphere of competition within family-of-origin, or, of being perceived as "different" than other family members (Card & Wise, 1978)
4. Power struggles and modeling of aggressive behavior in family-of-origin (Klein, 1978)
5. Low self-esteem (Nadelson & Notman, 1977)
6. Fear of rejection (Abernathy, 1974)
7. Low frustration tolerance (Vincent, 1961)
8. Poor impulse control and rebelliousness (Daniels, 1969)
9. Role reversals in parenthood (Osofsky & Osofsky, 1978)

B. CONTEXTUAL VARIABLES

1. Overrepresentation of lower socioeconomic status groups (Lincoln et al., 1976; Reiss, 1976)
2. High enemployment (Moore, 1978; Nye, 1976)
3. Lowered educational aspirations and accomplishment (Moore & Waite, 1977; Nye, 1976)
4. Youthfulness at birth of first child (Lincoln et al., 1976)
5. Overrepresentation of single parent female-head-of-household families (Hertz, 1977)
6. Large numbers of children born in close succession (Trussell & Menken, 1978)
7. High rates of relationship disruption (Lorenzi et al., 1977; Card & Wise, 1978; Spanier & Glick, 1981)
8. Product of adolescent parent in family-of-origin (Baldwin & Cain, 1981)
9. Likelihood of welfare dependency (Hertz, 1977)
10. Ignorance of child-care techniques and practices (Furstenburg, 1976)
11. Isolation (Klerman, 1975)
12. Lack of knowledge of child development and unrealistic expectations (Vincent, 1961; DeLissovoy, 1973)
13. Role reversals as a parental practice (Osofsky & Osofsky, 1978)

C. CHILD VARIABLES

1. Complications of pregnancy (Ryan & Schneider, 1978)
2. Disproportionate rates of birth defects (Nye, 1976)
3. Disproportionate rates of neurological problems (Menken, 1972)
4. Disproportionate prematurity rate (Minde, 1980; McAnarney, 1978; Hunter, Kilstrom, Kraybill, & Loda, 1978)
5. Disproportionate low birthweight and small-for-gestational-age rates (Cooper, 1977; Mitchell, Gorle, & Greenberg, 1980)
6. Disproportionate handicapping conditions rate (Drotar, Baskiewicz, Irvin, Kennell, & Klaus, 1975)
7. Disporportionate mental retardation rate (Pasamanic & Lilienfield, 1956)
8. Cognitive functioning and school behavior problems (Hardy, Welcher, Stanley, & Dallas, 1978)
9. Poor nutrition and generalized poor health (Wallace, 1970; Plionis, 1975)

Developmental History and Personality of the Parent

Clinicians working with and studying maltreating families have repeatedly observed that parents who mistreat their offspring report a history of maltreatment in their own childhood (Kempe, Silverman, Steele, Droegemueller, & Silver, 1962; Spinetta & Rigler, 1972; Steele & Pollack, 1972). Researchers are considerably less sanguine in their acceptance of this "intergenerational transmission hypothesis" (Belsky, 1979; Jayaratne, 1977; Parke & Collmer, 1975). The fact that several prospective studies do document an association between the rearing of individuals and their subsequent parenting provides additional support, though, for claims that a parent's socialization history can be influential (Butterfield, Van Doornick, Dawson, & Alexander, 1979; O'Connor, Altemeier, Sherrod, Sandler, & Vietze, 1979). It is important to note that, although influence of childhood experiences may have been overstated in the adult maltreatment literature (Straus, Gelles, & Steinmetz, 1980), the link may be stronger when adolescent parents are concerned (Bolton, 1985). At least one recent study of adolescent parents who maltreated their child during its first 2 years of life found that getting pregnant to escape a violent family-of-origin discriminated those adolescent parents who maltreated from those who did not (Bolton, Charlton, Gai, Laner, & Shumway, 1985).

Both maltreating and adolescent parents often grow up in families characterized by emotional deprivation, rejection, and exposure to violent behavior (Cheetham, 1977; Klein, 1978; Straus et al., 1980). This experience suggests unresolved dependencies and a psychological immaturity often represented within both groups of parents (Blumberg, 1974; Daniels, 1969). The unmet psychological needs of childhood can lead to overdependence on a child (Daniels 1969), which may manifest itself in the role reversal frequently identified in both maltreating adult and adolescent mother–child dyads (Osofsky & Osofsky, 1978).

The Child's Contribution

The frequent observation that a single child within a family is often selected as the target of maltreatment raises the possibility that there is something particular about that child that contributes to his/her maltreatment (Brown & Daniels, 1968; Friedrich & Boriskin, 1976; Milowe & Lourie, 1964). Consequently, it has been suggested that maltreated children differ from their siblings and peers prior to their maltreatment (Birrell & Birrell, 1969; Gil, 1970; Johnson & Morse, 1968). These findings are confounded, again, by the overrepresentation of childhood problems (e.g., prematurity) in the lower socioeconomic status groups most frequently reported for maltreatment but must be considered important potential contributors nevertheless.

Prematurity, low birth weight, and small-for-gestational age births are all frequently reported within samples of maltreated children (Martin, Conway, Beezly, & Kempe, 1974). Fontana (1973), Elmer and Gregg (1967), and Klein and Stern (1971) all have reported high rates of low birth-weight children, ranging from 23 to 30%, in their studies of maltreatment. Because the normal incidence of low birth weight in the population at large is between 7 and 8%, it would seem that children with this problem are at some increased risk. Similarly, premature children, whether because of lethargy and lack of responsiveness, oversensitivity, or difficulty in parent–child interaction, seem to be dispropor-tionately at risk for child maltreatment (Beckwith & Cohen, 1976; Bolton, 1983; Brown & Bakeman, 1979; Field, 1977) and interaction problems with parents (DeVitto & Goldberg, 1983; Goldberg, 1978).

In many respects, we might think of the premature infant as having a more difficult temperament or behavioral disposition. And whereas the evidence con-cerning the effects of difficult temperament in the population of nonrisk children is mixed (Bates, 1980), select evidence supports the notion that difficult tem-perament can undermine parental functioning. Campbell (1979) reported, for example, that when mothers rated their infants as having difficult temperaments at 3 months, they interacted with them less and were less responsive to their cries at 3 and 8 months than were a set of matched controls. Similarly, Bates (1980) found that there was more conflict between mothers and 2-year-olds rated as difficult, with mothers displaying more power assertion, including frequent use of controlling actions, frequent repetition of prohibitions and warnings, and more frequent removal of objects from their children. Consistent with these data, Gamble and Belsky (1984) reported that mothers' reports of their 3- and 4-year-olds' temperaments accounted for almost 50% of the variance in independent evaluations of the growth-promoting nature of the home environment, with mothers of more difficult preschoolers providing less stimulating, affectionate, and responsive care.

The child of the adolescent parent may present all the previously mentioned problems—and more. Problems such as complications of pregnancy (Ryan & Schneider, 1978), handicapping conditions (Drotar, Baskiewicz, Irvin, Kennell, & Klaus, 1975), low birth weight (Mitchell, Gorle, & Greenberg, 1980), mental retardation (Passamanic & Lilienfield, 1956), neurological dysfunctions (Men-ke, 1972), and prematurity (Minde, 1980) may not be direct casual factors in child maltreatment (Caplan, Watters, White, Parry, & Bates, 1984), but they may affect the parent's confidence and/or make the concrete tasks of child care more difficult for the adolescent parent. These child-related pressures do not decrease for the adolescent parent as the child gets older, because school prob-lems, cognitive limitations, and behavior problems tend to persist (Baldwin & Cain, 1981; Hardy, Welcher, Stanley, & Dallas, 1978). Given the stresses of the adolescent parent's environment, it is not difficult to understand how an ex-plosive or frustrating child could help produce an explosive parent.

Contextual Sources of Stress and Support

Lower socioeconomic status is probably the most frequently reported charac-teristic of abusive and neglectful families (Elmer 1967; Gil, 1970; Polansky, Holly, & Polansky, 1975). In addition to being poor, abuse appears in families suffering from unemployment and labor market shrinkage (Gil, 1971; Steinberg, Catalano, & Dooley, 1981). When this level of stress and potential for crisis is added to the marital discord (Elmer, 1967; Green, 1976; Young, 1964) and isolation attributed to maltreating families, the stage is set for problems (Bennie & Sclar, 1969; Giovannoni & Billingsley, 1970; Light, 1973; Zalba, 1966).

In general, women who bear children during adolescence and males who father these children tend to complete fewer years of schooling than peers who delay childbearing (Card & Wise, 1978; Elster & Panzarine, 1980; Furstenberg & Talvitie, 1980). Related to this, both men and women who become parents as adolescents have poorer employment status (Moore, 1978; Nye & Berardo, 1973). In addition to being poor and under or unemployed, it is the rare adolescent parent who escapes the pressures of single parenthood (Caplan et al., 1984). And, even when a partner is present, the same relationship stresses that characterize the maltreating adult parent (Helfer, 1975) produce high rates of dissolution in the relationship between adolescent parents (Spanier & Glick, 1981).

Like maltreating adult parents, adolescent parents have difficulty resolving conflict and crisis (Straus et al., 1980). Early studies based on small clinical samples of parents also suggested that both adult parents who maltreat their children and adolescent parents in general may have unrealistic expectations of the child, be ignorant of child care/development, and have a low tolerance for the types of frustration often imposed by parenthood (DeLissovoy, 1973; Steele, 1975).

For the adolescent male or female who has entered parenthood, dealing with the stressful context may be too much. The socially isolated (Klerman, 1975) and welfare-dependent (Hertz, 1977) adolescent female who has only had her own adolescent mother as a model from which to develop positive marital and/or parent–child relationships (Baldwin & Cain, 1981), is clearly at risk. More recently, however, research on the adolescent father reveals that he, too, may play a role in the increase or reduction in the risk of child maltreatment (Bolton, 1984).

The Etiological Model and the Adolescent Father

Although less is known regarding adolescent fathers, their apparent "fit" with the risk factors described by the model guiding our analysis is as disquietingly matched as is that of their female partners (See Table 8.2).

Psychological and contextual stressors confront the adolescent father from all sides (Elster & Lamb, 1982). Educational termination is premature and employment opportunities are consequently limited (Lorenzi, Klerman, & Jekal, 1977). Whether married or not, relationship instability is the rule and abandonment remains a common outcome (Babikian & Goldman, 1971). Obviously, the poverty that follows from educational and occupational curtailment predicts greater environmental deprivation. What is often overlooked, however, is the frustration that may be directed at the child for "doing this to me."

In addition to "real world" economic pressures the adolescent father may find isolation more real than his parental partner. Should the adolescent mother

TABLE 8.2
Child Maltreatment Risk: Critical Variables in the Adolescent Father

A. DEVELOPMENTAL HISTORY / PSYCHOLOGICAL VARIABLES

1. Role confusion (Elster & Lamb, 1982)
2. Immaturity (Elster, McAnarny, & Lamb, 1983; Montemayor, 1983)
3. Fear of emotional rejection (Fry & Trifiletti, 1983)
4. Inadequate family life in family-of-origin (Price, 1981)
5. Generalized perception of being out-of-control and overwhelmed (Robinson & Barret, 1983)

B. CONTEXTUAL VARIABLES

1. Generalized lack of support of overt rejection from social network (Elster & Lamb, 1982)
2. Isolation from adolescent parental partner and their child (Furstenburg, 1981, Hendricks, 1984)
3. Premature termination of educational aspirations (Kerckhoff & Parrow, 1979)
4. Employment difficulty (Lorenzi et al., 1977)
5. Financial stress (Brown, 1984)
6. Marital relationship instability and abandonment (Babikian & Goldman, 1971)
7. Lack of adequate knowledge in childcare, child development, parenthood skills, and relationship responsibilities (Elster et al., 1983; Elster & Panzarine, 1980; Russell, 1980)

return to her family-of-origin with the child, it is not at all unusual for the adolescent father to be kept at a distance from her and his child (Furstenberg, 1981). This distancing may also be the response of the adolescent father's own family and peers (Elster & Lamb, 1982). Added to the other-initiated isolation is the reality that service agencies—presumed sources of help—often fail to include the adolescent father in their programming. This psychologically immature young man will often interpret these isolating factors as overt and personal rejections (Elster & Lamb, 1982, in press)—correctly so!

The adolescent father is often underprepared for the role(s) he will soon be asked to play. Developmental immaturity impairs this preparation (Montemayor, 1983). His expectations of the relationships with a partner and child are distorted (Price, 1981). He may present himself as one "in control," whereas he experiences the reverse on an emotional level (Elster, McAnarney, & Lamb, 1983; Robinson & Barret, 1983). The psychological strategies necessary to deal with this life change are often beyond this young man's grasp (Vaz, Smolen, & Miller, 1983).

In sum, psychological immaturity and environmental restrictions imposed by both formal and informal networks increases stress and thereby frustrates the adolescent father. Truly wanting to help, he is likely to terminate educational plans in order to contribute more directly to mother and child (Kerckhoff & Parrow, 1979). This sacrifice is met with extreme difficulty in locating substantive employment (Lorenzi et al., 1977), and financial distress is the outcome (Brown, 1984). Paternal responsibilities are pointed up to him but he is allowed few opportunities to respond. Frequently, positive expectations of the impending relationship with mother and/or child are crushed, and abandonment of both may be the result (Babikian & Goldman, 1971). This is more the result of a restrictive social context than the lack of necessary parenthood knowledge to which the abandonment is more commonly attributed (Elster & Panzarine, 1980). Thus, the stresses of adolescent parenthood for the father, and the path to maltreatment, may be either direct or indirect.

What little preparation this father has for his new role, what little confidence he can muster in himself, and whatever desire he has to play a role in his child's life are seldom reinforced by others. Consequently the child suffers the deprivational effects of father absence. This deprives the child of both a potential protective buffer and the opportunity for a meaningful attachment relationship.

More directly the experience of having his role diluted or destroyed entirely by the stresses of the situation and the others involved generates great frustration. In essence, the adolescent father feels himself disappearing from the situation entirely. This sudden thrust into parenthood has changed all his relationships, caused him to lose a previous identity, and denied his presence. The frustration and anger that grows out of this state has no point of release nor target. Unfortunately, one of the primary targets may be the only individual he feels capable of dominating at this moment in his life—the child. Whether that dominance takes the form of rejection or overt acting out against the child, the consequences can be severe and enduring.

Summary

In sum, several key elements are worthy of restatement. First, the high rates of child maltreatment anticipated for adolescent parent–child dyads have not materialized in empirical study. Yet, adolescent parents share the preponderance of characteristics known to be present disproportionately often in adults parents who maltreat their children. Second, virtually all the research in all aspects of adolescent parenthood has focused on the mother–child relationship. Finally, what little is known about the adolescent father has not been applied to the maltreating event, although it is known that he, too, shares the characteristics of abusive adult parents. Obviously, the risk for maltreatment is related, as it is in the adult parent, not to the mere presence of these risk factors but to the degree to which they are present at any given point in the relationship. Results of a preliminary study of maltreating and nonmaltreating adolescent parents appears to support this supposition.

THE ABUSIVE ADOLESCENT PARENT

A population of 960 adolescent mothers who delivered their child during a 16-month period in 1980–81 has been followed by Bolton and his colleagues in Arizona. Of these adolescent mothers, 190 were assessed as "high risk" within

24 hours of delivery based upon the match between their own personal psychological/social context/child characteristics and those of the etiological model presented earlier. Recently, a follow-up study of these mothers, the fathers in the situation, the males involved with the mothers at this point (if different), and the health/behavioral characteristics of the children by age 2 years was conducted. The goal of this study was to identify the characteristics that discriminated between those adolescent parents and children who were involved in substantiated child maltreatment reports in the first 2 years of the child's life and those who were not (Bolton et al., 1985).

Only 9.5% of the adolescent mothers initially assessed as at "high risk" had been reported for substantiated child maltreatment during the 27 months since the birth of the child. In all known (from official records) cases, the mother was the perpetrator. These represented only about 10% of the group thought to be at extreme risk, and approximately 2% of all the adolescent mothers assessed for risk-generating variables—a rate that is about what would have been expected in the community from which the mothers were drawn (1.5%). However, it is important to note that more time needs to elapse before an accurate picture can be obtained. In other samples of adolescent mothers in Arizona, the mean age of the child victims seems to be about 5 years of age. Importantly, however, there were differences within the "high-risk" group between adolescent mothers who maltreated and those who did not.

The adolescent mothers who engaged in child maltreatment had greater experience with violence in their past than the nonmaltreating mothers and had experienced family victimization of some type. Slightly more than 1-in-10 of the nonabusive mothers had also experienced some form of violence (11%); a rate still higher than that found in other studies of the population areas from which these adolescents were drawn (7.5%). This would confirm the presence of negative childhood experiences in the life of high-risk adolescent mothers.

Consideration of other contextual factors reveals that the maltreating adolescent mothers had more frequent experience with physical illness than their nonabusive counterparts. In fact, 31% of the abusive mothers presented with a significant disease (e.g., diabetes, pyelonephritis, hypertention) at delivery, as compared to about 18% of the nonmaltreating mothers. Fatigue and illness, if continued through early child care, may increase risk for these mothers. In related fashion, few of the maltreating adolescent mothers reported pregnancy as an enjoyable experience, whereas most of the nonmaltreating adolescent mothers were able to identify positive points. The maltreating mothers required a greater number of special procedures at delivery (e.g., ultra sonography, ABD/pelvic, X-ray, Creatinine clearance, and Non-Stress testing). Eighty-six percent of the maltreating mothers required some special procedure as compared to 32.1% of the nonmaltreating mothers, although the reader is cautioned that the numbers are small. In somewhat contrary fashion, it was the nonmaltreating adolescent mothers who demonstrated more labor and delivery complications (cord problems, sphincter ext., rectal wall tearing, sulsuc tears, and cervical laceration). Two-thirds (64.2%) of the nonmaltreating mothers had such problems as compared to about one-quarter (27.5%) of the adolescent mothers who later maltreated their children.

Child rearing was of lower quality in the first year of the children's lives for mothers who later maltreated. Both in the hospital during the early postpartum period, and at biweekly visits for up to a year, the maltreating mothers had less eye contact, did less touching, were less accepting of their children's need for reciprocal interaction, and failed to demonstrate a positive understanding of the children's needs. Feeding difficulties did not seem to discriminate between problem mothers and successful mothers, however.

The mothers who became abusive were about four times more likely to be the sole child-care provider than mothers not yet abusive by the child's second birthday. This in-home isolation was confounded, however, by the fact that the maltreating adolescent mothers were twice (44.4%) as likely to be married than were the nonmaltreating counterparts (21.5%). The marriages seemed to encourage the already tenuous families-of-origin to pass responsibility of the adolescent mother and child on to the adolescent father. Apparently, this was not a responsibility that was readily accepted, because 20% of these married fathers did not live with the mother and child and only 50% contributed to the financial support of mother and child. Interestingly, two-thirds of the fathers had frequent contact with their children regardless of the level of the contact with the mother. Additionally, neither financial support nor contact with the child appeared to influence the adolescent mother's self-reported perception of the stability of their relationship—a factor that may speak to the power of denial in adolescence.

The maltreating adolescent mothers were also more likely to be Anglo than from an ethnic group, possibly indicating that they left the hospital to enter an environment that was less well prepared for premature parenthood than sometimes demonstrated in the minority cultures of the Southwest. This point illustrates a caution to the reader. The fact that 61.1% of the maltreating mothers were Anglo (compared to an expected 45%) illustrates that these mothers are a special group and generalization is ill advised. This sample is drawn from the lowest income area of a large Southwestern urban area of about 1.5 million. Some southwestern ethnic groups (e.g., Hispanic and Native Americans) are overrepresented while others more familiar to large urban areas (e.g., Blacks) are underrepresented. This is a study, then, that requires replication in other geographic areas.

The characteristics of the fathers in the high-risk group were also studied. Generally, within the "high-risk" group, fathers were young men (65% under 24) older than the mothers (85% of which were still under 21 as of the child's second birthday) and not usually adolescents (only 40% were adolescents at the child's birth). These young fathers were pressed by educational termination (mean achievement = 10th grade) and occupational obstacles (labor and blue-collar occupational status in 80% of the employed fathers). Although two-thirds of the fathers were employed at least part time, their mean income level was only about $700 monthly. The younger the fathers, the more likely they were to be minority group members in this "high-risk" group. Regardless of age or minority group membership, however, only 15% of the couples reported sharing any child-care responsibilities. In the "high-risk" group, 21.3% described alcohol abuse problems, 10.7% reported drug dependencies, 6.7% were reported by the mother to be violent, and nearly 1 in 10 (9.3%) had criminal records or had "done time." All these role factors were slightly more prominent among fathers paired with mothers who eventually maltreated the children (Bolton, MacEachron, Laner, & Gai, in press).

One buffer in the family situation seemed to be provided by the young fathers' families. No officially reported maltreatment has yet occurred among an adolescent parent pair living with the fathers' parents or receiving financial support from the fathers' parents. In the absence of this external support system, however, the presence of a male, at least in the "high-risk" group, appeared to increase risk. His presence could rarely be seen as beneficial.

Almost 40% (37.9%) of the infants who were later maltreated were born with a problem condition of some type (e.g., herpes, jaundice, sepsis). None of the nonmaltreated infants had comparable problems. Six in 10 (62%) of the later-maltreated infants (compared to 10.7% of nonmaltreated) required some therapeutic intervention (e.g., phototherapy, IV infusion, antibiotics, oxygen, transfusion). Only 44.8% of the maltreated infants were vaginal deliveries as compared to 92.8% of the nonmaltreated infants. And, 20.6% were low birth weight, as compared to 3.5% of their nonmaltreated peers.

Immediately following birth, almost 90% (89.3%) of the nonmaltreated infants were reported as "satisfactory." Only 65.5% of those later maltreated were given a similar clearance, and, almost 14% (13.8%) were still in the NICU. Overall, about 6 in 10 (58.6%) of the maltreated infants received a positive report upon leaving the hospital as compared to 96.4% of the nonmaltreated infants. It seems clear from these data that the infant at medical risk may also be the infant at increased risk for maltreatment at the hands of an adolescent parent during its first 2 years of life.

These data appear to confirm the hypothesis that adolescent mothers, fathers, and children all contribute to the risk for child maltreatment. As predicted by the etiological model, these risk factors seem to originate in their environment, in their personality, and in the physical characteristics (particularly with respect to the child) that accompany their entry to the family relationship. The adolescent parents who maltreated were also similar to abusive adult parents, in that they faced many problems of great intensity. Although all problems described by the etiological model may occur in families, (especially lower socioeconomic status families), their number, their intensity, and the parents' ability to cope with them seems to distinguish between potential maltreatment and the reality.

Conclusion

Ultimately, the risk within the adolescent parent–child relationship seems to have been overstated, at least as it pertains to adolescent mothers. Adolescent mothers and their children are, indeed, confronted by the same contextual/ personal and child-centered problems that are known to increase risk for maltreatment. However, as in the study of adult parents, the risk may not be translated in actual abuse. Importantly, the movement from risk to reality does not appear more likely among adolescent parents than among their adult counterpart. Less certain is the contribution of fathers.

From what little is known about adolescent fathers, it appears that the pressures they face may be greater than those faced by adolescent females. The fathers may be more personally violent, have difficulty with drug/alcohol abuse, and or have greater difficulty in controlling their temper. In an indirect fashion, they may have had their plans more severely curtailed by the births, may feel themselves to be more isolated from their children and support systems, and may be shackled by an overwhelming helplessness in seeking to contribute to their childrens' lives. Isolated from the children, these fathers not only fail to come to know the children, they fail to acquire the protective responses known to other parents. Most critically, indications are that they will participate in parenting if given the opportunity.

The adolescent parent–child relationship "seems" wrong. It violates social norms. When something appears to be broken, outsiders (e.g., service providers) attempt to fix it, but the attempt to fix something that is not broken may be a major obstacle in our work with adolescent parents. The information on adolescent parents is more positive than anticipated. Child maltreatment does not occur at record rates, buffers are available in the form of supportive families, and adolescent fathers do seem willing to play a part. From the past decade's experience, the wise decision may be to focus on those adolescent partnerships that are working.

REFERENCES

Abernathy, V. (1974). Illegitimate conception among teenagers. *American Journal of Public Health, 64*, 662–665.

Babikian, H. M., & Goldman, A. A. (1971). Study of teenage pregnancy. *American Journal of Psychiatry, 128*, 760–765.

Baldwin, W., & Cain, V. S. (1981). The children of teenage parents. In F. F. Furstenberg Jr., R. Lincoln, & J. Menken (Eds.), *Teenage sexuality, pregnancy, and childbearing*. Philadelphia: University of Pennsylvania Press.

Bates, J. (1980). The concept of difficult temperament. *Merrill–Palmer Quarterly, 26*, 299–319.

Beckwith, L., Cohen, S. E., Kopp, C. B., Parmelee, A. H., & Marcy, T. G. (1976). Caregiver–infant interaction and early cognitive development in preterm infants. *Child Development, 47*, 579–587.

Belsky, J. (1984). Determinant of parenting: A process model. *Child Development, 55,* 83–96.

Belsky, J. (1978). Three theoretical models of child abuse: A critical review. *International Journal of Child Abuse and Neglect, 2,* 37–49.

Belsky, J. (1979). The interrelation of parental and spousal behavior during infancy in traditional nuclear families: An exploratory analysis. *Journal of Marriage and The Family, 41,* 62–68.

Belsky, J. (1980). Child maltreatment: An ecological integration. *American Psychologist, 35,* 320–335.

Bennie, E., & Sclar, A. (1969). The battered child syndrome. *American Journal of Psychiatry, 125,* 975–979.

Birrell, R., & Birrell, J. (1969). The maltreatment syndrome in children: A. hospital survey. *Medical Journal of Australia, 2,* 1023–1029.

Blumberg, M. L. (1979). Psychopathology of the abusing parent. *American Journal of Psychotherapy, 28,* 21–29.

Bolton, F. G., Jr. (1980). *When bonding fails: Clinical assessment of the high risk family.* Beverly Hills, CA: SAGE.

Bolton, F. G., Jr. (1983). *The pregnant adolescent: Problems of premature parenthood.* Beverly Hills, CA: SAGE.

Bolton, F. G., Jr. (1984, May). *The father in the adolescent pregnancy at risk for child maltreatment: Helpmate or hinderance?* Paper presented to the Society for Research in Child Development Study Group on Adolescent Fathers, Heber, Utah.

Bolton, F. G., Jr. (1985). *The pregnant adolescent: Bi-lateral victimization.* Denver: American Humane Association.

Bolton, F. G., Charlton, J. K., Gai, D. S., Laner, R. H., & Shumway, S. M. (1985). Preventive screening of adolescent mothers and infants: Critical variables in assessing risk for maltreatment. *Journal of Primary Prevention, 5,* 17–25.

Bolton, F. G., Jr., Laner, R. H., & Kane, S. P. (1980). Child maltreatment risk among adolescent mothers: A study of reported cases. *American Journal of Orthopsychiatry, 50.*

Bolton, F. G., Jr., MacEachron, A., Laner, R. H., & Gai, D. S. (in press). The adolescent family and child maltreatment: Perspectives on father, mother, and child. *Journal.*

Bolton, F. G., & Laner, R. H. (1981). Maternal maturity and maltreatment. *Journal of Family Issues, 2*(4), 485–508.

Brown, F. E. (1980). Juvenile prostitution: A nursing perspective. *Journal of Psychiatric Nursing and Mental Health Services, 18,* 32–24.

Brown, J. V., & Bakeman, R. (1979). Behavioral dialogue between mothers and infants: The effect of prematurity. In *Selected readings in mother–infant bonding* (DHE# Pub. No (ohd#) 79-30225), Washington, DC.

Brown, J., & Daniels, R. (1968). Some observations on abusive parents. *Child Welfare, 47,* 89–96.

Brown, S. V. (1984). The commitment and concerns of black adolescent parents. *Social Work Research and Abstracts, 19,* 27–34.

Butterfield, P., Van Doornick, W., Dawson, P., & Alexander, H. (1979, March). *Early identification of dysparenting.* Paper presented at the meeting of the Society for Research in Child Development, San Francisco.

Campbell, S. (1979). Mother–infant interaction as a function of maternal ratings of temperament. *Child Psychiatry and Human Development, 10,* 67–76.

Caplan, P. J., Waters, J., White, G., Parry, R., & Bates, R. (1984). Toronto Multi-agency Child Abuse Research Project: The abuser and the abused. *The International Journal of Child Abuse and Neglect, 8,* 343–352.

Card, J. J., & Wise, L. L. (1978). Teenage mothers and fathers: The impact of early childbearing on the parent's personal and professional lives. *Family Planning Perspectives, 10,* 199–205.

Cheetham, J. (1977). *Unwanted pregnancy and counseling.* London: Routledge & Kegan Paul.

Cooper, T. (1977). Present HEW policies in primary preventing. *Preventative Medicine, 6,* 198–201.

Daniels, A. M. (1969). Reaching unwed mothers. *American Journal of Nursing, 69,* 332–335.

DeLissovoy, V. (1973). Child care by adolescent parents. *Children Today, 2,* 22–25.

DeVitto, B., & Goldberg, S. (1983). The development of early parent–infant interaction as a function of newborn medical status. In T. Field, S. Sostek, S. Goldberg, & H. H. Shuman (Eds.), *Infants born at risk.* Holliswood, NY: Spectrum.

Drotar, D., Baskiewicz, A., Irvin, N., Kennell, J., & Klaus, M. (1975). The adaption of parents to the birth of an infant with a congenital malformation: A hypothetical model. *Pediatrics, 56,* 710–717.

Elmer, E. (1967). *Children in Jeopardy: A study of abused minors and their families.* Pittsburg: University of Pittsburg Press.

Elmer, E., & Gregg, G. S. (1967). Developmental characteristics of abused children. *Pediatrics, 40,* 596–602.

Elster, A. E., & Lamb, M. E. (1982). Adolescent fathers: A group potentially at risk for parenting failure. *Infant Mental Health Journal, 3,* 148–155.

Elster, A. B., McAnarney, E. R., & Lamb, M. E. (1983). Parental behavior of adolescent mothers. *Pediatrics, 63,* 494–503.

Elster, A. B., & Panzarine, S. (1980). Unwed teenage fathers: Emotional and health educational needs. *Journal of Adolescent Health Care, 1,* 116–120.

Field, T. (1977). Maternal stimulation during infant feeding. *Developmental Psychology, 13,* 539–540.

Fontana, V. (1973). *Somewhere a child is crying: Maltreatment—causes and prevention.* New York: Macmillan.

Friedrich, W., & Boriskin, J. (1976). The role of the child in abuse: A review of the literature. *American Journal of Orthopsychiatry, 76,* 580–590.

Fry, P. S., & Trifiletti, R. J. (1983). Teenage fathers: An exploration of their developmental needs and anxieties and the implications for clinical-social intervention and services. *Journal of Psychiatric Treatment and Evaluation, 5,* 219–227.

Furstenberg, F. F. (1976). *Unplanned parenthood: The social consequences of teenage childbearing.* New York: Macmillan.

Furstenberg, F. F. (1981). Implicating the family: Teenage parenthood and kinship involvement. In T. Ooms (Ed.), *Teenage pregnancy in a family context: Implications for policy.* Philadelphia: Temple University Press.

Furstenberg, F. F., & Talvitie, K. G. (1980). Children's names and parental claims. *Journal of Family Issues, 1.*

Gamble, W., & Belsky, J. (1984). *Stressors, supports, and maternal well-being as determinant of mothering.* Unpublished manuscript, The Pennsylvania State University.

Gil, D. G. (1970). *Violence against children.* Cambridge, MA: Harvard University Press.

Giovanni, J., & Billingsley, A. (1970). Child neglect among the poor: A study of parental adequacy in families of three ethnic groups. *Child Welfare, 49,* 196–204.

Goldberg, S. (1978). Prematurity: Effects on parent–infant interaction. *Journal of Pediatric Psychology, 3,* 137–144.

Green, A. (1976). A psychodynamic approach to the study and treatment of child abusing parents. *Journal of Child Psychiatry, 15,* 414–421.

Hardy, J. B., Welcher, D. W., Stanley, J., & Dallas, J. R. (1978). Long range outcome of adolescent pregnancy. *Clinical Obstetrics and Gynecology, 88,* 1215–1232.

Helfer, R. E. (1975). *The Diagnostic Process and Treatment Programs.* DHE Publication No (OH#) 75–69. Washington, DC: Superintendent of Documents, U.S. Government Printing Office.

Hendricks, L. E. (1983). Suggestions for reaching unmarried black adolescent fathers. *Child Welfare, 6,* 141–146.

Hertz, D. G. (1977). Psychological implications of adolescent pregnancy: Patterns of family interaction in adolescent mothers-to-be. *Psychodynamic, 18*, 73–79.

Hunter, R. S., Kilstrom, N., Kraybill, E. N., & Loda, F. (1978). Antecedents of child abuse and neglect in premature infants: A prospective study in a newborn intensive care unit. *Pediatrics, 61*, 629–635.

Jayaratne, S. (1977). Child abuser as parents and children: A review. *Social Work, 22*, 5–9.

Johnson, B., & Morse, H. (1968). Injured children and their parents. *Children, 15*, 147–153.

Kempe, C. H., Silverman, F. N., Steele, B. F., Droegemueller, W., & Silver, H. K. (1962). The battered child syndrome. *Journal of the American Medical Association, 181*, 17–24.

Kinard, E. M., & Klerman, L. V. (1980). Teenage parenting and child abuse: Are they related? *American Journal of Orthopsychiatry, 50*, 481–488.

Kerchoff, A. C., & Parrow, A. A. (1979). The effect of early marriage on the educational attainment of young men. *Journal of Marriage and the Family, 41*, 97–107.

Klein, L. (1978). Antecedents to teenage pregnancy. *Clinical Obstetrics and Gynecology, 32*, 1151–1159.

Klein, M., & Stern, L. (1971). Low birth weight and the battered child syndrome. *American Journal of Diseases of Childhood, 122*, 15–18.

Klerman, L. V. (1975). Adolescent pregnancy: The need for new policies and new programs. *Journal of School Health, 45*, 263–267.

Light, R. L. (1973). Abused and neglected children in America: A study of alternative policies. *Harvard Educational Review, 43*, 556–598.

Lincoln, R., Jaffe, F. S., & Ambrose, A. (1976). *11 Million teenagers.* New York: Guttmacher Institute.

Lorenzi, M. E., Klerman, L. V., & Jekal, J. F. (1977). School age parents: How permanent a relationship? *Adolescence, 12*, 13–22.

Martin, H., Beezely, P., Conway, E., Kempe, C. H. (1974). The development of abused children, Part I: A review of the literature: Part II: Physical neurologic and intellectual outcome. *Advances in Pediatrics, 21*, 25–73.

McAnarney, E. R. (1984). *The adolescent family: Report of the fifteenth ross roundtable on critical approaches to common pediatric problems.* Columbus, OH: Ross Laboratories.

Menke, T. C. (1972). Teenage childbearing: Its medical aspects and implications for the U.S. population. In C. Westcal & R. Parks (Eds.), *Demographic and social aspects of population growth.* Washington, DC: U.S. Government Printing Office.

Miller, S. M. (1983). *The influence of adolescent childbearing on the incidence, type, and severity of child maltreatment* (mimeo). New York: Child Welfare League of America.

Milowe, D., & Lourie, R. S. (1964). The child's role in the battered child syndrome. *Journal of Pediatrics, 65*, 1079–1081.

Minde, K. L. (1980). Bonding of parents to premature infants: Theory and practice. In P. M. Taylor (Ed.), *Parent–infant relationships.* New York: Grunn & Stratton.

Mitchell, W. G., Gorlee, R. W., & Greenberg, R. A. (1980). Failure to thrive: A study in a primary care setting, epidemiology, and follow-up. *Pediatrics, 65*, 971–977.

Montmayor, A. Q. (1983). Parents and adolescents in conflict: All families some of the time; some families all of the time. *Journal of Early Adolescence, 3*(1–2), 83–102.

Moore, K. A. (1978). Teenage childbirth and welfare dependency. *Family Planning Perspectives, 10*, 233–235.

Moore, K. A., & Wait, L. J. (1977). Early childbearing and educational attainment. *Family Planning Perspectives, 9*, 20–40.

Nadelson, C., & Notman, M. T. (1977). Treatment of the pregnant teenager and the putative father. *Current Psychiatric Therapy, 19*, 81–87.

Nye, F. I., & Berardo, F. M. (1973). *The family: Its structure and interaction.* New York: Macmillan.

Nye, F. I., & Berardo, F. M. (1976). *School age parenthood.* Extention bulletin 667. Pullman: Cooperative Extention Service, Washington State University.

O'Connor, S., Altemeier, W., Sherrod, K., Sandler, H., & Vietze, P. (1979). *Prospective study of non-organic failure to thrive.* Paper presented at the meeting of the Society for Research in Child Development, San Francisco.

Osofsky, J. D., & Osofsky, H. J. (1978). Teenage pregnancy: Psychosocial considerations. *Clinical Obstetrics and Gynecology, 21,* 1161–1172.

Parke, R., & Collmer, C. (1975). Child abuse: An interdisciplinary review. In E. M. Hetherington (Ed.), *Review of child development research* (Vol. 5). Chicago: University of Chicago Press.

Pasamanic, B., & Lilienfield, A. (1956). The association of maternal and fetal factors with the development of mental deficiency: (II) Relationship to maternal age, birth order, previous reproductive loss and degree of mental deficiency. *American Journal of Mental Deficiency, 60,* 557–569.

Polansky, N., Holly, C., & Polansky, N. (1975). *Profile of neglect.* Washington, DC: U.S. Department of Health, Education, and Welfare.

Price, J. V. (1981). Problems of adolescent fathers. *American Journal of Orthopsychiatry, 41.*

Reiss, I. L. (1976). *Family systems in America.* Hinsdale, IL: Dryden Press.

Robinson, B. E., & Barret, R. L. (1983, April). Locus of control of unwed adolescent fathers versus adolescent non-fathers. *Perceptual and Motor Skills, 56.*

Ryan, G. M., & Schneider, J. M. (1978). Teenage obstetric complications. *Obstetrics and Gynecology, 21,* 1191–1197.

Spanier, G. B., & Glick, P. C. (1981). Marital instability in the United States: Some correlates and recent changes. *Family Relations, 31,* 329–338.

Spinetta, J. J., & Rigler, D. (1972). The child-abusing parent: A psychological review. *Psychological Bulletin, 4,* 296–304.

Steele, B. F. (1975). *Working with abusive parents from a psychiatric point of view.* Washington, DC: Government Printing Office (DHE Publications Number {OH} 75-70).

Steele, B. F., & Pollack, C. (1972). A psychiatric study of parents who abuse infants and small children. In R. E. Helfer & C. H. Kempe (Eds.), *The battered child* (2nd ed.) Chicago: University of Chicago Press.

Steinberg, L., Catalano, R., & Dooley, D. (1981). Economic antecedents of child abuse and neglect. *Child Development, 52,* 975–985.

Straus, M. A., Gelles, R. E., & Steinmetz, S. (1980). *Behind closed doors: Violence in the American family.* New York: Anchor/Doubleday.

Trussell, J., & Menken, J. (1978). Early childbearing and subsequent fertility. *Family Planning Perspectives, 10,* 209–218.

Vaz, R., Sole, P., & Miller, C. (1983). Adolescent pregnancy. *Journal of Adolescent Health Care, 4,* 246–250.

Vincent, C. (1961). *Unmarried mothers.* New York: Free Press of Glenco.

Wallace, H. (1970). Factors associated with perinatal mortality and morbidity. *Clinical Obstetrics and Gynecology, 13,* 13–43.

Young, L. R. (1954). *Out of wedlock.* New York: McGraw–Hill.

Zalba, S. (1966). The abused child: A typology for classification and treatment. *Social Work, 12.*

9 Clinical Issues in Adolescent Fatherhood

James S. Kahn
University of Utah

Frank G. Bolton, Jr.
Arizona Department of Economic Security

> When we dicided to get married we were both still in high school. We thought we couldn't be teenagers anymore and gave up most of our friends, besides we didn't think we had anything in common with them anymore. The only problem was, we didn't know how to be adults or parents either. Now that our son is 2 and I'm 18 my wife and I have separated as we both want the chance to be teenagers again.

Implicit in this quotation is evidence of the premature role transition and potential role conflicts that confront the adolescent male facing fatherhood. In this chapter we hope to sensitize the scientist–practitioner to these conflicts and their psychosocial implications. A rationale and model for addressing the needs of this clinical population is provided.

WHY SERVE ADOLESCENT FATHERS? A RATIONALE FOR SERVICE DELIVERY

Adolescent fatherhood is a topic of study that has been more than simply neglected. Adolescent fathers have been avoided both in research and clinical practice. This avoidance has impeded not only research but service delivery as well.

As this volume attests, increasing empirical and clinical attention is being directed towards the special needs of the partners (boyfriends, husbands) of adolescent mothers. Intervention programs directed towards adolescent fathers are now being encouraged (Barret & Robinson, 1982, Sander, 1982). Federally funded adolescent pregnancy programs sponsored by the Office of Adolescent

Pregnancy Programs are urged to address the psychological and vocational-educational needs of these young fathers. A joint effort by the Ford Foundation and Bank Street College has resulted in the formation of the Teen Father Collaboration (see chapter by Klinman et al.).

Because social service providers cannot address the needs of all adolescents nor all fathers, one must ask: Why serve adolescent fathers at all? Examination of this issue (Sander, 1982) has aided the development of our current rationale for the provision of mental health services to adolescent fathers. Among the reasons for actively involving these young fathers in social service programs are the following:

1. To promote active decision making among adolescent fathers regarding pregnancy, child care, and vocational-educational decisions.

2. To promote the involvement of young fathers, when appropriate, in the pregnancy and parenting process.

3. To increase the socioeconomic independence of adolescent families, many of whom now rely on federal assistance programs. Unfortunately, many of these young fathers are undereducated and have great difficulty financially supporting their young families (see chapter by Marsiglio).

4. To decrease the repeat pregnancy rate. Compliance with contraceptive use among adolescent females has been demonstrated to be related to their level of involvement with their partners (Gebbhart & Wolf, 1977).

5. To promote the psychological, social, and vocational-educational competence of these young men, their partners, and their children.

Previously, adolescent fathers have been made to shoulder total blame for the erratic and less-than-helpful response to the situation that typified their behavior. In early descriptive accounts, adolescent fathers were portrayed as lacking maturity, having a penchant for ignoring responsibilities in favor of self-gain, and tending to run from the situation (Pannor, Massarik, & Evans, 1971). They were said to be self-centered, irresponsible, and lacking stable life goals. It is little wonder that attitudes toward young fathers were judgmental and punitive (Barret & Robinson, 1982). The most frequent response to this stereotype by agencies serving adolescent mothers was to ignore adolescent fathers completely (Hendricks, Howard, & Caesar, 1981).

Recently, however, Elster and Panzarine (1979) have described young fathers as the "missing keys" to the reduction of psychosocial risk associated with adolescent pregnancy and suggest that adolescent mothers find increased emotional stability when the father is present during the pregnancy and early parenthood period. Contrary to the expectation that adolescent fathers avoid the pregnancy, clinical experience and empirical research suggest that they often wish to be involved, to contribute both financially and emotionally, and are seriously and realistically concerned about their obligations and responsibilities (Hendricks,

1984; Kahn & Elster, 1983). Adolescent fathers remain interested in their child's future and often describe themselves as ''in love'' with their adolescent partners (Hendricks, 1984). Realistically, we know that the involvement between adolescent mothers and adolescent fathers may lessen as time goes on (Lorenzi, Klerman, & Jekel, 1977). In the short term, however, the young father's involvement can be beneficial to himself, the teen mother, and their child (Ventura & Hendershot, 1984) and should be reinforced.

Psychological Considerations in Service Delivery

Clinicians should reflect on the various developmental roles of the adolescent as they bear upon what we are just coming to know, the adolescent father. Understanding the juxtaposition of these potentially conflicting roles can facilitate the conceptualization and implementation of informed intervention strategies.

Contradictory Roles: Adolescent and Father

Adolescence is characterized by both intra and interpersonal psychological conflicts. A certain extent of adolescent conflict is normative and may be beneficial in facilitating the adolescent's transition to adulthood (Montemayor, 1983). The sudden introduction of external change in the form of fathering a child can serve to alter critical features of this developmental period and may exacerbate the normal conflicts of adolescence.

Adolescent fathers are faced with struggles at nearly every point in their daily existence. They may be confronted with rejection from family and friends, may face barriers to contact with their partners and children, and may struggle with their desire to contribute in some meaningful way to the new family and life that they and their partners have begun. Because there are no clear roles for adolescent fathers, the full range of adolescent behavioral testing can be anticipated.

Adolescent fathers must reconcile the contradictory roles of both adolescence and fatherhood. As adolescents these young men seek to establish their own identities in personal and professional realms and resolve vocational-educational decisions and often conflictual peer and familial relationships. Cognitively, increases in their fund of knowledge and capacity for abstract reasoning allow them to begin thinking critically about their multiple roles as students, employees, friends, boyfriends, athletes, sons, and brothers. Cognitive reformulations of values, attitudes, and moral judgments would also be expected.

Adolescent fathers must reevaluate their identity as adolescents in light of their new roles as parents and perhaps as partners in heterosexual relationships. Premature role transitions occur as these young men seek to develop and/or learn new ''adult'' roles and behaviors as fathers, husbands, and sons-in-law. Adolescent fathers are also expected to negotiate health care systems, public assistance programs, low-income housing programs, and legal services. These roles demand continued self-sacrifice as health care, living situation, alternative education, and financial decisions are navigated.

Conflicts between adolescent roles and values and the demands of adolescent fatherhood are obvious. Clinical experience indicates that, whereas some young fathers may utilize parenthood to successfully resolve the conflicts of adolescence, others may not. Role conflicts become exacerbated as adolescent fathers are torn between commitments to themselves and to their partners and children. As adolescents, there is a desire to achieve a positive self-image and strong sense of personal control. Adolescent fathers, however may experience a lack of personal control as parents on both sides, and the adolescent mother herself, make pregnancy and parenting decisions independent of the adolescent father's thoughts and feelings. Adolescent fathers find themselves in the uncomfortable position of wanting to make a difference and not knowing how.

When involved, physical and psychological distress may occur as adolescent fathers seek to allocate their limited time, financial, and emotional resources to meet the demands of these conflicting roles. Attending school and working during the evenings while simultaneously attempting to nurture their partners and children may lead to increased feelings of futility and helplessness. As a result, adolescent fathers may come to resent their partners and their children.

The ability to invest in tomorrow is a parental mandate, and tomorrow does not have great meaning for the adolescent. Parental sacrifice is more comfortable for the individual who recognizes that he is not giving a part of himself away forever in making sacrifices for a spouse or child. Clinically, these role conflicts may be manifested by wide swings in behavior. Diminished self-efficacy, dysphoric and labile moods, depression and poor impulse control may become evident. Unrealistic appraisals of marriage and parenthood may compound the negative impact of the conflicting roles confronting these young fathers.

In summary, adolescent fathers are ill prepared for the intimacy and sexuality implied by their too rapid role transition. Misconceptions and limited knowledge are the hallmark of their approach to contraception, sexuality, and pregnancy (Elster & Panzarine, 1980). Parallel misconceptions mark their initial forays into career and educational realms. Adolescent fathers thrust prematurely into conflicting roles through the prospect and reality of fatherhood are thus predisposed to a number of psychological stressors.

PRACTICAL APPROACHES IN OUTREACH
TO ADOLESCENT FATHERS

Providing clinical services to adolescent fathers is clouded by the absence of a clear nosology. However, in our clinical experience adolescent fathers have two basic service needs. First, there is a need to introduce concrete, problem-specific interventions directed at reducing immediate psychological distress, aiding the decision-making process regarding relationship or pregnancy outcomes, and facilitating the acquisition of basic life needs (e.g., employment). Second, there is a need to assist adolescent fathers in developing the knowledge and skills necessary to cope with the multiple new roles that they must assume.

The provision of concrete help and psychoeducational assistance is likely to prove difficult. It must be reocgnized, for instance, that a recent study (Hendricks, 1984) indicated whereas only 7% of adolescent fathers would in general seek help from a service delivery agency, a majority would seek help from such an agency if it were offering something concrete (e.g., information regarding legal rights of adolescent fathers to their children). Clearly, tangible services are a key ingredient in helping adolescent fathers.

Initial contacts with adolescent fathers should focus on the establishment of trust and rapport while simultaneously providing practical and tangible help. Adolescent fathers are likely to be anxious, suspicious, and fatalistic or unrealistic about their future. They may be unlikely to believe anyone, especially someone ''who wants to help him.'' Fear of agency sponsorship, legal responsibilities, the clinical setting, and even the authority of the service provider are all real concerns to adolescent fathers that present barriers in developing a therapeutic relationship.

Clinical interventions with adolescent fathers are also difficult because of the complex nature of the problems that these youths are experiencing. The crisis of pregnancy and parenthood are intertwined with each adolescent father's own developmental issues and the denial of overt pathology. Recruitment, assessment, and intervention strategies should reflect a reocgnition of adolescent development, as well as this individual variability among basic psychological and demographic characteristics.

Assessment

Prior to addressing the clinical needs of adolescent fathers a comprehensive data base is required. Broad-band, standardized assessment protocols that acknowledge the adolescent father's service needs in light of their multiple roles are warranted. Demographic data, personal and family data, a medical history if appropriate, and, most importantly, psychological and vocational-educational data are essential. The Teen Mother and Child Program (TMCP) at the University of Utah Health Sciences Center employs the intake format presented in Appendix I. This is utilized in conjunction with a stress checklist (Appendix II). Interviews are best carried out over two sessions and should be conducted in part with the adolescent mother and other family members present and, in part, individually with the adolescent father. Clinicians are offered the opportunity to establish rapport with their often skeptical clients and provide psychological support while simultaneously providing basic information and help. It should be remembered, however, that the relationship between adolescent fathers and their partners may be too deeply strained to initially withstand these joint interviews. Adolescent fathers may feel more comfortable if seen individually by a male clinician, at least in the early visits (Hendricks, 1984).

Fathers outreach counselors should be proficient in evaluating adolescent fathers ongoing perceptions of, and reactions to, the multiple new roles that confront them. Disposition of the pregnancy should be addressed, as should the nature of the adolescent father's decision-making process itself. Research suggests that not all adolescent fathers perceive themselves as being involved in this decision-making process (Vaz, Smolen, & Miller, 1983). It may be useful to review these pregnancy-related decisions, noting positive and negative consequences, as well as intervention strategies adolescent fathers may use to express their thoughts and feelings to significant others.

Premarital and marital assessments should be provided to those adolescent fathers seeking to maintain ongoing relationships with their partners. Standardized assessment protocols and treatment models (Spanier, 1976; Stuart, 1980) will prove valuable in evaluating and facilitating informed decision making among adolescent fathers with regards to such decisions as whether or not to marry or separate, and about behaviors that might improve the clarity and quality of the adolescent couple's relationship. Similarly, clinicians should assess initial and ongoing parental reactions to the pregnancy and the couple's relationship.

Assessment of the young father's knowledge of fetal and child development is warranted, as is an evaluation of their knowledge regarding pregnancy and contraceptive use (Elster & Panzarine, 1980; Rivara, Sweeney, & Henderson, 1985). In the area of formal education and vocational training, adolescent fathers educational status and vocational aspirations should be assessed. Intellectual, academic, and career evaluations are appropriate.

It is important that practitioners remain sensitive to the extenuating circumstances of each adolescent pregnancy. These might include familial rejection, educational stagnation, or a previous history of psychological or physical disorders. Comprehensive psychological evaluations with adolescent fathers addressing such clinical pathologies as intellectual handicaps, learning disabilities, depression and other affective disorders, conduct and personality disorders, and substance and alcohol abuse may be warranted.

Interventions

Psychological, social, and educational interventions based upon the multiple new roles of adolescent fathers are essential. Assessment interviews and psychoeducational evaluations should aid the therapist and his young clients in the formulation of clinical goals.

Tangible assistance should include information about employment, vocational-educational training programs, low-income housing, financial subsidies, legal information regarding paternity and marriage, and health care services. In the TMCP we have found it useful to have a liaison relationship with community-based agencies providing these services, as well as having written programmatic materials from these agencies on hand.

Consultation and coordination between fathers outreach workers and local school psychologists, social workers, and admissions counselors at career guidance and job training facilities will prove valuable. The need to take action and provide tangible results is paramount in the alleviation of immediate crises, and in the enhancement of the therapeutic relationship between adolescent fathers and clinicians.

Adolescent fathers may benefit from interventions facilitating the identification and communication of their cognitions and affects surrounding the disposition of the pregnancy. Information and counseling regarding parenting, adoption, and abortion alternatives should be provided. Social skills training and the use of modeling and role-play techniques and cognitive rehearsal may aid adolescent fathers as they seek to communicate their thoughts and feelings to their partners, parents, peers, and perhaps school officials. Specific, accurate information will foster realistic appraisals and active decision making regarding pregnancy and parenting.

Joint sessions with adolescent fathers and their partners may be held when judged to be necessary and appropriate by all concerned. Relationship, marital, and divorce counseling may be warranted on both an individual and couple basis. Joint sessions with adolescent fathers and their partners do hold the potential for destruction, however, unless clinicians are scrupulously careful to uphold confidence gained in individual sessions. Error in this direction is quick promise of adolescent fathers leaving the service scene.

A similarly cautious approach in reaching out to the extended families of adolescent fathers is demanded. Not all adolescent fathers immediately inform their extended family of the pregnancy (Vaz, Smolen, & Miller, 1983). When informed, not all families respond positively. When their response is negative, its force may be directed toward the adolescent father. In other cases, the adolescent father's family rallies around him and seeks to provide "protection" through the seeking of legal recourse against paternity. Still others may discharge frustration and anger by deprecating the adolescent mother (Pannor, Massarik, & Evans, 1971). This collage of action and reaction on the part of extended families, an unpredictable pattern that varies across the course of the pregnancy and parenthood, demands flexibility from the clinician.

Service to extended families may demand joint visits with either or both of the adolescents, as a family unit, a parental marital pair, or as individuals. Topical issues may range from relationship status to living situation, work, school, and child care. The only true promise is the expression of a wide range of emotions that are certain to include frustration, anger, and occasional bewilderment. As difficult as it may be, clinicians are encouraged to highlight any and all positive outcomes in the situation (increased responsibility, increased maturation, and increasing goal directedness) to offset the possibility of familial surrender and collapse.

Clinical interventions in light of the novel role transition to adolescent fatherhood may target childbirth and parenting. Clinicians should facilitate the active involvement of the adolescent father, when appropriate, in the pregnancy and parenting process. Adolescent fathers should not be left in the waiting room when they accompany their partners to prenatal appointments or well-child visits. Adolescent fathers should be directly involved in teaching and diagnostic work conducted by obstetric, pediatric, and nutritional providers. Structured group activities including budgeting, parenting, relationship, and shopping assignments will prove beneficial. Agency and home-based parent education programs may be especially effective for high-risk parents. Fathers outreach workers should also act as advocates linking adolescent fathers to day care, crisis nursery, and public health care services.

Clinicians should be prepared to provide crisis interventions in response to affective and conduct disorders that stem from either adjustment reactions, relationship discord, or pre and postnatal complications. Adolescent fathers, as well as adolescent mothers, who experience divorce, unemployment, spontaneous abortions, miscarriage, still birth, or neonatal complications may be at risk for acute psychological stress as a result of their social isolation and relatively poorer problem-solving skills. While working individually with adolescent fathers, the feeling of importance given to these adolescents through working exclusively with them may be an aid. This relationship should include the father in some basic decision making (i.e., appointment times and places). This is not a relationship that begins with the discovery of the pregnancy and ends with the birth of the child. The variety of concerns and width of needs will expand as gestation progresses (Elster & Panzarine, 1983) and even more as the young father watches his child grow and develop.

In summary, provision of outreach services to adolescent fathers requires the implementation of valuable and creative intervention strategies. Clinicians may be called upon to provide individual, couple, family, and group counseling and educational services. Peer counseling, fathers support groups, and fathers workshops may prove effective outreach strategies. Audiovisual and written materials can often be obtained through state and local Departments of Health, University systems, and parenting resource centers. In addition, programs such as the Bank Street Teen Father Collaboration have reference and material lists available for the practitioner.

Administrative Concerns

As cost-effectiveness and accountability issues become relevant, clinicians should triage their services to adolescent fathers with positive, as well as high-risk (e.g., arrest records, multiple pregnancies) prognostic indicators. Characteristics of those fathers most amenable to outreach services include maintaining an ongoing relationship with the adolescent mother, enrollment in high school or vocational training, relative psychological health, adequate social support networks, and an urban, stable home environment (Sander, 1982).

Characteristics of clinical staff members working with adolescent fathers should be addressed. The patterns of most fathers outreach programs suggest that male clinicians are most effective. Adolescent fathers may be predisposed to respond positively to same-sex adult and peer counselors. It is important that professional and paraprofessional staff members be sensitive to the unique cultural differences in their population as well as being provided with inservice and educational materials relevant to this clinical population.

The range of programs serving, and with the potential to serve, adolescent fathers is diverse. These might include university or hospital-based adolescent pregnancy programs, school-based programs, community mental health centers, church programs, or other community service agencies such as the YMCA, Boys Club, Explorer Scouts, or Parent Education Resource Centers.

CONCLUSION

As service providers we must accept some responsibility for the sometimes disturbing actions of adolescent fathers. That responsibility grows out of the fact that adequate programming for adolescent fathers has not yet been developed and implemented. However, the provision of services to these young men must reflect a genuine commitment to them, their children, and partners, rather than an administrative desire to boost "case counts." The problems of adolescent fathers (e.g., adolescence, being in need of parenting and relationship skills, and premature educational termination) may create "turf" issues for the separate services directed toward these individual problems. In that counting heads means more dollars next year, a fiscal tug-of-war may result. In such instances adolescent fathers are "wanted" by service delivery programs for the wrong reasons and frequently provided with inadequate and disjointed services.

The provision of clinical services to adolescent fathers can and should be part of comprehensive adolescent pregnancy programs, as well as being provided through community and educational institutions. Although a rationale, parameters, and models of service delivery were presented, the actual implementation and provision of these services is likely to be difficult and frustrating. This is true due to the very nature of the client: an adolescent and father. Service providers will be required to go beyond the scope of their academic training to meet the demands of this clinical population. However, it is felt that such efforts can have positive benefits to adolescent fathers, their partners, children, and to society as a whole.

REFERENCES

Barret, R. L., & Robinson, B. E. (1982). Teenage fathers: Neglected too long. *Social Work, 27,* 484–488.

Elster, A. B., & Panzarine, S. (1979). Adolescent pregnancy—Where is the unwed teenage father? *Pediatrics, 63,* 824.

Elster, A. B., & Panzarine, S. (1980). Unwed teenage fathers: Emotional and health educational needs. *Journal of Adolescent Health Care, 1,* 116–120.

Elster, A. B., & Panzarine, S. (1983). Adolescent fathers: Stresses during gestation and early parenthood. *Clinical Pediatrics, 10,* 700–703.

Gebbhart, G. O., & Wolff, J. R. (1977). The unwed pregnant adolescent and her male partner. The *Journal of Reproductive Medicine, 19,* 137–140.

Hendricks, L. E. (1984). *Outreach with teenage fathers: A preliminary report on three ethnic groups.* Paper presented at Harvard Medical School postgraduate course on Stresses and Supports for Families in the 1980's, Boston, Massachusetts.

Hendricks, L. E., Howard, C. S., & Caesar, P. P. (1981). Help-seeking behavior among select populations of black unmarried adolescent fathers: Implications for human service agencies. *American Journal of Public Health, 71,* 733–735.

Kahn, J. S., & Elster, A. B. (1983). Adolescent fathers—Can they be reached? *Journal of Adolescent Health Care, 4,* 215.

Lorenzi, M. E., Klerman, L. V., & Jekel, J. F. (1977). School-age parents: How permanent a relationship. *Adolescence, 12,* 13–22.

Montemayor, R. (1983). Parents and adolescents in conflict: All families some of the time and some families most of the time. *Journal of Early Adolescence, 3,* 83–103.

Pannor, R., Massarik, F., & Evans, B. (1971). *The unmarried father.* New York: Springer.

Rivara, F. P., Sweeney, P. J., & Henderson, B. F. (1985). A study of low socioeconomic status, black teenage fathers and their non-father peers. *Pediatrics, 75,* 648–656.

Sander, J. (1982). *Teenage fathers: Issues in service delivery.* Paper prepared for the Ford Foundation Meeting, Minneapolis.

Spanier, G. B. (1976). Measuring dyadic adjustment: New scales for assessing the quality of marriage and similar dyads. *Journal of Marriage and the Family, 38,* 15–28.

Stuart, R. B. (1980). *Helping couples change.* New York: Guilford.

Vaz, R., Smolen, P., & Miller, C. (1983). Adolescent pregnancy: Involvement of the male partner. *Journal of Adolescent Health Care, 4,* 246–250.

Ventura, S. J., & Hendershot, G. E. (1984). Infant health consequences of childbearing by teenagers and older mothers. *Public Health Reports, 99,* 138–146.

APPENDIX I:

Teen Mother and Child Program Intake Form

1. Date: _____   2. Who was present: _____
3. Age: ____   4. Marital Status: ____
5. Current Living Arrangements: _____
6. Referred by: _____
7. How far along in pregnancy: _____
8. Planned Pregnancy: Y   N   Expected Pregnancy: Y   N
9. Main Concerns:
10. Current plans for pregnancy: parent _____   adoption _____   undecided _____
11. Personal reaction to pregnancy: _____
12. Reaction of FOB: _____
13. Reaction of her parents: _____
14. Reaction of his parents: _____
15. How has relationship with her parents changed since pregnancy? _____

16. How has his relationship with his parents changed since pregnancy? _____

17. Relationship with FOB: Length of time known: _____

18. Relationship . . .   At Conception: At Entry:
    Married   _____   _____
    Engaged/living together   _____   _____
    Dating Regularly   _____   _____
    No Relationship/divorced   _____   _____
    Separated   _____   _____
    Other   _____   _____

page 5
F A T H E R   O F   T H E   B A B Y *
Name_____   Age _____   Phone Number _____
1. Medical History
   a. Allergies: Y ____   N ____   Type _____
   b. Current use of . . . alcohol   Y ____   N ____   How much _____
                            cigarettes   Y ____   N ____   How much _____
                            social drugs   Y ____   N ____   How much _____
                            medications   Y ____   N ____   How much _____
   c. Medical illness . . .   self   family
                                         current (x)   past (x)   relationship
       heart disease
       cancer
       liver/kidney disease
       congenital defects
       high blood pressure
       diabetes
       psychiatric
       sexually transmitted diseases
       asthma
       multiple births

page 6

2. Unusual childhood experiences: Y ____   N ____   If yes, describe: _____
    _____

3. History of Physical Abuse: Y ____   N ____   If yes, by whom: _____
    _____

4. History of Sexual Abuse: Y ____   N ____   If yes, by whom: _____
    _____

5. School
    a. Presently enrolled in school: Y ____   N ____
                                          Where: _____
                                          What grade: ____
                                          If no, last grade completed: ____
    b. Average G.P.A.: ____
    c. Plans to graduate: Y ____   N ____
    d. Vocational plans: _____
    d. Difficulties in school: Y ____   N ____
        If Yes:
        Learning Problems? (ADD/LD)   Behavior Prob? (Truancy, Expelled)
6. Employment History
    a. Currently employed: Y ____   N ____   Where: _____
                                                   Position: _____
                                                   Hours/Week: _____
                                                   Salary: _____
    b. Past employment: (type of job; note any patterns of problems with employers): ____
        _____

page 7

7. Social History
    a. religious preference _____   Active ____   Inactive ____
    b. relationship with peers: _____
    c. source of support: _____
    d. age began dating: ____
        age of onset of sexual activity: ____
        (1) use of contraceptives: Y ____   N ____   Type _____
        (2) other pregnancies: Y ____   N ____   If yes, outcome of other pregnancies
             _____
    e. arrests or judicial involvement (describe) _____
        _____
    f. strengths: _____
8. Expectations & Concerns
    a. description of relationship with MOB: _____
    b. desire a change in that relationship: Y ____   N ____
                                describe: _____
        _____
    c. has life changed since becoming aware of the pregnancy: Y ____   N ____
        (describe): _____
    d. expectancies/anxieties about becoming a parent: _____
        _____

page 8
9. Marital History
    a.   Number of times married: _____
    b.   Length of other marriages (other than current marriage): _____
10. Family History
    a.   Marital status of parents: _____ How long? _____

	Age	Occupation	Education	Preg. Prior to age 18
Father (natural)				
Mother (natural)				
Stepfather				
Stepmother				
Siblings (denote M or F)				

*NOTE: Similar information is gathered on the adolescent mother.

APPENDIX II:

Teen Parent Checklist

As young parents you may have a variety of concerns. We would like to help you identify and remediate these areas of concern. We would also like to help you identify positive aspects of this pregnancy. Please fill out the remainder of this checklist.

1. Mother's name: _____   Father's name: _____

   Date: _____   Status: _____

2. Please rank the severity of each of the following concerns from 1 (least stressful) to 5 (most stressful). Then rank order your top 3 concerns.

FOB's Rank	MOB's Rank	Stressor	Description
_____	_____	Deciding what to do about the pregnancy. MOB: 1 — 2 — 3 — 4 — 5 FOB: 1 — 2 — 3 — 4 — 5	
_____	_____	Relationship problems with girlfriend/wife. MOB: 1 — 2 — 3 — 4 — 5 FOB: 1 — 2 — 3 — 4 — 5	
_____	_____	Relationship problems with parents. MOB: 1 — 2 — 3 — 4 — 5 FOB: 1 — 2 — 3 — 4 — 5	
_____	_____	Problems with friends. MOB: 1 — 2 — 3 — 4 — 5 FOB: 1 — 2 — 3 — 4 — 5	
_____	_____	Financial concerns. MOB: 1 — 2 — 3 — 4 — 5 FOB: 1 — 2 — 3 — 4 — 5	
_____	_____	Legal problems. MOB: 1 — 2 — 3 — 4 — 5 FOB: 1 — 2 — 3 — 4 — 5	
_____	_____	Concerns about work. MOB: 1 — 2 — 3 — 4 — 5 FOB: 1 — 2 — 3 — 4 — 5	
_____	_____	Concerns about the health of the mother and baby. MOB: 1 — 2 — 3 — 4 — 5 FOB: 1 — 2 — 3 — 4 — 5	
_____	_____	Other MOB: 1 — 2 — 3 — 4 — 5 FOB: 1 — 2 — 3 — 4 — 5	

3. At this point, please comment on any positive influences this pregnancy has had on your life.

10

The Teen Father Collaboration: A Demonstration and Research Model

Debra G. Klinman
Joelle H. Sander
Jacqueline L. Rosen
Karen R. Longo
Bank Street College of Education

INTRODUCTION

> When I was raised, I was raised with my father and mother. My father always cared for me, showed us how to do the right thing. That rubbed off on us. I want to be the father my father was for me. My feeling is, if you've made something, you can't return it. You can't recycle it. Be the man you were when you made it.

John is eighteen. His girlfriend is pregnant; soon, he will join the ranks of adolescent fatherhood. Although he wants to help provide for his child, he has just been laid off at work. Because of his age, he lacks the education or training to find another job quickly. Under the circumstances, he is finding it hard to "do the right thing."

John's predicament is not unusual. Given that some 600,000 babies are born to teenage mothers every year, many thousands of young men face the responsibilities of fatherhood long before they are adequately equipped to cope with them. Many flee the responsibility; but others care deeply about their families and want to take an active role in helping to support them, psychologically and financially.

Although social service providers have a long history of outreach and assistance to teenage mothers, the male partner in adolescent pregnancy—stereotyped as a victimizer and abandoner—has been largely ignored. However, in recent years, three converging forces have prompted a great deal of interest in these previously neglected young men: new research which documents the impact of fathers on the development of their children; increasingly frequent requests by young parents of both sexes for service programs that include fathers; and the recognition by service providers themselves that programs which isolate young mothers from the potential support of their partners have been far from effective in solving the major national problems of adolescent pregnancy and parenthood.

By itself, this new interest in teen fathers is not enough. In spite of years of service to and research about teenage mothers, surprisingly little is known about effective strategies for reaching and serving the teenage father. The Teen Father Collaboration, a two-year national demonstration and research effort, was designed to provide this much needed information.

The Teen Father Collaboration is unusual in that it brings together many kinds of people—program administrators, service workers, community planners, researchers, and funders at several levels—all working together to accomplish several important goals: to develop effective methods for reaching out to young fathers; to provide these young men with services that successfully increase their responsibility as fathers; to document with care all aspects of program development and impact; and to focus local and national attention on the importance of including teenage fathers in any future attempts to overcome the many problems associated with adolescent childbearing.

HISTORY OF THE COLLABORATION

The Teen Father Collaboration grew out of a Ford Foundation initiative. In 1982, with the cooperation of the Council on Foundations, community foundations across the country were invited to select an issue of common concern, and then address the issue programatically through a funding partnership with Ford.

The issue which generated the most interest was adolescent pregnancy and parenting. Ford suggested two complementary directions for the funding partnership: the replication of Project Redirection, a program designed to assist economically disadvantaged young mothers; and the initiation of new services for the underserved teenage father.

Each community foundation chose one of these directions and selected a local service organization as its program site. Ford also invited two research organizations to participate: Manpower Demonstration Research Corporation (MDRC) to work with the Project Redirection sites, and Bank Street College of Education to collaborate with those sites interested in serving teenage fathers.

In all, eight program sites, with support from their funders and Bank Street, launched the Teen Father Collaboration in April, 1983.

PARTICIPATING ORGANIZATIONS AND THEIR RESPECTIVE ROLES

Bank Street College.   Bank Street staff offer technical assistance to all eight program sites, both in person during annual visits, and through ongoing telephone contact. Bank Street also encourages cross-site networking by facilitating direct contact among sites with common issues, publishing a triannual newsletter, and organizing annual working conferences.

In its role as documentor of the Collaboration, Bank Street implements an extensive plan of data collection and analysis (described in detail in a later section of this chapter). Two major research questions concern the impact of service delivery on participating teenage fathers: First, which program interventions are most effective in increasing the participant's responsibility as a father? Second, what teen father characteristics are associated with positive programmatic outcomes? A final question concerns the process of program development and implementation: What strategies most successfully overcome the obstacles associated with outreach and service to adolescent fathers? Results are being used to formulate models and guidelines for assisting teenage parents in a variety of settings and communities all across the country.

Funding sources.   As already described, the Collaboration represents an unusual funding partnership. The Ford Foundation supports the process of research, documentation, and networking across all sites, provides ongoing leadership in the collaborative effort, and plays an important role in focusing national-level public attention on the needs of both partners in adolescent childbearing.

Eight community foundations (see Table 10.1) provide money for service delivery within their own communities. Each community foundation plays a major public advocacy role as well, encouraging the interest and support of other key resource people within its community.

Local service providers.   Eight local agencies, each with an established program of assistance to adolescent mothers, have expanded their efforts to include teenage fathers (see Table 10.1). These sites vary in several important ways. They serve racially and ethnically diverse populations, reflecting the varying compositions of their local communities. They define their service populations differently, most serving young men who are age 19 or younger, while a few include the somewhat older partners of adolescent mothers as well. Agencies are housed in different types of settings: hospitals, schools, and social service agencies. A few have relatively large staffs, several rely on the efforts of just one or two people. Depending on their resources and staffing, some target a small number of teen fathers each year, while others are able to serve many more.

TABLE 10.1

An Overview of the Eight Local Sites Participating in the Teen Father Collaboration

State	City	Community Foundation	Service Provider	Setting	Race and Ethnicity of Teen Fathers Served	Number of Teen Fathers Targeted per year
California	San Francisco	San Francisco Foundation	Teenage Pregnancy and Parenting Project of the Family Service Agency of San Francisco	School	41% Black 35% Hispanic 10% White 9% Asian 5% Other	120
Connecticut	Bridgeport	Bridgeport Area Foundation	YMCA of Greater Bridgeport	Social Service Agency	73% Hispanic 10% Black 10% Asian 5% White 2% Other	75
Kentucky	Louisville	Louisville Foundation	Teenage Parent Program of the Jefferson County Public Schools	School	79% White 20% Black 1% Other	20
Minnesota	Minneapolis	Minneapolis Foundation	Division of Indian Work	Social Service Agency	80% American Indian 9% Black 9% White 2% Hispanic	35
Minnesota	St. Paul	Saint Paul Foundation	Face to Face Health and Counseling Service, Inc.	Social Service Agency	90% White 1% Black 1% Other	15
New York	Poughkeepsie	Area Fund of Dutchess County	YMCA of Dutchess County	Social Service Agency	46% White 41% Black 13% Hispanic/Latino	15
Oregon	Portland	Oregon Community Foundation	National Council of Jewish Women Insights	Social Service Agency	75% White 13% Black 4% Hispanic 4% Asian 2% American Indian 2% Other	25
Pennsylvania	Philadelphia	Philadelphia Foundation	The Medical College of Pennsylvania	Hospital	62% Black 38% White	50

Some offer most of their services on-site; others function as referral centers, helping young fathers connect with service providers elsewhere in the community.

What all eight sites have in common is their commitment in reaching out to a previously neglected population and their creativity in designing a comprehensive range of services to meet the teen father's many needs. Typically, their programs include the following components: prenatal and parenting classes, family planning workshops, educational programs, vocational skills training, job placement services, individual and peer counseling, and couples groups.

The next section of this chapter presents a description of each local site, illustrating the variety and commitment which characterize the Collaboration as a whole.

Service Delivery at the Eight Local Sites

Each of the eight agencies has developed a unique program to combat the numerous difficulties teenage fathers face. The TEENAGE PREGNANCY AND PARENTING PROJECT (T.A.P.P.) of the FAMILY SERVICE AGENCY of San Francisco, the largest agency in the Collaboration, is a school-based program. Its far reaching and effective linkage system connects young black, latino, white, and Asian fathers with many organizations in their community: the San Francisco Department of Social Services, the San Francisco Public Health Department, and the Children's Home Society, to name only three major resources.

On-site service delivery staff at T.A.P.P. include peer counselors, continuous case counselors, an employment counselor, public health nurses, an outreach worker, and a project coordinator. These men and women offer teen fathers individual counseling at least once a month, a weekly peer discussion group of eight or ten young men, couples counseling, a well-baby care program, vocational guidance and some job placement services. An on-site nursery is available where young fathers can learn parenting skills—how to bathe, diaper, feed, and play with their children. As one 16-year-old father said:

> I didn't know anything about taking care of my child, and that's why I joined this program. Now they're teaching us how to hold and diaper a baby. Later on we'll learn how to fix formulas. I'm learning how to be a real father!

In addition to these services, T.A.P.P. also organizes group recreational outings for young fathers to reduce their feeling of isolation from their peers. As one 18-year-old put it:

> Being with people in the same position as I am really helps. Before this program, I felt like I was one in a million. I'm getting through this whole thing knowing other people are in the same boat.

Camping trips, baseball games, an evening at the circus—all serve to foster both a sense of comraderie and a social network among these adolescent fathers.

Although many teen fathers are recruited through the teen mother program at T.A.P.P., other young fathers enter the program through the committed efforts of an outreach worker whose main job is to scout neighborhood recreational centers and local teen hangouts and to "connect" with these young men. Newspaper articles, radio programs, television spots and fliers are among some of the other successful strategies that are attracting teen fathers to the T.A.P.P. program.

THE NATIONAL COUNCIL OF JEWISH WOMEN INSIGHTS, located in Portland, Oregon, serves pregnant teens as well as teen mothers and their male partners. Its service population is predominantly white, though blacks, hispanics, and Asians have also become clients. Through an active program of home visits, a small group of paid staff and trained volunteers come to know, first-hand, how these adolescent-headed families are faring. Special attention is paid to the children in these families and this has proven especially important in cases where child abuse is suspected. In several instances, abusing parents have been encouraged to join the agency's couples counseling service. Having the help of a neutral third party appears to have reduced the incidence of child abuse, alleviating the parents' sense of guilt and giving them more positive feelings about their parenthood.

The Insights program coordinator does a great deal of personal counseling, trying to help young fathers become skillful and satisfied in their role as parents. He also assists them in their search for jobs, helping them write resumes, fill out job applications, and scan want ads for appropriate job openings.

A couples group for mothers and fathers is co-led by a male/female team. This group deals with such issues as communication, child abuse, parenting styles, and sharing domestic and childcare responsibilities. In a population that is beset by a myriad of difficulties, the need to talk out problems—whether individually, as a couple, or in a group—is enormous. Many teen parents at Insights have stated that they feel less frustrated and desperate because they now have an interested and objective person helping them resolve some of their difficulties.

Insights receives a steady stream of teen father referrals from the young mothers enrolled in both the Insights Project and the Boys and Girls Aid Society of Oregon. Community nurses and youth service centers have also been excellent referral sources. In addition, Insights staff members have been instrumental in raising public awareness about the problems of adolescent parenting throughout their community.

Two Collaboration sites are located in Minnesota: THE DIVISION OF INDIAN WORK (DIW) in Minneapolis, and FACE TO FACE HEALTH AND COUNSELING SERVICE, INC., in St. Paul.

Operating under the auspices of the Greater Minneapolis Council of Churches, the Division of Indian Work is the first urban organization to provide direct services to the American Indian community throughout that state. The agency is located in South Minneapolis, an area which has the largest concentration of American Indian people in the United States—between 10,000 and 15,000. Fully half of the American Indian population is aged 18 and under, 50% are high school dropouts, 50% struggle with alcohol and chemical dependency, and an astounding 60 to 70% are unemployed. Furthermore, the rate of teenage pregnancy is 11 times higher than the state-wide average. Given all these problems, DIW has had to design a comprehensive program of much-needed services.

Three staff members comprise DIW's teen father component, all placing great emphasis on their home visit program. Because most young families do not have telephones, the male counselor must make repeated trips to reach them at home. Once he establishes a relationship with a teen father, they discuss a variety of personal issues: education, employment, domestic violence, cultural heritage, and what it means to be a father.

The counselor also offers job skills training, referring young fathers to local employment agencies for possible job placement. He administers a fathers support group and, with the female coordinator of the teen mothers program, co-leads a couples group. An important parent-child group rounds out the program, insuring that fathers and children have consistent and regular periods of time together, which helps the fathers become more skilled at childrearing. During these group activity times, issues of normal child development are discussed. This kind of education is particularly important in helping to moderate unrealistic expectations fathers may have about their children, thereby reducing the potential for abusiveness.

FACE TO FACE HEALTH AND COUNSELING SERVICE, INC. emphasizes employment skills in its efforts to help young fathers. In its first program cycle, over twenty hours of preemployment classes were attended by enthusiastic young parents. Classes in parenting skills and life management skills are also available to help young men become more effective and engaged as fathers.

To enhance its employment program, Face to Face is working hard to establish contacts within the private employment sector, engaging the support of community business leaders. The agency has already established important linkages with two federal job training programs (S.Y.E.T., Summer Youth Employment and Training and J.T.P.A., Jobs Training Partnership Act). These resources have helped young fathers obtain work experience through summer jobs as well as vocational training during the school year. Teen fathers are also encouraged to discover their own employment opportunities, putting to use what they have learned in job skills training classes. As one young man said:

> If I had never found this agency, I might never have gotten such a good job. If I had gotten an ordinary job, I would have continued to stay at home and would never have gotten married. Now, my job keeps me and my wife and baby away from welfare.

THE TEENAGE PARENT PROGRAM (TAPP) of the JEFFERSON COUNTY PUBLIC SCHOOLS, located in Louisville, Kentucky, is a school-based project which has worked with pregnant teenagers since 1970, and now offers services to teen fathers as well. Young fathers-to-be enroll in specially designed childbirth education classes which help them feel emotionally connected to their child before its birth. The, after the birth, they participate in well-baby care and parenting skills classes, learning to diaper, feed, and bathe their infants in a well-equipped home-like environment.

Another component of the program, the Vocational Explorer Unit, under the auspices of the Boy Scouts of America, offers teen fathers and fathers-to-be opportunities to learn about various kinds of occupations. Subsequently, they are placed in work settings where they receive 4 to 6 hours of closely supervised training each week for up to a full year.

A unique grandparents support group also operates at TAPP. Parents of both teen mothers and teen fathers meet together in their own informal network. Their goals are to help their children and grandchildren, and to work out their own feelings about becoming grandparents.

On the East coast, THE GREATER BRIDGEPORT ADOLESCENT PREG-NANCY PROGRAM, in Bridgeport, Connecticut, offers a multitude of services to a predominantly hispanic population: individual counseling and recreational services at the local YMCA, vocational services under the auspices of the Private Industry Council, and family planning instruction and medical services through the Bridgeport Community Health Center. This expanding network of services is coordinated by a staff of two at the YMCA.

The program's outreach worker scouts out teen males in their local hangouts. The success of the Bridgeport project, in great part, has resulted from the determination of this outreach worker and his skill in establishing an informal network among young fathers and fathers-to-be throughout the community. Since many of these young men share a common cultural heritage, they have been able to provide each other with a strong sense of community and support.

The Fathers' Outreach Component at the YWCA of DUTCHESS COUNTY in Poughkeepsie, New York, is the smallest program in the Collaboration. However, even with only two part-time staff members, this agency offers key services to teen fathers. Individual counseling is available to all participants. Many of these young men and their partners also take advantage of family planning education, parenting skills classes, and a couples group. A job skills training class has prepared several teen fathers for job placement, and appropriate referrals have been made to a G.E.D. program in the area.

THE TEEN FATHERS PROGRAM at THE MEDICAL COLLEGE of PENNSYLVANIA HOSPITAL in Philadelphia recruits teen fathers primarily through its prenatal and pediatric clinics. As soon as a young man enters the clinic with his female partner, he is introduced to the teen father counselor. This male counselor describes the range of services that are available: individual counseling, prenatal counseling and classes, and educational or vocational referrals. This immediate, on-the-spot, personal contact has proven invaluable. An 18-year-old expectant father related his experience this way:

> I only came to the clinic to hear my baby's heartbeat. But a social worker stopped me and told me about the program that was being given for teen fathers. Before I had a chance to say no, a counselor who was sitting right next door to the room I was in introduced himself to me. He was frank. He told me about the program. There were no strings attached. I have to be honest, if my counselor hadn't been there right at that moment, I might have told that social worker I'd come back, but I wouldn't have.

From the beginning of their contact with the hospital, the teen fathers and fathers-to-be know that the staff members have the best interests of both young parents in mind. Emphasis is placed on the young man's involvement with his partner's pregnancy from its initial stages, so that he can provide her with the support she needs. He, too, receives psychological help and information as he makes the transition to fatherhood. A number of teen fathers who participate in childbirth classes choose to be present at the birth of their children. As one father said, "Being there for my girl was real important to me, but seeing the birth of my daughter changed my life!"

Barriers to effective service delivery.   The relative success of these eight program sites tends to overshadow some of the problems that were encountered by the agencies in reaching and serving teenage fathers. During their first 3- to 6-months of operation, each Collaboration site faced a range of attitudinal, organizational, and structural barriers. Certain of these barriers were site-specific; others were more generic, and are likely to affect the potential success of most programs designed to serve adolescent fathers. They include:

1. Lack of agency-wide support for thinking about the male partner in adolescent parenthood as a primary client in his own right. This barrier has a long history rooted in the traditional female bias that pervades the social service profession.

2. Inadequate funding, assigning low priority to male clients in the competition for scarce resources (money, staff time, space, equipment), and failure to sustain funding for innovative programs over time.

3. Insufficient numbers of trained male service workers, and a less than optimal match between the particular characteristics of male clients and the characteristics, skills, and attitudes of the staff people who are selected to serve them.

4. Failure to attract adequate numbers of young fathers through the right combination of aggressive, "street-wise" outreach strategies and individualized followup.

5. Inability to retain reasonable numbers of young fathers by failing to build a comprehensive program of service delivery geared to their real-life needs. Com-

monly, young men will not enter a program unless it provides them with job-related skills and training; they will not stay in a program over time unless it helps them deal with their more personal, relationship-oriented problems.

Evaluating the relative merits of the strategies developed by agencies to overcome such barriers is one of several goals of the Collaboration's research component. Given the diversity among programs, the task of assessing the Collaboration's impact is a challenging one. What follows is an overview of this complex *in vivo* research component—its major questions and its multiple sources of data. A subsequent section presents some preliminary findings.

THE RESEARCH COMPONENT: MAJOR QUESTIONS

As described earlier, Bank Street College plays a multifaceted role in the Teen Father Collaboration, including the design and implementation of an extensive research agenda. More specifically, the research questions are:

1. What program interventions are most effective in increasing the teen father's responsibility with regard to economic support of his child, contribution to his child's social and emotional development, application of principles of well-baby care, and utilization of family planning information?
2. What teen father characteristics at program entry (for example, goals as a father, relationship to the child's mother, or family background) are associated with increases in responsibility along the dimensions cited above? Put into programmatic terms, is it possible to identify and screen for a population of teen fathers with whom agencies are most likely to succeed?
3. What are the obstacles to both reaching and working with teen fathers, and what strategies can agencies use to overcome these obstacles and develop successful programs of service?

Data Collection

Both quantitative and qualitative data are being collected to address these questions. Since the responsibility for data collection is shared by Bank Street and the eight local sites, Bank Street staff have conducted extensive training sessions to insure the comparability of data across sites. Data analyses are conducted by Bank Street. An overview of all data collection tasks is presented in Table 10.2.

Five sets of data focus on the impact that service delivery programs have on teen father participants.

(1) A *Background Information* form is administered by agency staff to all teen fathers who make initial contact with a program. The form consists of such basic information as age, ethnicity, religious background, living arrangements, educational and job status (and goals for these), relationship with partner and child (or

TABLE 10.2
Teen Father Collaboration Data Collection Plan

Impact Data On Teen Fathers	Data Source	Assessment Interval
1. Background Information	Agency and teen father	Teen father's first visit to agency
2. Baseline Data	Agency and participant	Entry date into ongoing program
3. Ongoing Log	Agency	Ongoing
4. On-Site Interviews	Bank Street and participant	Once a year
5. Outcome Data	Agency and participant	Exit data from ongoing program
Process and Implementation Data		
1. Characteristics, Resources, and Operation of Agency	Agency	Beginning of collaboration
2. Quarterly Summary of Agency Services	Agency	Quarterly
3. Prescheduled Telephone Interviews	Bank Street and Agency	As needed
4. Site Visit Interview	Bank Street and Agency	Once a year

expected child), and financial or in-kind contributions to the child (actual or anticipated). Analyses of these data will yield descriptive ''profiles'' of one of the largest samples of teenage fathers ever studied.

(2) A *Baseline Data* form is administered to all teen fathers who become enrolled in an ongoing program of agency services. This form, administered by an agency staff person soon after the teen father enrolls, is designed to assess his goals on entering the program, his knowledge of child development, his relationship with his child, his attitudes toward childrearing, and related items.

(3) An *Ongoing Log* records each enrolled participant's attendance, progress, and attitudes during his involvement in agency services. This record is kept by an agency staff person who knows about the teen father's progress in some detail. It contributes depth and richness to the assessment of program impact in individual cases.

(4) *On-Site Interviews* with teen father participants are conducted by Bank Street staff during annual site visits to each agency. These interviews explore systematically the young father's relationship to his partner and child, his concerns about their well-being and his own, and his hopes for the future. The interviews permit an indepth look at a sub-sample of teenage fathers who articulate where they feel the strengths and weaknesses of agency programs lie. They provide a much needed source of first-hand information about this population and the issues they confront in becoming parents so early in their lives.

(5) An *Outcome Data* form on enrolled participants is administered by an agency staff person to each teen father when his involvement in the agency

program is coming to an end. This form parallels the Baseline Data form and selected items in the Background Information form, permitting the measurement of change over time.

Process and implementation issues are the focus of four additional sets of data. They describe the participating organizations, the services they offer, and the obstacles and successes they encounter.

(1) *Characteristics, Resources, and Operation of Agency* was a form completed by each of the eight local sites at the beginning of the Collaboration. This form was used to record information on organizational structure, agency size, staffing, local client populations, range of services, and other aspects of agency operations.

(2) A *Quarterly Summary of Agency Services* is completed by agency staff four times a year. This form details activities on teen father recruitment, referrals, direct services, staff assignments, community development activities, external contacts, and related items.

(3) A *Prescheduled Telephone Interview* is conducted between Bank Street and agency staff. In advance of this interview, questionnaires are distributed to project directors so that they—and other relevant project staff—are well prepared to discuss issues pertinent to the documentation process. These include problems and solutions related to recruiting and serving teen fathers, staff attitudes, and community involvement. This interview tends to catalyze efforts and raise important issues at each local site.

(4) *Site Visits* to agencies and community foundations are conducted by teams of Bank Street staff. Interviews are held with service delivery staff, administrators, and data collectors to garner varied perceptions of each local program, its relationship to the larger service community and to the Collaboration as a whole. Bank Street staff also observe services-in-action in order to gain firsthand knowledge of their physical setting, content, attendance, mode of delivery, and the response of participants.

Bank Street staff also interview representatives of each community foundation to explore the relationship between the agency and its sponsoring foundation, and the impact on the foundation of its participation in a national collaboration.

Preliminary Findings

Some interesting trends are suggested from preliminary analyses of selected elements from the first year of data collection.[1] Systematic analyses have focused on 245 young fathers and fathers-to-be who made initial contact with one of the Collaboration's eight service sites during its first year of operation, and who responded to the Collaboration's Background Information form. As pre-

---

[1]Rosen, J. L., & Sander, J. H. (1984, June). *Who is the Teenage Father? Preliminary Findings—Parts 1 and 2.* Paper presented at The Teen Father Collaboration/Project Redirection Conference, San Francisco.

viously described, this form is essentially descriptive in nature, and was designed to yield participant "profiles." These early findings are supplemented by the content analysis of indepth, systematic interview data on a sub-sample of 18 teen fathers selected by staff at each local site. Interviews were conducted by Bank Street staff during site visits in the fall of 1983 and the winter of 1984.

The 245 teen fathers and fathers-to-be who made contact with the Collaboration during its first year showed marked diversity in ethnic and religious background but similiarity in many other characteristics. Twenty-three percent of the young men were white, 33% were black, and 28% hispanic, including Chicanos, Puerto Ricans, and others from Central and Latin America. Small percentages of American Indians and Asians were also represented (5% and 8% respectively). In terms of religious background, most young men considered themselves either Protestant (39%, and this included several denominations) or Catholic (38%). Fifteen percent said they had no religious affiliation, with the remaining 7% stating that they belonged to one of a wide range of sects, including Muslim, Mormon, Rastofarian, Jehovah's Witness, and Mieng.

The vast majority of these young men (67%) were not enrolled in any type of educational program at the time they made contact with the Collaboration. Some had already graduated from high school; many more had dropped out because, as they reported, they were bored, did not like school, or needed a job. However, when asked if they had plans to return to school, three quarters of the respondents said yes.

The employment picture was particularly dismal. At the time they made their first contact with the Collaboration, two out of every three young fathers were unemployed. Of those who did hold jobs, about half worked full-time, half part-time. Not surprisingly, job training and placement services were of great importance in attracting many of these young fathers to the services provided by the Collaboration and in keeping them enrolled.

Other findings offer new perspective on the long-held stereotype that teenage fathers are "hit-and-run victimizers" who take advantage of young women. Clearly, this is not always the case. Since this self-selected sample includes only young men concerned enough with their children and partners to have joined a Collaboration service program caution, of course, should be used in applying these findings too broadly.

The vast majority (89%) of the young men who made contact with Collaboration services considered themselves and the mother of their child to be part of an intact couple (13% were married; 76% said the young women were their "girlfriends"). Furthermore, these relationships were unusually long-lasting for this age group: 62% of the young men said they had known their partners for 2 years or longer, while almost a quarter of the sample had known their partners for more than 3 years.

These findings would be less surprising if most of the young fathers said they had entered Collaboration programs at the urging of their female partners. But the majority (63%) reported entering by way of other agency outreach strategies:

presentations in the schools, public service announcements, and active recruitment efforts in local teenage hangouts. This finding has important implications for social service agencies, suggesting that they need not focus their recruitment efforts solely on the young mother in order to attract the young father as well.

The young men were very much of a presence in the lives of their children. Exactly half of the sample had already become fathers; the other half were fathers-to-be. Across both groups, the vast majority of young men (87%) were experiencing parenthood for the first time. The majority of the fathers (78%) said they saw their child every day; similarly, most of the fathers-to-be (83%) reported that they planned to see their child on a daily basis. Just over half of the fathers (55%), and fewer of the expectant fathers (40%), said they were able to make financial contributions to their children, but the majority of both groups indicated they could contribute to their child's well-being in other ways—by spending time with them and providing them with food, clothing, toys, or books.

Systematic, indepth interview data add another important dimension to the trends already described. The selection of the young men who were interviewed was made primarily on the basis of their availability during site visits and may therefore be biased. What these teen fathers have to say, however, suggests the wide range of reactions to fatherhood that exist in this population.

To date, analysis of a sample of first year interview data has focused on a set of issues with special relevance for program planners and service workers: the reactions of the young men when they first learned about their local agency's program for teen fathers, and their assessment of the services that were of greatest benefit to them.

Maurice, at 19, was afraid and dubious when his high school guidance counselor broached the subject of his enrollment in a teen father program:

> When she first told me about the program, I just freaked out. People say I'm really career oriented. And this, like, was just so much setback. The child—I hadn't fully accepted the idea. I personally really didn't want to think about the matter. But the more my counselor spoke to me, the more I began to accept the idea. 'What have I got to lose?' I thought. I realized I was just scared.

This reaction was not an uncommon one. Many of the young men were somewhat overwhelmed by their new responsibilities as fathers, and were reluctant to admit they needed help and support.

Other young fathers reacted quite differently, relieved to find out that help was available and eager to take advantage of it. Edgar, a 19-year-old father-to-be, explained his reaction this way:

> I found out about this program through my friend Pedro, who found out from his cousin. Right away, when Pedro told me, I thought it was a good idea. At the time I was desperate for any kind of help—any kind of support I could get. When something like this happens—having a baby—a lot of people back out. But I'm

here, right in the middle. I reached out. Right now I'm going to stick to this for what help they give me and what help I can give out to other guys.

Whatever their initial reactions—fear, denial, relief—the fathers we interviewed did eventually enroll in Collaboration services. What did they find most useful? Which program components kept them involved, motivated, and committed?

Often it was the one-to-one relationship between a young father and his counselor which made the crucial difference. Bill, 17, said this about his counselor:

> He is someone I can really talk to. I know what it's like to grow up without a father. My father was a bum. He was an alcoholic and took drugs. I have a very bad complex about not being able to be a good enough father. I don't want what happened to me to happen to my son. My counselor is someone I can trust to help me with this.

Once this kind of trusting relationship has been established, program staff can offer concrete help. In Bill's case, this meant referral to a job skills and employment placement program. Bill was then able to take an important step toward contributing to his son's financial wellbeing and becoming a "good enough father."

Other young fathers preferred peer counseling. Being part of a peer group mobilized these young men, encouraging them in their responsibility as partners and fathers.

Bob, for example, was the 18-year-old father of a 3-month-old daughter. For him the peer counseling group afforded a variety of important benefits. One of these was a lessening of the sense of isolation and social alienation that he and his teenage wife both felt. From this peer group, a network of adolescent parent couples formed, creating a support system that extended far beyond the agency's services. Bob said that the group helped him face his deep concerns about becoming a father; other young fathers in the group said they gained confidence and support from their participation in the group.

Parenting skills classes were described by several young fathers as particularly useful. Learning how to take care of their children gave them the confidence they needed to become actively involved as fathers. Walter, 19, felt unsure of himself and unable to play a useful role in the day-to-day care of his infant. He was grateful when he started to attend parenting classes with a group of comparably unskilled young men:

> I felt there was a lot of stuff that I needed to learn. When my baby was first born, I didn't know how to change the diapers or even let down the side of the crib. I'm learning so much now.

Similarly, classes and workshops in vocational training were critical for young fathers like James, 17, who wanted to develop the confidence to apply for and obtain jobs:

> I learned how to communicate with others in the program. It made me feel more confident about filling out applications and meeting employers because I got to practice doing these things so much before I went to the real place to try to get a job.

As described earlier, each of the Collaboration's local programs is able to offer teen fathers many different kinds of services. Therefore, the young father can take advantage of several new opportunities at the same time—gaining greater self-esteem, more social support, confidence as a parent, and higher level job skills according to his own individual needs.

SUMMARY

The Teen Father Collaboration, a two-year demonstration and research partnership, is aimed at discovering and documenting effective strategies for working with the male partner in adolescent childbearing. In this Collaboration, programs for teenage fathers have been implemented in eight cities around the country. Preliminary findings suggest interesting answers to important questions: Who are the young men who take advantage of services when they are offered? What first attracts these young fathers to programs, and which services encourage their continuing participation?

Other questions remain, and many will be addressed in the Collaboration's final report. Broadly, this report integrates both process and outcome data, generating models and guidelines that can be adapted for use in a variety of settings across the country. Along with the Collaboration's three major research questions, several issues are of particular interest: Are there specific components of service programs for teenage fathers that ought to be included any time this population is served? If so, do these components vary with variations in race, ethnicity, and cultural background? How can a community organize its resources and develop a program that meets its own local needs? Finally, from the varied perspectives of service providers, researchers, and funders, what is gained by addressing the issue of male involvement in adolescent parenthood—not in isolation, but as members of a collaborative network instead?

11 Young Fathers and Their Children: Some Historical and Policy Perspectives

Maris A. Vinovskis
The Institute for Social Research, University of Michigan, Ann Arbor

Although the role of the father in child development and care is usually slighted or even totally ignored, there are now indications of new interest among scholars and policy makers. Yet much of the recent discussions focuses narrowly upon the present without a proper appreciation of the changing role of the American father over time. In addition, many of the current studies concentrate on some particular facet of child development without considering the broader societal implications as well—especially from the perspective of policy makers.

This chapter explores some of the issues surrounding the role of fathers in the care and support of young adolescent mothers and their children from an historical and policy perspective. By analyzing the changing involvement of fathers over time in the raising of their children as well as the shifts in the perceptions and remedies for the problems associated with adolescent pregnancy, we are able to understand better the situation of the father today. To examine the attitude of policy makers towards fathers, we consider the evolution of the recent federal legislation for helping school-age mothers and their children from the perspective of the fathers.

THE ROLE OF THE FATHER IN THE PAST

Today the role of the father in the care and socialization of young children is seen by many Americans as secondary or peripheral compared to that of the mother. Indeed, there is a widespread belief that mothers are by nature more suited for the rearing of children. Even the function of the father as the main source of financial support for the young child is often seemingly challenged by the availability of federal, state, or local welfare assistance for single mothers as well as by the reluctance of many adolescent mothers and fathers to marry (Cath, Gurwitt, & Ross, 1982; Lamb, 1981; Lamb & Sagi, 1983).

The role of the father in the past was more central to the lives of young children than today (Moran & Vinovskis, forthcoming). In seventeenth-century New England, for example, not only was there strong religious and community pressure to avoid premarital sexual activity, but also to marry if an unintended pregnancy occurred. Because the financial burden of raising an out-of-wedlock birth ultimately fell upon members of the local community, every possible effort was made to ensure that the errant couple married and supported their child. Although mothers worked hard in their homes in colonial America, the father was seen as the primary and essential source of economic support for his family.

The father's role in seventeenth-century New England extended well beyond the economic support of the children and the mother. The Puritan father, as the undisputed head of the household, was given the task of catechizing the children as well as other members of that household (Axtell, 1974). Although the mother was regarded as an important assistant, it was the father who had the responsibility in the household for teaching young children to read and interpret the Bible. Although the father's role derived from more general Puritan and English views of the duties of the head of the household, they were reinforced by the fact that New England fathers were more literate than mothers (Auwers, 1980; Lockridge, 1974) and the belief that women could not be entrusted with the religious instruction in the home after the difficulties with Anne Hutchinson and her followers in Massachusetts in the 1630s (Hall, 1968). The father was also seen as essential for disciplining and guiding young children, as mothers were often viewed as too indulgent and lenient towards their children. Furthermore, whereas some scholars (Shorter, 1975; Stone, 1977) have questioned the emotional involvement of fathers with their young children, others (Demos, 1982) have pointed to its existence at least among some colonial fathers.

If our ancestors had an elevated view of the role of the father in the support and socializing of young children, they did not differentiate between the responsibilities of adolescent and adult fathers. Contrary to the situation today, Puritan Americans did not distinguish as sharply or clearly between adolescence and adulthood (Demos & Demos, 1969; Hiner, 1975; Vinovskis, 1983). Rather, the emphasis was on the transition from a period of economic dependency in youth (whether on their own family or on some other household) to one of being a full-fledged adult whose independent status was signaled by the ability to maintain one's own household (Kett, 1977). Only under the latter circumstances was one considered eligible for marriage. As a result, relatively few young adolescent females or males married in New England and if they did it was not cause for concern unless they were unable to support themselves and their offspring (Greven, 1970; Jones, 1981; Norton, 1981; Vinovskis, 1981b).

Thus, in seventeenth-century New England, fathers were the primary and necessary providers for their children. Mothers nursed and cared for the physical needs of the young child, but it was the fathers who were delegated the vital responsibility of catechizing and socializing the young children. Although early adolescent childbearing and rearing did occur, it was neither as widespread nor considered as problematic as today.

During the eighteenth century, we can observe some fundamental changes in the role of fathers. The strong and aggressive prohibition against any premarital sexual relations was eased during the eighteenth century. Premarital sexual relations became an expected if not accepted part of colonial courtship rituals. As a result, the number and rate of premarital pregnancies increased during the second half of the eighteenth century (Smith & Hindus, 1975). Whereas most of these led to a hastily arranged marriage, there was also a greater tolerance of out-of-wedlock births. Yet the community fears of being saddled with the care of indigent unwed mothers and their children persisted so that fathers were forced to support, whenever possible, their offspring even if they managed to avoid marrying the mother (Wells, 1980).

Perhaps the most important change in the role of the father was the relinquishment of his catechizing functions in the household. By as early as the mid-seventeenth century, males were much less likely to join the Puritan church than females (Moran, 1980). Because the duties of catechizing rested upon a religious foundation, many fathers were no longer able or willing to teach their children the Bible. Instead, community and church leaders experimented with a wide variety of other options for catechizing such as enlisting public school teachers, but reluctantly they accepted the larger role of the mother for this task because women continued to be active members of the church (Moran & Vinovskis, 1982, forthcoming). One consequence of this shift was the growing sentiment that women should be educated as they were now to be entrusted with the religious education of their children in the home (Malmsheimer, 1973; Ulrich, 1982). The mother's part in educating children was reinforced by the expansion of the roles of women as a consequence of the American Revolution (Kerber, 1980; Norton, 1980). As a result, by the eighteenth century, the mother's contribution to the physical and spiritual care of young children was considerably expanded, whereas the responsibilities of the father were gradually contracted in practice as well as in theory.

Thus, in eighteenth-century America, fathers were expected to support their offspring even if they did not marry the mother. Although there was little change in the attitudes towards adolescent parents because of their age, there was a dramatic shift in the relative roles of the mother and father. Whereas the seventeenth-century father was expected to be the primary religious instructor of his children in the home, the eighteenth-century family frequently delegated this task to the mother. Although some lamented the diminished role of the father in the socialization of the child, most others accepted it and concentrated on preparing the mothers for this new responsibility.

The nineteenth century witnessed another shift in attitudes toward premarital sexual activity and a further expansion of the role of the mother in the care and socialization of young children as that of the father receded or changed. It also saw the emergence of the concept of adolescence as well as the growth in the role of the state rather than the local community in the care of poor mothers and their children. Altogether, the nineteenth century was an important bridge in the changing attitudes and behavior towards the role and rights of fathers in the care of their children from the colonial period to the twentieth century.

Increasingly in the early nineteenth century, premarital sexual activity was regarded as sinful and shameful. Drawing upon the religious zeal from the Second Great Awakening as well as a more general redefinition of appropriate courtship behavior, women who became pregnant prior to marriage were treated as outcasts—especially if they did not marry the father. Not only was there a dramatic drop in premarital pregnancies in the nineteenth century, but also an apparent rise in abortions as single women increasingly tried to eliminate a potential source of great shame and rebuke (Mohr, 1978; Smith & Hindus, 1975). Respectability was more and more defined as being chaste prior to marriage or at the very minimum of marrying the father if one became pregnant (Rothman, 1984). Although most nineteenth-century Americans accepted these new values, some strongly resented the double standard that punished the behavior of the women much more than that of the men (Smith-Rosenberg, 1971).

Once a woman became a mother, the extent and complexity of her tasks multipled and expanded in the nineteenth century. Although popular advice literature often expressed the wish that fathers would take a more active role in the upbringing of their children, there was a reluctant acceptance of the fact that most fathers were too busy with their careers and jobs to play a large role in the socialization of their children beyond providing for their material needs (Kuhn, 1947). The increasing likelihood that the father would now work outside the home reduced the amount of time and opportunity that he would have to interact with his family—especially as the availability of transportation separated the home from the place of work by even greater distances (Warner, 1963). Although the evangelical press frequently exhorted fathers to pray with their families and children, women continued to be more active and involved religiously than males in the catechizing of children in the home (Ryan, 1981). The woman's role in the religious realm was also enhanced by the fact that most of the newly created Sunday schools were staffed by women rather than men (Sweet, 1983).

The mother's role in child development and education was stressed by the scientific and educational literature that emphasized her particular suitability for the care of young children (May & Vinovskis, 1976). This notion was strengthened by the nineteenth-century doctrines of ''separate spheres'' and the ''cult of domesticity,'' which asserted that women were especially competent to raise and educate young children whereas men were more suited for making a living outside the home (Cott, 1977; Degler, 1980). Almost all the nineteenth-century child-rearing manuals and advice books were directed to mothers with only passing references to the role of fathers (Demos, 1982).

Another important change was that after the mid-nineteenth century there was a growing disposition among judges in divorce cases to award the custody of children, especially the young ones, to the mother rather than to the father (Griswold, 1982; Grossberg, 1983; May, 1980; Zinaldin, 1979). Previously it had been assumed by the courts that in almost any divorce or separation the custody of the children should be given to the father rather than to the mother so that the pattern of male inheritance and dominance would be continued. In the second half of the nineteenth century, however, the interests and well-being of the child were increasingly taken into consideration while at the same time the number of divorces in the United States began to increase rapidly. Given the nineteenth-century view of the importance of the mother for the care and rearing of young children, it is not surprising that the fathers were now less likely to receive custody of the children. In the twentieth century, of course, this has evolved to the point where the mother, rather than the father, almost automatically receives the custody of young children unless she seems to be unfit or unwilling to raise them (Weitzman & Dixon, 1979).

During the second half of the nineteenth century there was also a growing awareness of a separate and distinct stage of adolescence and a tendency to treat young adolescents differently than adults. Although historians continue to disagree upon the exact timing of the emergence of adolescence as a phase of the life course, most of them now locate that development somewhere in the nineteenth century (Demos & Demos, 1969; Vinovskis, 1983). The emerging view of adolescence stressed the need for postponing marriage, even if the individual was economically self-sufficient, and for acquiring additional education or some other type of job training—especially for males who were expected to pursue careers. In addition, any early sexual activity was seen by medical authorities as extremely detrimental to the physical and mental development of the adolescent (Clarke, 1873). This distinction between adolescents and adults received practical reinforcement with the creation of special institutions such as juvenile courts and homes for unwed adolescent mothers (Brenzel, 1975; Schlossman & Wallach, 1980).

Finally, the nineteenth century witnessed the increasing involvement of the state rather than just the local community in the care of the poor (Rothman, 1971). This assistance was often provided through state institutions that became more common and specialized over time. As the distinction between the ''deserving'' poor and those unworthy of support grew among social reformers, special efforts were made to provide help for single mothers and their young children. Although these developments were still relatively modest by the end of the nineteenth century, they created the precedents and expectations for the expanding role of the state and then the federal government in these areas in the twentieth century.

By the 1950s the diminished role of the father in the rearing of the young child was an accepted fact. Fathers were viewed as necessary for the economic well-being of the family, but mothers were expected to be the primary caretakers of the young. Compared to the nineteenth century, the first half of the twentieth century saw a shift away from the strict prohibition against any premarital sexual activity. Yet if someone became pregnant, it was expected in the 1950s, especially among the white population, that the couple would marry (Cutright, 1972). Parents and educators cautioned children against becoming sexually involved or marrying too early, but their advice was frequently ignored as adolescent childbearing reached its peak of 97.3 births per 1000 women ages 15–19 in 1957 (Vinovskis, 1981a).

Although early childbearing was rising, it was not tolerated in most public schools. Pregnant girls, even those who were married, were usually forced to drop out of school and young mothers were discouraged from re-entering their regular high school classes (Stine, 1964). Among those pregnant girls who did not marry, many sought illegal abortions despite the considerable legal and health risks involved (Polgar & Fried, 1976). Those unmarried adolescents who decided to have their babies were often quietly sent to a maternity home in another community and were then encouraged to place the child up for adoption (Sedlack, 1980). Thus, teenage childbearing in the 1950s was very common but public attitudes toward the young mother and her child, especially if she was not married, were negative. Although some federal, state, and local welfare support was available to these young mothers, the stigma attached to the receipt of this assistance was considerable and the amount of funds furnished was minimal.

During the 1960s and early 1970s, some important changes were underway that led to the reconsideration of the treatment accorded to pregnant adolescents. Premarital sexual activity was becoming more common and accepted as approximately one out of four unmarried teenage girls ages 15–19 had experienced intercourse in 1971 (and almost half of those ages 18 or 19) (Zelnik & Kantner, 1977). Although the rate of teenage childbearing was diminishing, the total number of children born to adolescents rose as well as the likelihood of having an abortion—especially after the Supreme Courts liberalization of abortion laws in 1973 (Moore & Burt, 1982).

Even more disturbing, for many Americans, was the alarming rise in out-of-wedlock births among teenagers. Whereas fathers in the 1950s typically married the pregnant adolescent, about a third of the children born to teenagers in the early 1970s were out-of-wedlock (Moore & Burt, 1982). Americans were not particularly concerned about the lack of paternal care for these children, but they were upset by the increased welfare costs as the amount and types of public assistance available increased during these years (Moore, 1978).

While many people were worried about the "epidemic" of adolescent pregnancy and looked for ways of curtailing it, a few individuals also looked for ways of helping the young mother and her child (Vinovskis, 1981a). Reflecting the growing stress placed upon high school graduation in the 1960s as well as the expectation that many of these young mothers would eventually enter the labor force, efforts were made in demonstration sites such as the Webster School in Washington D.C. in the 1960s and early 1970s to help adolescent mothers to continue their education. In addition, these programs emphasized the need for comprehensive medical and social services for the adolescent's child in order to ensure its healthy development and to minimize any of the problems associated with births to teenagers (Klerman, 1981). Although the role of the father was mentioned from time to time by these concerned citizens, the mother and the child received the primary if not exclusive attention.

POLICY MAKERS AND THE ROLE OF THE FATHER

So far we have considered the changing role of the father in the care and support of young children from the seventeenth to the twentieth centuries. Going from a position of centrality in the socialization of the children in colonial America, the father by the 1970s was seen as increasingly peripheral either as a source of paternal interaction with the child or even as the main source of economic support. In order to find out whether policy makers also saw the father as less important, we review the efforts to create a federal program of comprehensive care for adolescent mothers and their children in 1975, 1978, and 1981 and see what role, if any, was envisioned for the young father.

School-Age Mother and Child Health Act, 1975

During the late 1960s and early 1970s a small group of individuals concerned about the plight of school-age mothers sought to alleviate their difficulties by persuading the federal, state, and local authorities to develop and fund comprehensive care services for adolescent mothers and their children. It soon became obvious to these advocates that without substantial federal involvement and aid it would be impossible to help but a small handful of these adolescents. Therefore, the National Alliance Concerned with School-Age Parents (NACSAP), with the indispensable help of Eunice Shriver of the Joseph P. Kennedy Jr. Foundation, persuaded Senator Edward Kennedy (D-MA), chairman of the Subcommittee on Health of the Senate Committee on Labor and Public Welfare, to introduce a "National School-Age Mother and Child Health Act" (U.S. Congress, Senate, Committee on Labor and Public Welfare, 1975). Although there was little chance that this legislation would pass in the closing days of that session, the extensive hearings on the bill on November 4, 1975 were seen by its supporters as an opportunity to publicize the needs of school-age mothers and their children as well as to lay the foundation for future legislation in this area.

Throughout the nearly 900 pages of testimony at the hearings as well as in the bill itself, there are only a few scattered references to the role of the fathers in the support and care of the young children (U.S. Congress, Senate, Committee on Labor and Public Welfare, 1975). The legislation mentions the need to help adolescent parents, yet the details of the proposed bill reveal that the focus is almost exclusively on the needs of the adolescent mother and her child. Among the 11 comprehensive services to be provided under this legislation is counseling for both the mother and the father of the child. But for other services such as educational or vocational training provided for the adolescent parent, only the school-age mother is eligible for assistance.

The neglect of the father's role in the proposed Kennedy bill is not surprising because its proponents usually assumed that the recipient of this assistance would be an unmarried pregnant adolescent. The draft Kennedy bill did state that adolescents would be eligible for these services regardless of their marital status, but most witnesses assumed that unmarried adolescents were the target population and that there was little need or opportunity to involve the father.

Dale Sopper, Acting Deputy Assistant Secretary for Legislation (Health), Department of Health, Education, and Welfare (DHEW), testified on behalf of the Ford Administration against the proposed legislation as being unnecessary and duplicative of existing federal progress (U.S. Congress, Senate, Committee on Labor and Public Welfare, 1975, p. 23). In his testimony as well as that of other Administration officials, the emphasis was on the services for adolescent mothers and their children with almost no apparent awareness of the existence or importance of the father.

Despite the growing problem of out-of-wedlock adolescent births that concerned many Americans, most of the supporters of this legislation did not argue that fathers should be encouraged to marry the pregnant adolescents or that efforts should be made to support teenage marriages. Instead, most witnesses as well as several Senators denounced the punitive attitude and behavior toward unmarried pregnant adolescents by Americans and the public schools and looked for ways of overcoming this handicap, because the stigma attached to adolescent out-of-wedlock pregnancies and births was seen as one of the major reasons for the increasing number of abortions as well as for the high rate of school dropout among these girls.

Although most witnesses simply ignored the role of the father in the support or care of the child, some even questioned the advisability of involving fathers at all. James Jeckel, Associate Professor of Public Health at Yale University (U.S. Congress, Senate, Committee on Labor and Public Welfare, 1975), testified that:

> Many people talk about the importance of including the fathers in the programs. Whereas I do not think they should be categorically excluded from programs (and

the bill does not), we have some data (as yet unpublished) that shows relatively few of these young mothers eventually marry the putative fathers, and that those adolescents who marry early tend to have more children than those who do not, and their marriages are unstable. It is my judgment that we are not yet ready to encourage the inclusion of fathers in most phases of specific programs for the mothers. (p. 380)

The only real dissent from the position of virtually ignoring the involvement of fathers came in written testimony submitted to the Senate by the Illinois Association for Comprehensive Services to School Age Parents Inc. Most of their 12 pages of testimony is focused on documenting the extent and nature of adolescent pregnancy and childbearing in Illinois communities, but in their section of recommendations they urged the amending of the legislation in order to provide all the relevant comprehensive care services for fathers as well as mothers. As they put it (U.S. Congress, Senate, Committee on Labor and Public Welfare, 1975):

We urge that the scope of the Bill be expanded to include the school-age father. He is often forgotten as a person with needs, and is often sought out for punitive action. Observations of professionals and research has pointed out that he can be a source of support to the mother and child and often truly interested in the fate of the offspring. Curtailment of services will more likely discourage him from active involvement and interest in the welfare of the mother and child. (p. 595)

This effort to recognize the special needs and contributions of the school-age father was ignored and forgotten. The "School-Age Mother and Child Health Act of 1975" itself was not enacted, but it did provide the intellectual and political context for subsequent debates over these same issues in 1978.

Adolescent Health Services, and Pregnancy Prevention Care Act of 1978

The creation of federal programs for the care of pregnant adolescents and young mothers received much more attention in 1978 when the Carter Administration made the issue of teenage pregnancy and childbearing one of its highest domestic priorities for FY1979 by proposing an additional $148 million to deal with these problems—including the new $60 million "Adolescent Health, Services, and Pregnancy Prevention Act of 1978." The proposed legislation was an outgrowth of the earlier unsuccessful "School-Age Mother and Child Health Act" as well as of the recommendations from the Administration's so-called "Alternatives to Abortion" interagency task force (Vinovskis, 1981a).

The discussions about this legislation in the U.S. Congress were more extensive than those 3 years earlier as four different committees debated the Administration's proposal. The legislative leadership for the "Adolescent Health, Services, and Pregnancy Prevention Act" again came from Senator Edward

Kennedy (D-MA), still Chairman of the U.S. Senate Subcommittee on Health of the Committee on Labor and Public Welfare, who cochaired two days of detailed hearings on the bill before the full Committee (U.S. Congress, Senate, Committee on Human Resources, 1978). In the House the legislation was assigned jointly to the Subcommittee on Health and the Environment of the Interstate and Foreign Commerce Committee and the Select Committee on Education of the Committee on Education and Labor, but only brief hearings were held by each of these subcommittees because neither group was particularly enthusiastic or supportive of this legislation (U.S. Congress, House, Committee on Human Resources, 1978; U.S. Congress, House, Committee on Education and Labor, 1978). The most extensive analysis of the entire problem of adolescent pregnancy was conducted by the recently created U.S. House Select Committee on Population, which only could examine the problem but could not enact legislation because it did not have any legislative jurisdiction (U.S. Congress, House, Select Committee on Population, 1978a).

During most of the testimony on this legislation, it became apparent that the bill was intended almost exclusively for adolescent girls and their children. Although there were some indications that a comprehensive service such as counseling might be available for fathers as well as mothers, the testimony of Joseph Califano, Secretary of DHEW, as well as those of other members of the Administration made it clear that the primary focus was on the adolescent girl and her child. Indeed, most witnesses ignored almost entirely the existence or the involvement of the father (U.S. Congress, Senate, Committee on Human Resources, 1978).

Because the Administration legislation included both prevention and care services, there were some witnesses who stressed the need for male involvement in the prevention of unintended adolescent pregnancies. The U.S. House Select Committee on Population, which emphasized prevention, even chastized the Administration for not involving more males in family planning clinics. Yet when that Select Committee Report discussed comprehensive care services for pregnant teens or young mothers and their children, it did not acknowledge or mention the role of the father (U.S. Congress, House, Select Committee on Population, 1978b).

Although only a few individuals discussed the need for involving fathers in the support or care of the adolescent mother and child, several of the existing service program descriptions submitted did mention that fathers could receive counseling services. Furthermore, a dramatic illustration of the problems of the adolescent father was provided by testimony before the Senate Subcommittee on Health (U.S. Congress, Senate, Committee on Human Resources, 1978) by a young man about his reactions and experiences after discovering that his girlfriend was pregnant:

> Well, I imagine my original reaction was one of fear—I was scared, along with Joanne. We both had tremendous fears of what the future would bring for us. We

knew that our lives would be changed dramatically within the next couple months, the rest of our lives.

I was greatly worried about our making it as a family; would we be able to possibly make a go of it. At the time, I was working on a part-time basis and I knew there was no way I could finance a family of three. So, luckily, we got a lot of support from our parents and we were able to move in with them until I could graduate from school. At that time, I got a job as an apprentice and from there, I completed the apprenticeship program.

Also emotionally, it is very difficult to adjust. As Joanne was saying, you are completely isolated. I had no activities of my own. I went to school and immediately after classes I went to work. I worked until late at night, and then I would come home and it was time for homework. Consequently, you just have no other time for anything else. It is very difficult. (p. 128)

This moving testimony demonstrated the problems faced by young fathers and evoked considerable sympathy from the few Senators present at the hearing. But the larger issue of the role of the father for the development of the young child was not pursued. Indeed, although several experts later testified about the developmental problems facing children of adolescent parents, they did not acknowledge the father's role in raising a young child.

Most references to fathers in the hearings in 1975 and 1978 were favorable and frequently alluded to the stresses experienced by them as result of the unintended pregnancy. But some witnesses, especially those before the House Select Committee on Population, implicitly if not explicitly, even questioned the importance of the involvement of the father—especially if it meant a "shotgun" marriage. Wendy Baldwin, from the Center for Population Research of NICHD (U.S. Congress, House, Select Committee on Population, 1978b), argued that society should not necessarily encourage pregnant teenagers to marry:

Adolescents who marry may not be better off and, in some ways, worse off than their peers who don't marry. The rates of marital disruption among young teenagers are high and there appears to be a greater likelihood of an earlier second pregnancy among those who marry. It is not clear that marriage is really a solution especially for the very young teenager. (p. 10)

Rather than marrying the father, many of the social scientists recommended that the pregnant adolescent girl stay with her parents and continue going to school. As Harriet Presser, a sociologist from the University of Maryland (U.S. Congress, House, Select Committee on Population, 1978a), observed:

I might add, in reference to the earlier discussion, that one of the reasons that girls do not marry the father of their child, based on my study, is that the girl's parents can often be more supportive than the father in enabling them to return to school. If the young woman is living with her family, her mother might help take care of her child while she returns to school. If, instead, she leaves the household and gets married, the father of the child is not likely to do this. She may, therefore, trade off marriage for going back to school. (p. 27)

The question of whether or not pregnant teenagers should be encouraged to marry is a very important one that did not receive adequate discussion and consideration at these hearings. Even if the pregnant teenager is more apt to remain in school if she does not marry, what are the costs of this strategy to her parents or the public? What are the disadvantages to the child of being raised out-of-wedlock? On the other hand, if she does marry, what are the effects of this not only upon her own educational development, but that of her husband as well? And are any of the advantages of paternal involvement for the development of the young child lost several years later if the couple divorces?

If several of the social scientists testifying in the House were convinced that pregnant adolescents, especially young ones, should not necessarily be encouraged to marry, Senator S. I. Hayakawa (R-CA) disagreed in the other chamber. He angrily denounced young fathers for their lack of involvement and responsibility (U.S. Congress, Senate, Committee on Human Resources, 1978):

Now, the one thing that I miss in all of this legislation, all the concern, I miss concern with the fathers of these children. They do not seem to have any responsibility in any of this, and what is to prevent, therefore, these young men or these boys from going on to produce, one after the other, out-of-wedlock babies, while cheerfully continuing with their studies, finishing high school, finishing college, leaving behind a whole trail of unmarried mothers and fatherless children to be taken care of by HEW and local agencies.

Is there within this program, or within all the people who are thinking about it, any concern with making the young men involved face some of the responsibilities that they are placing upon society? I see none. I see evidence, on the other hand, of a male-dominated society that wants to let the boys off free, wherever possible, while we cluck, cluck, cluck, over the girls. And, Mr. Chairman, I want to protest this absence of concern with the male parties to this social problem. (p. 90)

Senator Edward Kennedy angerly responded not by denying Hayakawa's assertions, but by reminding him that a similar protest against the lack of male responsibility could be made in regard to federal support of family planning programs or abortions. As Kennedy put it (U.S. Congress, Senate, Committee on Human Resources, 1978): "I would have been interested in my good friend and colleague from California raising those same issues on that issue (family planning), rather than targeting out this issue here, trying to deal with a particular problem" (p. 91).

Senator Kennedy then went on to say that "as I understand a very significant part of the parenting aspects of this bill that are included in there, it would also try to bring that special responsibility to young men, as well" (p. 91). Although Secretary Califano had up to then almost totally ignored the role of fathers in either the legislation or his own testimony, he quickly concurred with Senator Kennedy's observation.

Perhaps this sharp exchange between Senators Hayakawa and Kennedy helps to explain why DHEW, which had paid scant attention to the role of fathers, suddenly seemed to reverse itself in subsequent answers to written questions from the House Subcommittee on Health and the Environment. Replying to the question of ''why have the needs and responsbilities of the young adolescent male been generally ignored by the Administration's program,'' the Department responded at considerable length (U.S. Congress, House, Committee on Interstate and Foreign Commerce,1978):

> Although a few programs have begun to include some type of male strategy, there is not wide agreement on how teenage males should be approached. Current efforts in family planning programs have not been particularly successful, although there is male involvement in some comprehensive programs . . .
>
> Comprehensive Adolescent Pregnancy Programs involve males in the following kinds of activities:
>
> 1. Counseling sessions about pregnancy prevention and sexual responsibility. These sessions are held with males alone, and also with males and females together.
> 2. Group ''rap'' sessions with both fathers and non-fathers regarding pregnancy prevention.
> 3. Social workers assist the males in continuing with their education, enrolling in vocational education and manpower training programs, finding and holding jobs, budgeting their personal funds, etc.
> 4. Prospective fathers participate in the following kinds of activities:
>   a) The mother's preparation for childbirth
>   b) His presence in the delivery room itself
>   c) Parenting instruction
>   d) Relationship between adolescent mother and father
>   e) Family problems that may result from pregnancy
>   f) Legal concerns of the male
>   g) Financial responsibilities to the child.
>
> Under our new legislation, we will be asking each program to describe how they propose to deal with adolescent males. The legislation has been drafted with a broad mandate for innovative program development to allow communities to experiment and develop approaches to adolescent males which best work in their communities. From these experiences as well as what we learn from the limited number of programs already involved in this area, we will work to stimulate interest in expansion of this area and to share with communities the results of various program approaches. (p. 37)

Thus, the Carter Administration, which had not paid much attention to the role of the father in dealing with adolescent pregnancy, now endorsed a more comprehensive and ambitious approach for helping them—but the policy makers did not, and could not, escape from the original dilemma posed by different perspectives on the father at the hearings. Whereas almost all the individuals who mentioned the young father sought ways of helping him to cope with his own difficulties or of minimizing the extent of his involvement by discouraging marriage, a few others such as Senator Hayawaka wanted fathers to assume a larger moral and financial responsibility for their out-of-wedlock births and advocated more punitive measures to increase paternal involvement. Almost no one at the Senate and House hearings argued that increased paternal involvement should be encouraged because it might enhance the early development of the child

The Adolescent Family Life Program of 1981

Although the legislation establishing the Office of Adolescent Pregnancy Programs (OAPP) was not signed by President Carter until November 9, 1978, Secretary Joseph Califano announced the appointment of Dr. Lulu Mae Nix, the Director of the Delaware Adolescent Program, to manage the teenage pregnancy initiative within the Department of Health and Human Services (DHHS) on April 13, 1978—the same day that he had announced the transmission of the "Adolescent Health, Services, and Pregnancy Prevention Care Act of 1978" to the Congress. When OAPP was formally established, Dr. Nix became its first director.

At first glance, it seemed that the Office of Adolescent Pregnancy Programs (OAPP) was in an excellent position to carry out its mandate—including paying attention to the needs of adolescent males and young fathers. The legislation in November had just authorized $50 million for FY1979 and the Carter Administration committed itself to staffing OAPP adequately even in the event of a job freeze because this initiative was regarded as one of the highest priorities in the Department. Yet a series of unexpected events occurred that severely hampered the functioning of OAPP.

Because the legislation was not enacted until the closing days of the 95th Congress, it was not part of the regular FY1979 appropriations process. Instead, the Carter Administration included OAPP in the supplemental budget request, but only at a level of $7.5 million instead of the $50 million authorized by the Congress. The situation for OAPP became even more cirtical when Congress did not approve the supplemental budget until July 1979 and then provided only $1 million. In addition, despite the assurances that a sizable staff would be provided for this undertaking, the Administration, partly reacting to the greatly reduced budget for OAPP, allocated less than one-fourth of the promised positions. Whereas in subsequent years the amount designated for OAPP increased to $7.5 million for FY1980 and $10.0 million for FY1981, the program never achieved the size and scope intended for it by the original legislation (Vinovskis, 1981a).

In FY1979 only 4 comprehensive care projects were funded and another 23 new grants were added in FY1980. Partly as the result of the reduced funding and partly as a reflection of the orientation of the Director toward care programs for pregnant teens or young parents, the prevention aspects of the original legislation were ignored by OAPP during Nix's tenure in office. Because male involvement is usually emphasized more in pregnancy prevention than in pregnancy care programs, the neglect of this area undoubtedly minimized the number of young teenage boys reached by the OAPP funded programs.

In describing the goals of OAPP to the public and potential grantees, the initial emphasis was clearly on the needs of the female adolescent and the child. Yet the young father was not categorically excluded. Indeed, when Dr. Nix requested that grant applications provide a step-by-step explanation of how services will be delivered, she stated that "I would like to pick up an application and see clearly how each adolescent, infant, father, and family will be processed through that program." In addition, when she called for community involvement (Office of Adolescent Pregnancy Programs, 1980), she urged the applicants to "Remember, this is a man's issue, too, and it crosses all economic lines. Include men as well as women on your boards and committees."

Although males and young fathers were not excluded from the original OAPP plans for programs, their participation was not emphasized and usually it consisted only of the provision of counseling for the teenage fathers as part of the general services for any member of the extended family. A few programs under this Title VI legislation did try to make some special efforts to involve males, but most of these operations assisted males only if they had arrived on their own initiative. As a result, the Urban Institute evaluation of OAPP programs (Burt, Kimmich, Goldmuntz, & Sonenstein, 1984) found that only about 10% of the clients were males because, as they put it, "the primary focus has been on mothers and mothers-to-be" (p. 25). Because the numbers of males served were so low and their involvement was viewed as peripheral by the programs, the Urban Institute evaluation decided not to even analyze the effects of their participation under the Title VI legislation.

The election of Ronald Reagan resulted in major changes in OAPP. In March 1981 Marjory Mecklenburg replaced Lulu Mae Nix as the Director of OAPP and the new Administration proposed and succeeded in having the Title VI program placed into a block grant. At the same time, Senators Jeremiah Denton (R-AL) and Orrin G. Hatch (R-UT) introduced the Adolescent Family Life bill as Title XX of the Public Health Service Act of 1981 (U.S. Congress, Senate, Committee on Labor and Human Resources, 1981b). Although many of the goals and the intended scope of the Adolescent Family Life bill were different from those of its predecessor, there was also considerable continuity—in large part as the result of the need to obtain the cooperation and active support from Senator Edward Kennedy (D-MA), who continued to insist on maintaining the comprehensive care portions of the earlier legislation without any major changes.

The Title XX Adolescent Family Life legislation was intended as a small federal program to develop model demonstration projects and to encourage basic research. At least two-thirds of the funds were to be expended for service providers who were developing model care programs for pregnant adolescents and young mothers or for prevention projects designed to discourage early sexual activity among teens. Up to one-third of the funds could be used for primary research on the problems associated with adolescent sexuality, pregnancy, and early childbearing.

Unlike the situation in 1978, there was very little opportunity for supporters or opponents of the legislation to discuss its merits. The House did not hold hearings on the proposed legislation and the sessions devoted to the problems of adolescent pregnancy in the Senate focused largely on issues involving the provision of family planning services to teenagers (U.S. Congress, Senate, Committee on Labor and Human Resources, 1981a). As a result, there was very little mention or discussion of the role of adolescent males in the hearings on the Adolescent Family Life legislation. Similarly, although the Title XX legislation allows for the inclusion of males in the prevention or care projects, it did not emphasize their participation or detail the manner in which it should be enhanced. Issues such as family involvement and adoption, for example, received much more attention in the new legislation than the topic of fathers.

If the legislative process in 1981 did not pay much attention to the role of males and young fathers, some of the programs funded by OAPP, especially those emphasizing prevention, tried to involve them (U.S. Congress, House, Committee on Energy and Commerce, 1984). Terrence D. Olsen, for example, is developing an Alternative National Curriculum that tries to prevent early sexual activity and is now being tested on male and female students at selected public schools in Utah, California, and New Mexico. The Youth Health Services of Elkins, West Virginia also provides services such as vocational education to young fathers. The work of Arthur Elster of the University of Utah College of Medicine with adolescent fathers in a comprehensive teenage pregnancy program is particularly innovative and interesting. Thus, whereas most OAPP grantees still focus mainly on the needs of the adolescent girls and their children, a few are trying to develop and evaluate the provision of special services for young males and teenage fathers.

The interest of OAPP in fathers is also reflected in its research agenda. On May 10, 1984, OAPP requested proposals on "The Characteristics and Family Involvement of Fathers of Adolescent Premaritally Conceived Births." Because the details of the announcement are an indication of the interests of OAPP in fathers, the six items listed in that request (U.S. Federal Register, 1984) are reproduced below:

1. What are the demographic, social, ethnic, and economic characteristics of the fathers of babies born to single teenage women? To what extent are they different than fathers of babies born to married teenagers?

2. In what ways and to what extent are the fathers of out-of-wedlock teenage births involved in the lives of the mothers and children, socially and financially? Is their involvement different from that of fathers of babies born to married teenagers?

3. What are the social, economic, health, and developmental consequences of fathers' involvement in the lives of their out-of-wedlock children? Are those consequences different from the consequences of involvement with fathers of babies born to married teenagers?

4. Are the problems of teenage fathers of children born to single adolescent mothers very different from those of older fathers of adolescent mothers?

5. What can be done to alleviate some of the difficulties facing fathers of children born to adolescent women while at the same time increasing their involvement with and responsibility for the young mother and child?

6. What are the advantages and disadvantages of fathers not marrying the pregnant adolescent from the point of view of the young mother, the child, the father, and society as a whole? (19897)

The Reagan Administration's interest in fathers is much more extensive and broader than its predecessor's. Significantly, OAPP's focus is not only on the interaction of the father with the child or on his own problems and needs, but also on the father's economic responsibility to the mother and child. As OAPP's request for research put it (U.S. Federal Register, 1984):

> Whether or not fathers are socially involved, they may be economically involved with the unwed mother and her child. It is often assumed that the fathers of out-of-wedlock adolescent births are adolescents themselves, and therefore are unable to contribute financially to the support of the unwed mother and child. But the fathers tend to be several years older than the mothers, old enough for many of them to have completed high school and found jobs. Many are capable, therefore, of contributing financially at the time of the pregnancy and birth, many become able to do so at some time during the infancy of the child. Furthermore, if the father cannot contribute, his family (the paternal grandparents of the out-of-wedlock birth) may be able to do so. Of course, financial support from any paternal source at any time may have an important impact on the economic circumstances of the unwed mother and her family; also, it might reduce the burden of public welfare. (19896)

Whereas many practitioners in the field of adolescent pregnancy concentrate only on the problems or needs of the teenage father, the recent OAPP initiative is equally interested in the older males involved with adolescent girls—especially because the latter may be in a much better position to contribute to the support of the young mother and child. The Reagan Administration also does not accept the notion, advanced by several scholars at the hearings on adolescent pregnancy, that teenage marriages are necessarily disadvantageous for the pregnant adolescent. Indeed, one of the first research contracts funded by OAPP under the new

Title XX legislation was to the Human Affairs Research Centers of the Battelle Memorial Institute to analyze the effect that marriage has on the pregnant adolescents, their children, partners, and families.

Thus, although the role of fathers in adolescent pregnancy has not been a primary consideration among most congressmen and witnesses in 1975, 1978, or 1981 or among most researchers and practitioners in this field, the involvement of fathers is being highlighted by the Office of Adolescent Pregnancy Programs under Marjory Mecklenburg. Whereas the importance of the father in the development of the child as well as his own problems and needs are acknowledged, much of the recent thrust of the federal effort reflects the attempt to reduce out-of-wedlock births and to increase the father's economic contributions to the mother and child. Though it is too early to judge the impact of this new orientation, especially because the results from these demonstration programs and research initiatives are not available at this time, it is likely that much more attention will be paid to the role of the father in teenage pregnancies in the future.

CONCLUSION

In the past, the role of the father was central to the well-being of the family and the socialization of its members. During the colonial period, the father was expected not only to provide for the child'e economic needs, but also for its spiritual education. Puritans regarded the mother as an essential assistant to the father in caring for the child but placed the primary responsibility for support and education upon the father. No distinctions were made in the assignment of these tasks between adolescent and adult fathers. If the father failed to live up to his obligations to his wife and children, the state was quite willing to intervene in the affairs of that family to ensure that the welfare of society as a whole would not be endangered.

Today, after a series of historical developments that have tended to minimize the father's role in the care and support of his children, the mother is now seen as "naturally" suited for raising the children—although recently there are some indications that the importance of the father in the upbring of the children is being rediscovered. Therefore, it is not altogether very surprising that when policy makers confronted the issue of adolescent childbearing in the 1970s there was little thought or attention given to the responsibilities or needs of the father—especially if he was also a teenager. Indeed, in the attempts to help the young mother and her child, little effort was made to involve the father and many even suggested that encouraging these adolescents to marry was counterproductive.

The legislators who initially developed federal programs for assisting pregnant adolescents or young mothers and their children were not particularly concerned about forcing the putative fathers to support their offspring, but others in the Congress were calling for more effective and coercive child-support programs (Chambers, 1979). Although there was little overlap between the efforts to help pregnant teens and to make fathers support their children during the Carter Administration, there are some preliminary indications that this may be changing under the Reagan Administration as the Office of Adolescent Programs is exploring ways of involving fathers in the care and support of their children. Whether that involvement will consist mainly of forcing the fathers of the children of adolescent mothers to contribute financial support or of encouraging them to help in the rearing of their offspring is not clear at this time. Nor are there any clear indications of how the Adolescent Family Life programs would have to be altered to take into consideration both the interests of the Reagan Administration in having fathers involved in the upbringing of their children and in defraying the societal costs associated with early childbearing. In any case, the role of the father in the care and support of the children of adolescent mothers is likely to re-emerge in the 1980s and contribute to the more general re-examination of the rights and responsibilities of fathers in our society today.

REFERENCES

Auwers, L. (1980). Reading the marks of the past: Exploring female literacy in colonial Windsor, Connecticut. *Historical Methods, 4,* 204–214.

Axtell, J. (1974). *The school upon a hill: Education and society in colonial New England.* New Haven, CT: Yale University Press.

Brenzel, B. (1975). Lancaster Industrial School for Girls: A social protrait of a nineteenth-century reform school for girls. *Feminist Studies, 3,* 40–53.

Burt, M. R., Kimmich, M. H., Goldmuntz, J., & Sonenstein, F. L. (1984). *Helping pregnant adolescents: Outcomes and costs of service delivery.* Final report on the evaluation of adolescent pregnancy programs. Urban Institute.

Cath, S. H., Gurwitt, A. R., & Ross, J. M. (1982). *Father and child: Developmental and clinical perspectives.* Boston: Little Brown.

Chambers, D. L. (1979). *Making fathers pay: The enforcement of child support.* Chicago: University of Chicago Press.

Clarke, E. H. (1873). *Sex education: or, a fair chance for the girls.* Boston: J. R. Osgood.

Cott, N. F. (1977). *The bonds of womanhood: "Woman's sphere" in New England, 1780–1835.* New Haven, CT: Yale University Press.

Cutright, P. (1972). The teenage sexual revolution and the myth of an abstinent past. *Family Planning Perspectives, 4,* 24–31.

Degler, C. N. (1980). *At odds: Women and the family in America from the revolution to the present.* New York: Oxford University Press.

Demos, J. (1982). The changing faces of fatherhood: A new exploration in American family history. In S. H. Cath, A. R. Gurwitt, & J. M. Ross (Eds.), *Father and child: Developmental and clinical perspectives* (pp. 425–445). Boston: Little Brown.

Demos, J., & Demos, V. (1969). Adolescence in historical perspective. *Journal of Marriage and the Family, 31,* 632–638.

Greven, P. J., Jr. (1970). *Four generations: Population, land, and family in colonial Andover, Massachusetts.* Ithaca, NY: Cornell University Press.

Griswold, R. L. (1982). *Family and divorce in California, 1850–1890: Victorian illusions and everyday realities*. Albany, NY: State University of New York.

Grossberg, M. (1983). Who gets the child? Custody, guardianship, and the rise of a judicial patriarchy in nineteenth-century America. *Feminist Studies, 9*, 235–260.

Hall, D. D., Ed. (1968). *The Antinomian Controversy, 1636–1638: A documentary history*. Middletown, CT: Wesleyan University Press.

Hiner, N. R. (1975). Adolescence in eighteenth-century America. *History of Childhood Quarterly, 3*, 253–280.

Jones, D. L. (1981). *Village and seaport: Migration and society in eighteenth-century Massachusetts*. Hanover, NH: New England Press.

Kerber, L. (1980). *Women of the republic: Intellect and ideology in revolutionary America*. Chapel Hill: University of North Carolina Press.

Kett, J. F. (1977). *Rites of passage: Adolescence in America, 1790 to the present*. New York: Basic Books.

Klerman, L. V. (1981). Programs for pregnant adolescents and young parents: Their development and assessment. In K. G. Scott, T. Field, & E. Robertson (Eds.), *Teenage parents and their offspring* (pp. 227–248). New York: Grune & Stratton.

Kuhn, A. L. (1947). *The mother's role in childhood education*. New Haven, CT: Yale University Press.

Lamb, M. E., Ed. (1981). *The role of the father in child development* (2nd ed). New York: Wiley.

Lamb, M. E., & Sagi, A., Eds. (1983). *Fatherhood and family policy*. Hillsdale, NJ: Lawrence Erlbaum Associates.

Lockridge, K. A. (1974). *Literacy in colonial New England: An enquiry into the social context of literacy in the early modern west*. New York: Norton.

Malmsheimer, L. M. (1973). *New England funeral sermons and changing attitudes towards women, 1672–1792*. Unpublished doctoral thesis, University of Minnesota.

May, E. T. (1980). *Great expectations: Marriage and divorce in post-Victorian America*. Chicago: University of Chicago Press.

May, D., & Vinovskis, M. A. (1976). A ray of millenial light: Early education and social reform in the infant school movement in Massachusetts, 1826–1840. In T. K. Hareven (Ed.), *Family and kin in American urban communities, 1800–1940* (pp. 62–99). New York: Watts.

Mohr, J. C. (1978). *Abortion in America: The origins and evolution of national policy*. New York: Oxford University Press.

Moore, K. A. (1978). Teenage childbirth and welfare dependency. *Family Planning Perspectives, 10*, 233–235.

Moore, K. A., & Burt, M. R. (1982). *Private crisis, public cost: Policy perspectives on teenage childbearing*. Washington, DC: Urban Institute Press.

Moran, G. F. (1980). Sisters in Christ: Women and the church in seventeenth-century New England. In J. W. James (Ed.), *Women in American religion*. Philadelphia: University of Pennsylvania Press.

Moran, G. F., & Vinovskis, M. A. (1982). The Puritan family and religion: A critical reappraisal. *William & Mary Quarterly* (3rd Series), *39*, 29–63.

Moran, G. F., & Vinovskis, M. A. (Forthcoming). The great care of Godly parents: Early childhood in Puritan New England. In J. Hagen & A. Smuts (Eds.), *Research in child development in the past*.

Norton, M. B. (1980). *Liberty's daughters: The revolutionary experience of American women, 1750–1800*. Boston: Little Brown.

Norton, S. L. (1981). *Age at marriage and marital migration in three Massachusetts towns, 1600–1850*. Unpublished doctoral thesis, University of Michigan.

Office of Adolescent Pregnancy Programs, Department of Health and Human Services. (1980). *Information Bulletin*.

Polgar, S., & Fried, E. (1976). The bad old days: Clandestine abortions among the poor in New York City before liberalization of the abortion law. *Family Planning Perspectives, 8,* 125–127.

Potter, J. (1984). Demographic development and family structure. In J. P. Greene & J. R. Pole (Eds.), *Colonial British America: Essays in the new history of the early modern era* (pp. 123–156). Baltimore: Johns Hopkins Press.

Ryan, M. P. (1981). *Cradle of the middle class: The family in Oneida County, New York, 1790–1865.* New York: Cambridge University Press.

Rothman, D. J. (1971). *The discovery of the asylum: Social order and disorder in the New Republic.* Boston: Little Brown.

Rothman, E. K. (1984). *Hands and hearts: A history of courtship in America.* New York: Basic Books.

Schlossman, S., & Wallach, S. (1980). The crime of precocious sexuality: Female juvenile delinquency in the progressive era. *Harvard Educational Review, 48,* 65–94.

Sedlack, M. W. (1980). *The education of "Girls with Special Needs," 1865–1972.* Unpublished paper presented at Theacher's College Conference on History of Urban Education.

Shorter, E. (1975). *The making of the modern family.* New York: Basic Books.

Smith, D. S., & Hindus, M. S. (1975). Premarital pregnancy in America, 1640–1971: An overview and interpretation. *Journal of Interdisciplinary History, 5,* 537–570.

Smith-Rosenberg, C. (1971). Beauty, the beast, and the militant woman: A case study in sex roles and social stress in Jacksonian America. *American Quarterly, 23,* 562–584.

Stine, O. C. (1964). School leaving due to pregnancy in an urban adolescent population. *American Journal of Public Health, 54,* 1–6.

Stone, L. (1977). *The family, sex, and marriage in England, 1500–1800.* New York: Harper & Row.

Sweet, L. I. (1983). *The minister's wife: Her role in nineteenth-century American Evangelicalism.* Philadelphia: Temple University Press.

Tate, T. W., & Ammerman, D. L., Eds. (1979). *The Cheasapeake in the seventeenth century: Essasy on Anglo–American society and politics.* New York: Norton.

Ulrich, L. T. (1982). *Good wives: Image and reality in the lives of women in Northern New England, 1650–1750.* New York: Knopf.

U.S. Congress, House, Committee on Education and Labor. (1978). *Hearings, Adolescent Health, Services, and Pregnancy Care Act of 1978* (95th Cong., 2d Sess.).

U.S. Congress, House, Committee on Energy and Commerce. (1984). *Hearings, Adolescent Family Life Act Reauthorization* (98th Cong., 2d Sess.).

U.S. Congress, House, Committee on Interstate and Foreign Commerce. (1978). *Hearings, Adolescent Health, Services, and Pregnancy Prevention and Care Act of 1978* (95th Cong., 2d Sess.).

U.S. Congress, House, Select Committee on Population. (1978a). *Hearings, Fertility and Contraception in America* (II, 95th Cong., 2d Sess.).

U.S. Congress, House, Select Committee on Population. (1978b). *Fertility and Contraception in the United States* (95th Cong., 2d Sess., Serial B).

U.S. Congress, Senate, Committee on Human Resources. (1978). *Hearings, Adolescent Health, Services, and Pregnancy Prevention and Care Act of 1978* (95th Cong., 2d Sess.).

U.S. Congress, Senate, C ommittee on Labor and Human Resources. (1981a). *Hearings, Oversight on Family Planning Programs under Title X of the Public Health Service Act of 1981* (97th Cong., 1st Sess.).

U.S. Congress, Senate, Committee on Labor and Human Resources. (1981b). *Report on Adolescent Family Life Act of 1981* (97th Cong., 1st Sess.).

U.S. Congress, Senate, Committee on Labor and Public Welfare. (1975). *Hearings, School-Age Mother and Child Health Act of 1975* (94th Cong., 1st Sess.).

U.S. Federal Register. (May 10, 1984). *Announcement of Availability of Grants for Research on Adolescent Family Life, 49,* 19895–19898.

Vinovskis, M. A. (1983). American families in the past. In J. B. Gardner & G. R. Adams (Eds.), *Ordinary people and everyday life: Perspectives on the new social history* (pp. 115–137). Nashville, TE: American Association for State and Local History.

Vinovskis, M. A. (1981a). An "Epidemic" of adolescent pregnancy? Some historical considerations. *Journal of Family History, 6,* 205–230.

Vinovskis, M. A. (1981b). *Fertility in Massachusetts from the Revolution to the Civil War.* New York: Academic Press.

Warner, S. B., Jr. (1963). *Streetcar suburbs.* Cambridge, MA: Harvard University Press.

Weitzman, L. J., & Dixon, R. B. (1979). Child custody awards: Legal standards and empirical patterns for child custody, support and visitation after divorce. *University of California Davis Law Review, 12,* 472–521.

Wells, R. V. (1980). Illegitimacy and bridal pregnancy in Colonial America. In P. Laslett, K. Oosterveen, & R. M. Smith (Eds.), *Bastardy and Its Comparative History* (pp. 347–361). Cambridge, MA: Harvard University Press.

Welter, B. (1966). The cult of true womanhood, 1820–1860. *American Quarterly, 18,* 151–174.

Zelnik, M., & Kantner, J. F. (1977). Sexual and contraceptive experience of young unmarried women in the United States, 1976 and 1971. *Family Planning Perspectives, 9,* 55–71.

Zinaldin, J. S. (1979). The emergence of a modern American family law: Child custody, adoption, and the courts, 1796–1851. *Northwestern University Law Review, 73,* 1038–1089.

Epilogue: Research Priorities

Arthur B. Elster
Michael E. Lamb
University of Utah

Readers of this book, like the participants in our study group, may well have reached two conclusions: (1) We know much more about adolescent fathers than was thought, and (2) there remain many crucial but unanswered questions concerning adolescent fatherhood. In this epilogue, we list topics identified by the study group participants as fertile areas for future investigation.

Who Are Teen Fathers?

1. Do they differ with respect to social and psychological adjustment from teens who are not fathers?

2. Do those who remain involved with their partners and/or children differ from those who do not?

3. Can one distinguish subgroups of teen fathers on the basis of psychological adjustment, prospects for achieving financial independence, or prepregnancy behavioral characteristics?

4. If so, do these differences facilitate decisions regarding intervention and counseling, allowing for more effective intervention?

Do Teen Fathers Differ from Adult Fathers?

1. Do the perceptions and conceptions of parenthood change with age?

2. Does the transition to parenthood affect teen fathers and adult fathers differently?

3. Are teen fathers more or less involved in parenting than adult fathers, and are the determinants of paternal involvement different for teen and adult fathers?

4. Do aspects of psychological development or maturity influence parental behavior?

5. Do teen and adult fathers behave similarly in interaction with their children?

6. Do similar or different sociological factors influence the parental behavior of teen and adult fathers?

7. Does the father's age directly or indirectly affect child development?

What are the Effects of Social Change and Public Policy on Teen Fathers?

1. How have new child custody and child support laws, AFDC (Aid for Families with Dependent Children) regulations, federal regulations regarding population affairs, and Medicaid regulations affected the relationships between teen fathers and their infants?

2. What effect has the poor job market had on teen fathers and their new families?

3. Has the change from a preponderance of blue-collar factory jobs to a preponderance of jobs in the fast-food industry affected teen fathers and the exercise of their parental responsibilities?

4. Would elimination of the minimum age for teenagers adversely or positively affect the economic circumstances of teen fathers?

What is a Proper Clinical Approach for Teen Fathers?

1. Do clinical counseling services help teen fathers to adjust to their new roles and responsibilities?

2. Does vocational counseling help teen fathers occupationally and economically?

3. Can and should teen fathers be encouraged to provide more financial support for their children when they are not married?

4. How much effort should be devoted to clinical outreach if teen fathers resist intervention?

5. What factors impede the ability of clinical programs to contact and serve teen fathers?

6. Does the provision of clinical services to teen fathers adversely affect the provision of services for teen mothers?

7. Are there subgroups of teen fathers who need different types and degrees of service?

8. With what service providers should successful programs for teen fathers be staffed?

Public Data Sets

Some of these questions could be addressed using data from one or more of the large composite data sets now available. These include the National Longitudinal Study of Work Experience, from which the data presented in Dr. Marsiglio's chapter were drawn, and various data sets catalogued and made available by Sociometrics Corporation of Palo Alto, California. Many of the earlier studies concerned with the reproductive success and morbidity of teenage mothers used data from the national Collaborative Perinatal Project funded by NINCDS. This data set contains little information about fathers, however, and is in any event quite outdated. Because the data were gathered before the liberalization of abortion laws in 1973, the findings are not easily generalizable to the pregnant adolescents of today.

The other available data sets would support many insightful analyses, despite some evident deficiencies. Foremost among these is the failure to distinguish age of father using categories more refined than ''under 20 years of age.'' Just as researchers have come to realize that the outcomes for teen mothers and their infants vary greatly depending on maternal age, so too many outcomes vary depending on paternal age. We hope that when new data sets are prepared and made public they will provide as much detailed information as possible.

Author Index

Page numbers in *italics* refer to reference pages.